French
Faux Amis
The Combined Book

Learn why Frenchmen wear *slips*,
and why you'll <u>never</u> find *préservatifs*
in French food

by

Saul H. Rosenthal

French Faux Amis—The Combined Book

Published by Wheatmark®
610 East Delano Street, Suite 104, Tucson, Arizona 85705 U.S.A.
www.wheatmark.com

ISBN: 978-1-60494-220-0
LCCN: 2008941258

Also by Saul H. Rosenthal

The Rules for **the Gender of French Nouns**, (3rd revised edition)

Speaking Better French, **Faux Amis**

Speaking Better French, **more Faux Amis**

Speaking Better French, **still more Faux Amis**

Speaking Better French, **The Key Words and Expressions**

Speaking Better French, **More Key Words and Expressions**

French Key Words and Expressions, The Combined Book

et en français

Les règles du genre des noms *au masculin et au féminin*

Mieux parler anglais, **Faux amis**

Acknowledgements

It's difficult to remember to thank all of the people who helped me while I was writing the three books which are combined into this volume. I hope that I don't forget any of you.

Catherine Ostrow and Sylvie Shurgot read the manuscripts of all three original books, looking for errors and making suggestions. Jean-Claude and Marie-Jo Parfait, Brigitte Humbert, Jean-Marc Bard, John Moran, and Marie-Claire and Jean Lubaszka, all helped with at least one of the books, found errors and helped clarify complicated *faux amis*.

My daughter Sadie was always available for impromptu consultations and made great suggestions about current usage.

I also appreciated the encouraging words I received from Norman Shapiro, John Romeiser, Jonathan Walsh, Christiane Laeufer, Judy Baughin, A. G. Fralin, Marion Vergues, Roger Hawkins, and Steve Hedge.

My wife Cindy, in addition to suggesting several *faux amis*, was wonderfully patient while I spent enormous amounts of time writing these books, and I greatly appreciate her.

To all of you, and anyone else that I missed, thanks again very much.

Contents

Introduction

to

Faux Amis:
The Combined Book

These *faux amis* were originally included in three separate books:

Speaking Better French, Faux Amis

Speaking Better French, more Faux Amis

Speaking Better French, still more Faux Amis.

I felt you should have a chance to have all the *faux amis* in one place, for ease and simplicity. This book is the place, and in addition the *faux amis* have been updated, edited and rewritten, and additional *faux amis*, that weren't in any of the first three books, have been added.

As in the other books, the *faux amis* are purposely not alphabetized. This is not a dictionary after all! I want to give you the chance to make interesting discoveries, and stumble upon unexpected treasures, as you read through the book.

This book is meant to be fun to read. I hope that it'll be as much fun for you to read as it was for me to write.

What follows next is the introduction I wrote for the first book in this series, which explains the whole idea of faux amis and also my methods and goals in writing these books. I believe that you'll find it interesting...

Introduction

to

the first book in this series
Speaking Better French, Faux Amis

I wrote this book to help you avoid possible awkward misunderstandings when you encounter *faux amis*, those confusing word pairs which appear the same in French and English, but which unfortunately have different meanings.

You can find lists of *faux amis* in many places. This is not a list. What I have tried to do is to write an easy-to-read book in conversational language. It's not meant to be a textbook. I want you to be able to read it for fun, and I hope that you will find it fascinating.

I have tried to explain the nuances and to give lots of examples so that you will understand the differences in usage between the French and the English. The examples will help you understand how the words <u>can</u> be used, but I have also tried to make clear how they <u>shouldn't</u> be used. I've included a bit of history of a number of the words, with the aim of making your reading more interesting.

When you have finished reading this book, I hope that you will have learned most of the *faux amis* without having had to consciously memorize them.

Now let's go on and discuss a little more about what *faux amis* are:

Faux amis, or "false friends", are "friends" because they look the same in English and in French. They have similar spelling. Frequently they may be spelled exactly the same!

They are "false" friends, however, because they don't mean the same thing! The French word may look just like the English word, but it may mean something else entirely.

These *faux amis* can cause you trouble if you misunderstand them when you hear them spoken or when see them written. It's easy to assume that a French word means the same when it looks and sounds pretty much the same as an English word.

However a *faux ami* can cause you even more trouble, and sometimes even considerable embarrassment, when you use it in conversation and it means something different than what you expected. You assume that you know what it means because it looks just like an English word. Unfortunately, it may mean something else entirely than what you actually meant to say.

My wife likes to recount a classic example that happened to her personally. She was discussing organic food with French friends and mentioned that there are often preservatives in the food that you buy at supermarkets. She used the word *préservatifs.* However *préservatifs* doesn't mean preservatives in French, it means condoms! You can imagine the looks on the faces of her friends upon hearing that there are often condoms in supermarket food.

This problem of *faux amis* is pretty much restricted to French. You won't find the same thing if you are studying Russian or German, for instance. There are so many every-day French and English words that are almost identical that you come to expect that similar words mean the same thing. After discovering that *similar* means similar, *différent* means different, *stupide* means stupid, and *intelligent* means intelligent, it comes as a surprise when *sensible* doesn't mean sensible.

Faux amis are words like *préservatifs* and *sensible*. They are words that are recognizible as English words, and that we welcome as old friends, but which turn out to have different meanings in French. They can leave French people looking very perplexed when we erroneously use the French word with an English meaning.

In order to be fooled by "false friends" you have to have the legitimate expectation that a French word which looks and sounds like an English word will actually have the same meaning as the English word. The truth is that that's a very legitimate expectation. In conversation I have often used an English word, pronounced it with a French accent, and successfully had it understood by my French friends. In fact, they sometimes remark on how good my French vocabulary is because I use words that they wouldn't expect a foreigner to know. I can't take credit for it honestly, so I explain that the rather literary French word that I just used is actually an English word too.

To demonstrate how many words do mean the same thing, and why it is easy to be fooled when a French word does not have the same meaning as the English, here is a short list of paired words which do mean the same thing. I found them just by starting at the letter A of my dictionary :

abandon – abandon
abandonné – abandonned
abandonner- to abandon
abaque – abacus
abattoir – abattoir
abbaye – abbey
abbesse – abbess
abcès – abcess
abdication – abdication
abdiquer – to abdicate
abdomen – abdomen
abdominal – abdominal
abducteur – abductor
aberrant – aberrant
aberration – aberration
abhorrer – to abhor
abject – abject
abjuration – abjuration
abjurer – to abjure
ablation – ablation
ablution -ablution
abnégation – abnegation
abolir – to abolish
aboli – abolished
abolitionniste – abolitionist
abominable – abominable
abomination – abomination
abominer – to abominate
abondance – abundance
abondamment – abundantly

Believe it or not, this whole list came <u>from just the first two</u>

<u>pages</u> of the A's in my dictionary! We are still in words starting with Ab.

Imagine the length of the list if I had gone through all the rest of the A's, never mind the whole dictionary (which had over 900 pages). It gives you an idea how related the two languages are.

There's a good reason for the similarity between English and French. It's important to remember that after the conquest of England in 1066 by William the Conqueror, the language of the ruling classes and the court remained French for hundreds of years. Richard the Lionhearted, for example, although a famous King of England, didn't speak a word of English. His language was French and his name was *Richard, Coeur de Lion.* English was the language of the conquered Anglo-Saxons, the lower classes and the rural people.

Because the ruling classes spoke French for some hundreds of years, a great many French words became incorporated into English. Indeed, what we now call English is an amalgam of the original Anglo-Saxon language and the French of the conquerors (plus a lot of other miscellaneous words that were added later, like pizza and taco).

In fact, when talking of these English words that are identical, or almost identical to French, we say that they come from French. However, they don't just "come from" French! They <u>are</u> French, as we have just seen. Some of my French friends joke that English is just French mispronounced.

Then why are some words *faux amis*? Why do they look like English words but have different meanings. The answer comes from the fact that these French words entered English such a long time ago. They have often had hundreds of years to grow apart. Sometimes the English meaning of a word has gradually changed, sometimes it's the French meaning that's changed.

Many, many words are still practically overlapping in meaning in French and in English. That is to say, they still mean just about the same thing, and you can use the French word almost every time you would use the English word. For example, *abhorrer* and to abhor.

Some words have parted ways only slightly. Words like this still tend to overlap in some usages even though parts of their sense now differ.

There will be other words that have grown apart over the centuries so that their meanings are now different, but it's still evident that they came from the same ancestor.

Other words, although they may be written identically, or almost identically, may now have taken completely different meanings, for example *sympathique* and sympathetic.

Other words, as you will discover, may look and be spelled exactly the same and have come from the same (French) stem, but may now have completely different --- or even opposite --- meanings. For example *inhabitable* and inhabitable.

Finally, some words, although they look alike, will have come from different directions and different stems, and have unrelated meanings. For example, *dérider* and to deride.

English speakers usually recognize recently transplanted words like rendez-vous and entrée as French words. However, they are often not aware that so many of the common words they use in everyday speech are also French.

It's also interesting to reflect on the fact that numerous English words are just fragments of French word complexes, washed up on the shore of our language, so to speak.

For example, consider the English word "lassitude" which doesn't seem related in stem to any other English word with a similar meaning. Where does it come from?

It makes more sense when you know that in French there is a transitive verb *lasser*, which means to tire out or weary. *"Cela me lasse"* means "That tires me out". The adjective *las* or *lasse (fem)* means tired or weary, and *lassant* means tiring.

Finally, in this group of French words, is the noun *lassitude*, which, not surprisingly, means lassitude in French as well as in English. Thus, it's not a mysterious word, coming out of nowhere. It comes straight from French, a little orphan which got into English without the company of the rest of its family of *lasser, las, lassant,* etc.

There are many similar orphan words all around us. Some are fairly obviously French sounding, and have come relatively recently into English --- like *sabotage* and *saboteur*, members of the French family of words related to the verb *saboter*. Others are more like lassitude, words you would think of as pure English words. Think of important, for instance. It's hard to think of a more English sounding word. However, important is just the present participle of the French verb *importer* which means to matter, or to have importance. The rest of the verb didn't make it into English in this sense.

(*Importer* and to import are discussed in this book as partial *faux amis*).

It's interesting to reflect that in recent years there has been a reversal in the direction of word migration. As English has become the "global language," many English words have been incorporated into French. For example *parking, shopping* and *weekend* are now all in common use in France, and the stop signs in France say STOP, rather than AR-RÊTEZ.

Let's go on now to investigate some of our *faux amis*.

Faux Amis

I have purposely not alphabetized these *faux amis*. I did this in order to make the book more interesting to read. It's not meant to be a dictionary after all, but rather an intriguing book of discovery.

My hope is that, while reading it, you will stumble unsuspectingly upon a multitiude of interesting words that you didn't expect to encounter. However, you will find an alphabetized index in the back for reference, if you should happen to need it.

Please note that some words have many, many minor meanings, both in English and in French, and that I don't try to include a discussion of all of them. I restrict the discussions for the most part to those senses of the word that important and are in common use.

I have not tried to include all the *faux amis* that exist in the two languages. That would be a never-ending task, in which discussions of what was actually a *faux ami* would get lost in small differences of nuance and meaning. What I have done instead is to try to include the most important *faux amis*, the ones that are most likely to cause you trouble. It is certainly possible that you will come across other *faux amis* not included in this book.

Now, let's get started.

sensible – sensible
insensible – insensible

In French, the word *sensible* means <u>sensitive</u>, either sensitive physically or sensitive emotionally.

Sensible isn't related to the idea of "making good sense" as it is in English. It's related to sensing and sensation and thus, coming from a different direction, it has a completely different meaning.

> *L'oreille humaine est moins sensible à certains sons* – The human ear is less sensitive to certain sounds.

> *Vous êtes trop sensible* – You are too sensitive.

> *Il est toujours sensible à son charme* – He's still sensitive to her charm.

Sensible also means <u>perceptible</u> as in "able-to-be-sensed."

> *La différence de coloration était à peine sensible* – The difference in color is hardly perceptible.

Sensible **does not** mean sensible in the sense of reasonable.

To translate the English word sensible into French, you should use *sensé* or *raisonnable*.

> *C'est une idée bien sensée / bien raisonnable* – It's a very sensible idea.

Conversely, *insensible* means <u>insensitive</u> or <u>imperceptible</u>, as in:

> *Un homme dur et insensible.* – insensitive

> *Il est insensible au charme des femmes* – insensitive

> *La différence était presque insensible.* – imperceptible

la déception – the deception
décevoir – to deceive

These two words can really fool you. You think, for example, "How can *déception* not mean deception?" Well it doesn't!

The noun *la déception* means the <u>disappointment</u>.

> *Quand je suis revenu c'était une cruelle déception* – When I came back it was a cruel disappointment.

The verb *décevoir* means to <u>disappoint</u>.

> *J'étais très déçu.* – I was very disappointed.

Déception **does not** mean deception. **To translate** the English word deception into French, use *la tromperie* or *la supercherie.*

Décevoir **does not** mean to deceive. **To translate** "I was deceived" into French you'd use *J'ai été trompé.*

Interestingly, there **are** French words *désappointement, désappointer,* and *désappointé*, that exist and that do mean disappointment, to disappoint, and disappointed, respectively. However these words are rarely used compared to *déception, décevoir* and *déçu.*

terrible – terrible

In French, *terrible* can mean <u>dreadful</u>, <u>frightening</u>, or <u>awful</u>, as it does in English:

> *L'accident a été terrible* – The accident was terrible / It was a terrible accident.

However, in informal language it can also mean the opposite: <u>terrific</u>, <u>fantastic</u>. You can usually tell by context and tone of voice. If someone says about a meal or a wine,

> *Ce vin n'est pas terrible.*

or, in more casual language, what the French call *la langue familière:*

> *C'est pas terrible !*

it means he **didn't** like it.

Side Note: You are probably wondering why the French are using a word like *terrible* to mean fantastic. Let me remind you that we do a similar thing in English.

The English word "terrific" originally meant inspiring great terror and fear, frightening. My Webster's dictionary from the early 80's even lists inspiring terror as the first and preferred sense of the word.

Terrific has now changed in common usage to mean spendid, fantastic, wonderful or great. We ordinarily don't even think of the original meaning, and more recent dictionaries list "inspiring terror" as an archaic sense.

assister – to assist
l'assistance – the assistance

As you would expect, *"assister quelqu'un"* does mean <u>to assist someone</u>, as in:

>J'ai assisté mon père dans son travail.

>L'infirmière assiste le chirugien.

>Nous étions là hier pour assister Jean.

There is also the sense of <u>assisting someone emotionally</u>:

>J'ai assisté ma mère dans ses derniers moments.

However, the most common use of *assister* is for a different meaning. When it's *"assister à"* it means <u>to be present at</u> or <u>to attend</u>, as in:

> *J'ai assisté à une conférence hier.*

> *Nous allons assister à l'opéra.*

> *Comment connaissez-vous tous ces événements auxquels vous n'avez pas assisté ?*

Remember that "*J'ai assisté à une conference*" **does not** mean you assisted the conference in any way.

Similarly, *l'assistance* means the <u>audience</u> (opera) or the <u>people present</u> (conference), as well as <u>assistance</u> in the sense of "aid."

avertissement – advertisement

An *avertissement* is a <u>warning</u> or it refers to <u>alerting someone</u> or <u>letting them know in advance</u>. It comes from the verb *avertir* and has nothing to do with advertising.

> *Je ne faisais pas attention à ses sages avertissements* – I didn't pay attention to his sensible warnings.

To translate the word advertisement into French use *une réclame* or *une publicité*.

malicieux – malicious
malice – malice

In French, the meanings of *malicieux* and *malice* have changed to mean <u>mischievious</u> and <u>mischieviousness</u>, with an implication of cleverness and perhaps a little teasing. Thus:

> *C'est un enfant vif et malicieux* – He's a child who is lively, clever and mischievious.

> *un chaton malicieux* – a mischievious kitten

Malice and *malicieux* used to mean malice and malicious, but the French language has evolved and those meanings have mostly become obsolete in modern French, although you still may encounter the old meanings in classical works.

It's interesting to note that in this *faux ami* the meaning has changed in French while the original meaning endures in English. We'll encounter other *faux amis* like this, where it's the French meaning that has changed, some where it's the English meaning that has changed, and some where the meanings have changed in different directions in both languages.

To translate the English word malicious into French, use *méchant* or *malveillant avec préméditation*.

To translate malice into French use *méchanceté* or *malveillance*.

There is malice in her remarks – *Il y a de la malveillance dans ce qu'elle a dit.*

He's malicious – *Il est méchant.*

chagrin – chagrin

In French, *chagrin* means <u>sorrow</u> or <u>grief</u>.

In English, chagrin means annoyance, disappointment, frustration, and even humiliation.

Thus **to translate** the English word chagrin into French, try something like:

He was chagrined at his failure – *Il était déçu, contrarié et humilié à son échec.*

Historical Note: Many year ago, *chagrin* in French also had the meaning of irritation and annoyance, but this meaning has become obsolete in current usage. It's interesting though, because, like so many other examples, it demonstrates the common ancestry of the two words.

hardi – hardy

Hardi means <u>bold and daring</u> in French.

Hardy used to have the same meaning in English but that meaning has largely dropped out of current usage. In English, as you know, hardy now means strong, resilient and capable of withstanding stress.

To translate the English word hardy into French, you'd say *robuste* or *résistant.*

"Foolhardy", meaning foolishly or overly bold, is left over from when hardy meant bold in English, too. It comes from the Old French *folhardi.* (*fol* = crazy or foolish, *hardi* = bold)

Side Note: The Hardy Boys series of adolescent adventure stories was written from the 1920s to 1970s and featured the brothers Frank and Joe Hardy. (See Wikipedia).

The name was originally a *double entendre* on the name Hardy, which meant bold and daring at the time.

un préservatif – a preservative

Un préservatif in French is a <u>condom!</u>

If you want to talk about a preservative, in food for example, say *un agent conservateur,* or *un agent de conservation.* If you say, *Il y a un préservatif dans cette nourriture,* people will look at you very, **very** strangely!

pétulant – petulant
pétulance – petulance

In English, petulant means childishly irascible and sulky.

In French, however, *pétulant* means <u>bubbly and ex-</u>

huberant. (It may be related to *pétillant* or bubbly, as in *un vin pétillant*).

Similarly, in French, the noun *pétulance* means <u>exhuberance</u>.

To translate the English word petulant into French use *irascible*.

To translate the English word petulance into French use *irascibilité*.

sympathie – sympathy
sympathique – sympathetic

Sympathie doesn't mean sympathy in current French, it means <u>a warm spontoneous feeling of affinity that one person feels for another.</u>

Sympathique doesn't mean sympathetic, it means <u>likeable, warm, agreeable, nice, pleasant.</u>

If you say:

> *Je le trouve très sympathique.*

it means that you find him to be a very warm, likeable person.

Sympathique is a word which is very common in current usage. It's usually abbreviated in casual speech as "*sympa*". For example:

> *Il est très sympa.*

Sympathique is not restricted to talking about a person. It can also be used to refer to an object, as in:

> *Ce petit restaurant est très sympa* – This little restaurant is very pleasant, it has a nice feeling to it, it has a nice ambiance.

If you want **to translate** the English word sympathy into French, use *compassion*.

To translate the English word sympathetic into French, you can use *compréhensif* which means understanding, or try *compatissant*, which is stronger and more like actively sympathetic. Finally, you can say:

> *Il a de la compassion.*

To translate "sympathize with" into French, use *compatir à*.

Historical Note: In literary, historical French you may find *sympathie* used as a synonym for sympathy. This sense is archaic in modern French.

compréhensif – comprehensive

In English, the adjective comprehensive usually means <u>complete or exhaustive</u>.

In French, *compréhensif* is also an adjective but it relates to *comprendre,* or to the English word comprehension, and it means **understanding**.

Il est compréhensif et sympathique –
He's understanding and likeable.

To translate the English word comprehensive into
French, use *complet et exhaustif.*

l'occasion – the occasion

In French, *l'occasion* does mean the <u>occasion</u> or
<u>opportunity</u> just as the occasion does in English.

However, in French, *une occasion* has two other
meanings that the English word occasion doesn't
have:

First of all, *une occasion* means a <u>bargain</u>, as in:

J'ai trouvé une vraie occasion hier!

And secondly, probably the most common usage of
occasion in French is to refer to something <u>second
hand</u>. For example:

une voiture d'occasion – a used car

*Le camion n'est pas neuf, c'est une oc-
casion* – The truck isn't new, it's used.

une location – a location

The meanings of *une location* and a location are
completely unrelated.

In English a location is a place.

In French *une location* refers to a <u>rental</u>.

> *Location de voitures ici.* – Cars for rent here.
>
> une voiture de location. – a rental car
>
> *Nous avons trouvé une location pour nos vacances* – We found a rental (house) for our vacation.

Remember that *"C'est une jolie location"* **doesn't** mean that it's a pretty location. It means that it's a pretty rental. To say that it's a pretty location you'd say *un joli endroit.*

un raisin – a raisin

In French, *un raisin* is <u>a grape</u>.

In English, a raisin is a dried grape.

To refer in French to a dried grape, or what we would call a raisin, you should use *un raisin sec.*

une prune – a prune

This *faux ami* is similar to raisin and *raisin:*

In French, *une prune* is a <u>plum</u>.

In English, a prune is a dried plum.

To refer in French to what we would call a prune (a dried plum), the correct word is *un pruneau.*

As an aside, in French slang *un pruneau* can also refer to a bullet or "slug".

> *Gare aux pruneaux !* – Watch out for the bullets!

importer – to import

In English, to import means to bring goods into the country.

To import can have another meaning in a literary sense in English. This is to signify or mean. For example:

> The arrival of cheap steel imports trouble for the steel industry.

In French, *importer* does mean to <u>bring into the country</u>, as import does in English. However, *importer* **never** means to signify or mean.

On the other hand, the French verb *importer* frequently has another meaning altogether: to <u>be important or to matter</u>.

> *Il importe qu'il arrive à l'heure* – It's important that he arrives on time.

> *Peu m'importe* – It doesn't matter to me.

While import can be used as **a noun** with this meaning in English:

> It's of little import to me.

the sentence *Il importe qu'il arrive à l'heure* looks very foreign to us. That's because "to be important" is now archaic as a meaning for **the verb** "to import" in English.

inhabitable – inhabitable
inhabité – inhabited

You can't ask for a better example of a *faux ami* than this. *Inhabitable* and inhabitable are spelled exactly the same, but they are opposites!

The problem comes from the fact that the French word *habiter* means to live in. From this it follows that *habitable* means able to be lived in.

Thus, *inhabitable* doesn't mean inhabitable. It means the opposite: **not** *habitable,* **not** able to be lived in, **un**inhabitable.

To translate the English word inhabitable (able to be lived in) into French, you have to use *habitable.*

Similarly, *inhabité* doesn't mean inhabited, it means uninhabited.

To translate the English word inhabited (lived in) into French, use *habité.*

To review, as this is a bit confusing:

> To translate the English word inhabitable into French, say *habitable.*

To translate the English word **un**inhabit-able into French, say *inhabitable.*

To translate the English word inhabited in French, say *habité.*

To translate the English word **un**inhab-ited in French, say *inhabité.*

harassé – harassed
harassant – harassing

In French, *harassé* means <u>exhausted</u>, and *harassant* means <u>exhausting</u>.

Cette tâche est harassante.

Remember that *Je suis vraiment harassé* **does not** mean "I'm being really harassed." It means "I'm really exhausted."

To translate the English verb harass into French, use *harceler.*

To translate harassing into French, use *harcelant.*

actuel – actual
actuellement – actually
actualité – actuality

The French word ***actuel*** and the English word actual are real *faux amis*. *Actuel* doesn't mean actual at all. *Actuel* is an adjective and it means <u>current</u>, <u>existing now</u>.

La consommation actuelle est trois cent kilos – The amount consumed (used) as of now is three hundred kilos / The amount consumed as of now is....

La situation actuelle est grave – The current situation is grave.

Actuellement means <u>currently</u>, <u>presently</u>.

Il est actuellement à Paris – He is in Paris <u>right now</u>.

Note that this **doesn't** mean the same thing as:

He is actually in Paris – He is <u>really</u> in Paris

With a sentence like this you could easily think that in essence they mean the same thing, that he's actually in Paris means that he's in Paris now, and you could ask "What's the difference between being in Paris now and actually being in Paris?" Well, look at this sentence:

I thought he was in Paris last week but he was actually in Paris.

This doesn't say anything about "now". As you can see, the English word "actually" **always** means really, or in fact. It **never** means now or currently. Actual and *actuel* may look the same in some sentences but their meanings are **not** the same.

L'actualité has to do with the topicality or the currentness (of a bit of news, an idea, a book, etc.).

Les actualités are the news or the current events.

Remember that *en l'état actuel des choses* **doesn't** mean "in the actual state of things" or "in the real state of things." Those phrases in English imply a possibility of permanence: that that is the way things are, have been, and will continue to be.

On the other hand, *en l'état actuel des choses* means "in the present state of things." It thus describes a transient state, and allows for the possibility that it wasn't that way in the past and that it may not be that way in the future.

To translate the English word actual into French, use *réel.*

To translate the English word actually into French, use *en fait, en réalité,* or *réellement.*

cajoler – to cajole

In English to cajole means to persuade or seduce someone into doing something by coaxing and flattery.

In French *cajoler* means to surround someone with affectionate attention and tender words, to baby or cuddle someone. (Over the centuries it has lost its negative sense of attempting to persuade.)

To translate the English word cajole into French, use *enjôler*.

dérider – to deride

Dérider comes from an entirely different direction than to deride and thus it has a completely different meaning.

Dérider means to make someone less worried and sad, to cheer them up. (It comes from *dé-rider*, to remove the *rides*, or wrinkles, from the person's forehead.)

> *Je vais essayer de la dérider* – I'm going to try to cheer her up.

> *Il était triste hier, mais aujourd'hui il s'est déridé* – He was sad yesterday, but today he has cheered up.

If you want **to translate** the English verb "to deride" into French, use *ridiculiser, railler* or *se moquer de*.

dérivatif – derivative

In French, *un dérivatif* is a <u>distraction</u> or a <u>tension release</u>.

> *Il utilise le sport comme dérivatif.*

To translate the English word derivative into French, use *un dérivé*. *Un dérivé* comes from the verb *dériver de* (to derive from). For example:

C'est un dérivé du pétrole – It's a petroleum derivative / It's derived from petroleum.

vicieux / vicieuse – vicious

In English, vicious means cruel, violent, malicious, or even dangerous (a vicious animal).

In French *vicieux* is related to vice rather than to cruelty. *Vicieux* means <u>depraved</u> or <u>perverted</u>.

Il faut être un peu vicieux pour aimer ce film.

To translate the English word vicious into French use *méchant, malveillant,* or *violent* according to the sense that you are looking for.

Historical Note: Vicious used to mean depraved in English as well, coming from its French roots, but it has evolved a different meaning and the meaning "depraved" has long since become obsolete.

officieux / officieuse – officious
officieux / officieuse – official

In English, officious means pompous, bossy and petty.

In French, *officieux* doesn't mean anything like that.

In that case you might expect that *officieux* might

mean official. Actually, *officieux* means exactly the opposite. It means <u>unofficial</u>, as in:

> *une conclusion officieuse* – an <u>unofficial</u> conclusion

Remember that *une réunion officieuse* isn't an official meeting, it's an unofficial one.

Similarly, *officieusement* means <u>unofficially</u>, as in:

> *Je peux le dire, mais officieusement* – I could say it, but unofficially.

To translate the English adjective official into French, use *officiel*.

To translate the English word officious into French use something like *autoritaire, pompeux* or *suffisant*, (or a combination of similar words, depending on context).

Historical Note: Interestingly, in the past, the English word officious used to mean unofficial in diplomatic language, showing its derivation from *officieux*.

formel – formal
formellement – formally

In English, if you are talking about an occasion, <u>formal</u> means official, ceremonial, dressy and solemn. If you are talking about a person, formal can mean stiff, conservative, perhaps cold in demeanor, and perhaps pompous.

In French, *formel* doesn't have any of these meanings. *Formel* does not mean official, ceremonial, or stiff.

In English, formal can have other meanings in specific circumstances. If you are talking about a formal request, or formal training in a subject, formal means according to form. If you say "It's a purely formal arrangement", that means that it's just for form, just for outward appearance.

In French, *formel* **can** have these same general meanings as well. For example:

> *C'est un arrangement purement formel* – It's a purely formal arrangement.

However, the way *formel* is <u>usually</u> used in French is to describe an order, a denial, a statement, a proof, etc, and it means <u>unequivocal</u>, clear, precise, categorical, certain, incontestable, undeniable, or irrefutable, (as in a categorical denial, a strict proof, or a precise order).

> *un démenti formel* – a total denial, a flat denial, an unequivocal denial

> *une preuve formelle* – a strict proof / an incontestable proof

> *Je suis formel.* – I'm absolutely certain.

> *Défense formelle d'entrer* – Entrance is strictly forbidden.

Similarly, **in English**, the word <u>formally</u> usually means ceremoniously or officially, (although it can mean according to form as in "I'd like to formally request...").

In French, however, *formellement* means <u>unequivocally</u>, strictly or categorically.

> *Il est formellement interdit de fumer / entrer* – It is strictly forbidden to smoke / to enter.

To translate:

- If you are referring to something like an occasion or a restaurant, and you want to say in French that it is formal in the sense of dressy and ceremonial, use *cérémonieux* or *solennel*.

- If you are talking about a person and you want to say that he or she is formal, or has a formal style or a formal air about him, use *compassé, guindé, empesé,* or *formaliste*.

- If you are talking about clothes or a style of dress, and you want to say they are formal in the sense of "dressy", use *habillé*.

  (Note that *habillé* doesn't mean "formal" like tuxedos and formal gowns, it just means "dressy". *Plus habillé* means dressier, and you can use other terms like *un peu habillé* or *très habillé*.)

- If you want to say that the clothes are dressy

and that you especially like them, say that they are *chic* or *élégant*.

caméra – camera

In French, the word *caméra* refers just to a movie or TV camera. For a personal camera that we are most likely to call a "camera," the French say *un appareil photo*, or *un appareil* for short.

> *Je ne peux pas trouver mon appareil* – I can't find my camera.

The French will probably understand if you say camera, but it's not the right word.

consistant – consistent
inconsistant – inconsistent

In English, the word consistent can have at least three shades of meaning.

The first meaning is <u>unchanging</u>, as in "consistent results," or "a consistent approach."

The second meaning is <u>in agreement with</u> or <u>compatible with,</u> as in "results consistent with the theory," or "symptoms consistent with the diagnosis."

The third meaning is logical and <u>not self-contradictory</u>, as in "a consistent argument."

In French, the word *consistant* **doesn't** have any of these meanings at all. *Consistant* means <u>having</u>

substance, firm, solid, substantial. It usually refers to a substance, a food or a meal. If used for a sauce it would be translated as thick. It can also be used figuratively for a film plot, for instance, meaning that the plot has substance to it.

Likewise, *inconsistant* means insubstantial or lacking substance.

When it refers to a sauce or a cream, *inconsistant* could be translated as thin or runny. For a plot, a film, a novel, or an accusation, it is used figuratively, and also means flimsy and without substance. It is **not** a synonym for the English word inconsistent, which means not holding together logically.

reporter – to report
le report – the report

In French, the verb *reporter* **never** means to report. It is related in stem to *porter*, (to carry). It means *reporter*, thus to carry back or to bring back an object.

More often, reporter has a figurative meaning and means to carry back in time, as in:

Cela me reporte à ma jeunesse.

Reporter can also mean to put off, postpone, or carry into the future as in:

La réunion a été reportée à jeudi prochain.

It can also mean to <u>transfer</u> (literally: carry to), as affection:

> *Après le décès de sa femme il a reporté toute son affection sur sa fille.*

Finally, in accounting, it can mean to <u>carry forward</u>, as in:

> *Il faut reporter cette somme* – It's necessary to carry that sum forward.

Similarly, the noun ***le report*** doesn't mean the report. It refers to the carrying forward of a sum in accounting, or the postponement of a meeting or *rendez-vous*.

To translate the English noun report into French, use *le rapport*.

intoxication – intoxication
intoxiquer – to intoxicate
intoxiqué – intoxicated

In English these words most usually refer to drinking an excess of alcohol.

In French, on the other hand, *intoxication* comes from "toxin" or "toxic" and means <u>poisoning</u>. In familiar speech it also means <u>brainwashing</u>, such as by the press or the media.

> *une intoxication alimentaire* – food poisoning

Similarly, *intoxiquer* means to <u>poison</u>, or to <u>brainwash</u>.

The adjective *intoxiqué* means <u>poisoned</u> or suffering from poison. it can also mean <u>addicted</u>.

When used as a noun, *un intoxiqué* is an <u>addict</u>.

To translate:

Remember, *intoxication* does **not** refer to drunkenness. If you want a French equivalent to the English word drunk, use *ivre, soûl* or *gris.*

If you want to translate drunkenness, in the sense of the state of having had too much to drink, use *ivresse.* For chronic drunkenness use *ivrognerie.*

Although in English you can say "intoxicated with love" or "intoxicated with the beauty of the countryside" meaning drunk or euphoric with love or beauty, those expressions **don't work** in French. In French *intoxiqué* has a definite negative connotation. On the other hand you can say "drunk with love" as in English, by using *ivre* or *grisé.*

disgracieux / disgracieuse – disgraceful

This is fairly straightforward:

Disgracieux means <u>ungraceful</u> or <u>awkward</u>. *Disgracieux* does **not** mean disgraceful.

To translate the English word disgraceful into French, use *honteux, scandaleux* or *infâme.*

However, just to confuse things, *une disgrâce* **does** mean a disgrace in French, and *disgracié* **does** mean disgraced or in disgrace, but it is a little used word.

Il est tombé en disgrâce.

gracieux / gracieuse – gracious

Similarly, while the French adjective *gracieux / gracieuse* can mean <u>gracious</u>, it usually means <u>graceful</u>. There is a third possible meaning, as well. When someone says *à titre gracieux,* it means free, gratis, complimentary.

To translate the English word gracious into French, there are other non-ambiguous words that you can use. For example: *charmant, poli, affable* or *courtois.*

As an adverb, *gracieusement* means either gracefully or graciously.

And there is a noun, *la grâce,* which means grace, or charm, or gracefulness, all three.

marron – maroon

The color *marron* in French is <u>chestnut brown</u>, while the color maroon in English is in the red family. (The French word comes from *un marron,* which is a chestnut).

suffisant – sufficient

The French word *suffisant* **does** mean sufficient.

C'est plus que suffisant pour nous.

However it has a second meaning. It also means self-important, arrogant, conceited.

Il parle avec un air très suffisant – He talks with a very self-important, conceited air.

mondain / mondaine – mundane

Mondain is a French adjective that means fashionable or having to do with high society. For example:

une soirée mondaine

un homme mondain

The English word mundane is almost the opposite as it means ordinary and down-to-earth.

The noun *un mondain* or *une mondaine* means a person in the world of high society.

And, as an odd euphemism, *la police mondaine* is **the vice squad!**

Historical Note: There was a second meaning of *mondain* in French which is now fairly obsolete. In an old religious context, *mondain* meant worldly or earthly as opposed to sacred. (Referring to earthly pleasures, for example). It derived undoubtedly from the word *le monde* or the world.

It is interesting to speculate that the English word mundane probably came from this older meaning of *mondain*, as worldly. This was likely to have been the original sense of the word which migrated into English, while "having to do with high society" is probably a later evolution in French.

demander – to demand
une demande – a demand

As you probably already know, **demander** means simply to ask or request. It has none of the implication of insistence, authority, or harshness that it has in English. Thus:

> *Je lui ai demandé son avis.*

> *Puis-je vous demander de parler plus lentement ?*

Demander can also mean to need or require, but with a much softer connotation than in English:

> *Cela demande toute mon attention.*

To translate, if you want a French equivalent for the English verb "to demand", use *insister*, or, even better, use *exiger*, which is stronger.

Similarly, **une demande** is usually a simple request:

J'ai fait une demande de renseignements – I made a request for information.

Il l'a demandée en mariage – He asked for her hand in marriage.

Cela est cuisiné sur demande – That dish is prepared on demand.

In <u>economics</u>, *la demande* is the demand from "supply and demand".

La demande d'acier a diminué.

In <u>law</u>, *une demande* is a petition (for divorce, for example) or a claim (for damages, etc).

Son mari a fait une demande de divorce.

Il a fait une demande de dommages et interêts.

To translate, if you want a French equivalent for the English noun "a demand," use *une exigence*.

brave – brave

The French adjective *brave* can mean <u>brave</u>. However, this is an uncommon meaning for *brave*.

Thus, the English word brave would usually not be translated into French by *brave,* but by either *courageux* or *intrépide*.

In French, when *brave* does mean brave it is placed <u>after</u> the noun, as in:

> *C'est un homme très brave* – He's a very brave man.

On the other hand, *brave* is most often placed <u>before</u> the noun, in which case it means <u>good</u>, <u>honest</u>, <u>simple</u>, and <u>kind</u>.

> *C'est un brave homme* – He's a good, honest, simple guy.

> *Ce sont de braves gens.*

> *Son frère est un brave garçon.*

In modern speech this is by far the most common usage.

vexer – to vex
vexations – vexations
vexant – vexing

Let's look at **vexer** first. It's odd to have *vexer* and to vex as *faux amis*. *Vexer* is such a recognizable word that you would certainly guess that it means the same thing as its English counterpart. Unfortunately, it doesn't.

In English, to vex means to annoy, to irritate, to anger, to frustrate.

In French, *vexer* means to <u>hurt someone's feelings</u> or to <u>offend</u> them.

Se vexer means to <u>take offense</u>, <u>get upset</u> or <u>have your feelings hurt</u>.

> *Elle se vexe facilement* – She gets her feelings hurt easily.

> *Il se vexe pour un rien* – He gets his feelings hurt over nothing

> *Il m'a beaucoup vexé* – He really hurt my feelings / He really offended me.

Now let's look at vexation and **vexation**. In English, vexations are irritations. In French, *vexations* are <u>humiliations</u>, <u>hurt feelings</u>.

> *Elle est trop sensible pour supporter cette vexation* – She is too sensitive to put up with this humiliation, to put up with having her feelings so hurt.

And **vexant** means hurtful, wounding, <u>humiliating</u>.

Historical Note: In one French dictionary I did find *vexant* listed with a secondary meaning of irritating and annoying, (as in English). This meaning was listed as obsolescent in French.

Similarly, I did find to vex, in an English language source, with a secondary definition meaning to upset (as in French). This meaning was listed as obsolete in English.

I mention these not to confuse you but to demonstrate the common archaic source of the two words, even though they have now grown apart.

Remember that if someone says *"Je suis vexé!"*, it doesn't mean that they are angry, it means they are hurt or upset.

To translate, if you are looking for a French equivalent of the English word "to vex," try *irriter, agacer, ennuyer, embêter, contrarier,* or *mettre en colère.*

éditer – to edit

The French verb *éditer* does mean to <u>edit</u>. However, it also means to <u>publish</u>, inspite of there being another perfectly good French word, *publier*, which also means to publish.

This second meaning of *éditer,* meaning to publish, is a *faux ami* and can be confusing.

versatile – versatile

Although these words are spelled exactly the same they have completely different meanings.

In English, versatile means that something or someone is <u>able to adapt</u> to different usages or functions, or is able to serve in different ways.

In French, on the other hand, *versatile* refers only to a person or a mood and refers to the quality of being <u>changeable</u> or <u>fickle</u> and likely to change opinions or moods rapidly. You can see from the examples which follow that this is an entirely different meaning than the English meaning.

Cette foule peut être très versatile – That crowd could change moods quickly.

Elle a un caractère versatile – She changes moods and opinions easily.

To translate the English word versatile into French, use *polyvalent* if you are talking about a tool, a room, or some other object.

If you are talking about a person, though, you can say something like *"Elle a des talents variés,"* or *"Il a un esprit universel."* (*Universel* in this sense means all embracing, or covering everything.) Or just use *polyvalent* which is roughly translated as multipurpose.

Historical Note: My English language dictionary lists the origin of versatile, as coming from French in the early seventeenth century, with the meaning at the time being "inconstant" or "fluctuating". Since then the meaning has apparently stayed roughly the same in French, but evolved and changed in English.

une injure – **an injury**
injurier – **to injure**

In French, the noun *une injure* is an <u>insult</u> or <u>verbal</u>

abuse and the verb *injurier* means to insult or verbally abuse.

> *Ils en venaient aux injures* – They came to insults over it.

> *Il m'a fait injure* – He insulted me. (literary usage)

> *Il m'a injurié* – He insulted me. (current usage)

Une injure is **not** an injury or a wound.

To translate the English noun injury into French, use *une blessure*.

To translate the English verb to injure into French, use *blesser*. To injure oneself is *se blesser*.

prétendre – to pretend
prétendu – pretended

In English, the most common meaning for "to pretend" is to make believe.

In French, *prétendre* **does not** mean to make believe.

Prétendre à means to claim as one's right, as in:

> *Il prétend à un meilleur salaire.*

Or it can mean to simply to claim or assert as in:

Elle prétend pouvoir le guérir – She claims to be able to cure him.

Elle prétend être fort habile.

Il prétend être de la noblesse – He claims to be of the nobility. (Note that in English this would mean he's making believe to be of the nobility, which is not at all the same thing.)

My French friends tell me that in current usage there can be a note of skepticism implied by the speaker who uses the word *prétendre*. In other words: "She claims to be able to cure him but who knows?" or "He claims to be of the nobility, but who knows?"

This brings it a little closer to the English word pretend, but it's not the same. If one pretends in English, it's <u>not true</u>, it's make-believe. If one uses *prétendre* in French, the claim <u>may be true</u>, but you have doubts.

Note that there is a vestige of these usages in English as in "the pretender to the throne" meaning someone claiming the throne. However, in English, "he pretended to" is an archaic usage, and practically the only time you'd use it is in a historical context.

The past participle and adjective **prétendu** is used when something is claimed or asserted, but when one is skeptical about it. It's best translated as <u>supposed</u>, <u>alleged</u> or <u>so-called</u>, as in cette *prétendue cantatrice* – that so-called singer

When translating, if you are looking for a French eqivalent to "He is pretending", use *"Il fait semblant"*.

Side Note: As an interesting aside, the English and French words pretension / *prétention* and pretentious / *prétentieux* come from the French *prétendre* (to claim or assert).

un délai – a delay

In French, the word *délai* means something like the <u>time allowed</u>, or the <u>deadline for</u>, or the <u>period allowed</u>. In some phrases it can look as if it has the same meaning as delay (*sans délai,* for example), but it's not really the same. Here are some examples:

Je vais livrer dans les délais. – I will deliver on time, in the time allowed.

Il faut compter un délai de trois semaines. – You must allow three weeks.

délai d'attente – waiting period

délai de garantie – term of guarantee, guarantee period

sans délai – without any waiting period allowed, without delay

It's clear that the two words started off with a common ancestor but drifted apart over the centuries.

To translate, if you want to say in French that "There has been a delay", use *un retard*.

To translate the verb "to delay" use *retarder, reporter* (to postpone) or *repousser*.

large – large

These words are deceptively similar in French and English but do not mean the same thing.

In English, large means big. If you say a large man you mean someone both tall and broad. If you are talking about an animal or a building you mean big. If you refer to "a large number of" it means "lots of".

In French, *large* doesn't usually have **any** of those meanings. In French, *large* usually means <u>wide</u> or <u>broad</u>.

> *dix mètres de large* – ten meters in width
>
> *C'est une large route* – It's a wide road.
>
> *C'est plus haut que large* – It's higher than it is wide.

In translating into French, if you want to say large in the sense of big, use *grand* or *gros*. If you want to say large in the sense of tall, for a person use *grand*. For a building use *haut*.

If you want to say "a large number of...," say "*beau-coup de...*"

All that said, there are some cases where *large* and large overlap, especially when you are referring to something extended either literally or figuratively. For example:

> *un large cercle*
>
> *une large majorité*
>
> *dans une large mesure*
>
> *un esprit large*
>
> *un projet de large envergure* – a project of large scope

Also, *un pantalon large* is a baggy pair of pants.

Side Note: There is also a French noun, *le large*, which means the <u>open sea</u>.

Consequently, *au large de* means "off the shore of", and the idiom *prendre le large* means to run off or to escape, literally, "to take to the sea".

assumer – to assume

Assumer and to assume have meanings that are like the partially overlapping circles that I discussed in the Introduction. The circles probably were originally totally superimposed, and identical in meaning, but they have slipped apart over the years.

In English, the most common meaning of to assume is to suppose, to take for granted, to believe without evidence. *Assumer* **does not** have any of these meanings in French.

In both languages to assume means to take on (a responsibility, a debt, a role, an identity, a name, a pose, etc). This is the intersection of the two circles:

> *Je vais assumer la responsabilité.*

> *Il assume la dette.*

> *Il a assumé le rôle.*

In French, *assumer* also means to accept a consequence or a situation. To assume **does not** have this meaning in English.

> *Je m'assume comme je suis* – I accept myself as I am.

> *Cette nouvelle doit être difficile à assumer* – That news will be difficult to accept.

> *J'assume les conséquences de mes actions* – I accept the consequences of my actions.

librairie – library

This is a *faux-ami* that always confuses English speakers when they see it for the first time. *Une librairie* is a bookstore. *Le libraire* is the person who runs *la librairie:* the bookseller.

If you want to refer to an actual library in French, it's *une bibliothèque*, which, to add to your perplexity, also means a bookcase.

To summarize:

a bookstore = *une librairie*

a library = *une bibliothèque*

a bookcase = *une bibliothèque*

la lecture – the lecture

In English, a lecture is an educational talk or speech. It can also mean a scolding.

In French, *la lecture* doesn't have either of these meanings at all. *La lecture* refers to the act of <u>reading</u> (but it doesn't imply that it's out loud, as it would in English).

> *la lecture d'un livre* – the reading of a book

> *Elle est absorbée dans la lecture d'un roman* – She's absorbed in reading a novel.

> *la lecture d'une partition (de musique)* – the reading of a piece of music

> *la lecture silencieuse ou à voix haute* – reading silently or out loud

Il essaie de donner le goût de la lecture aux étudiants – He tries to give his students a taste for reading.

un patron – a patron

In English a patron of a store is a customer, especially a regular customer. A patron of a hotel is a (frequent) guest.

A patron can also be someone who gives frequent support, financial or otherwise. For example: a patron of the arts.

In French, *un patron* doesn't have either of these two meanings. *Un patron* is a <u>boss</u>, or a <u>proprietor</u>, of a business.

> *Le patron d'un restaurant.*

> *Il faut demander à la patronne.*

> *La patronne d'un hôtel.*

> *Salut, patron !* (Hi Boss!)

Finally *un patron* or *un saint patron* can refer to a patron saint as in English.

To translate: If you want to refer to a patron of a store in French, use *un client* or *un client régulier*. For a patron of the arts use *un mécène*.

incohérent – incoherent

In English, the adjective incoherent refers to speech (or possibly writing) that is disjointed and doesn't make sense. Incoherent speech can be secondary to illness, fever, brain injury, or even emotional upset, as in: "He was babbling incoherently".

A secondary usage, which is much less common, uses incoherent for a policy or theory that doesn't hold together logically, or is self-contradictory.

In French, as well, the dictionary definition of *incohérent* is <u>illogical and inconsistent,</u> and from that you would think it means pretty much the same thing as the English word incoherent. However the overlapping circles of meaning have slipped a bit. *Incohérent* is used in ways that would jar the ear if they were in English. For example:

> *Qu'il ait fait cela n'est pas impossible mais c'est incohérent.*

This means that for him to have done that is not impossible but it's either illogical or inconsistent with what one would expect. In English we would use "illogical" or "inconsistent" (depending on which we meant) instead of incoherent.

> *Elle est d'une humeur incohérente, qui produit parfois des baisers, parfois des coups.*

Here again we can figure out the meaning (inconsistent), but it sounds strange to us because it's a way of using incoherent that would not at all be normal usage in English.

A translation for the above sentence that would come pretty close is: She has inconsistent moods, producing kisses at some times and blows at others, or: She has an inconsistent temperament which produces...

What is different is that in English, incoherent has come to be used primarily for speech, or in a pinch for a policy or theory, which is disjointed or illogical. In French *incohérent* is used much more generally to mean inconsistent or illogical. And, it is used specifically for behavior or moods in ways that are foreign to us, as you saw above.

abuser – to abuse

In English, to abuse power or authority means to take advantage of it and use it in a wrong or harmful way. To abuse alcohol or drugs means to use them to excess, to go beyond the limits. To abuse a person or child means to take advantage of a position of power to mistreat the person physically (or verbally), or to force oneself sexually on them.

in French, the verb *abuser* can be used in all these same ways:

> *Il abuse de son pouvoir, de son autorité.*

> *Elle abuse de l'alcool.*

On croit qu'il a abusé de sa propre fille.

However, *abuser* can also be used in a couple of senses which would be foreign to English. First of all it can mean to <u>go too far</u> in a social sense, or <u>surpass the limits of politeness,</u> as in:

> *Je ne vais pas rester longtemps. Je ne veux pas abuser.*

Abuser can also mean to <u>fool someone</u>, usually, but not always, by taking advantage of their credulity. (French synonyms: *tromper, duper, berner*).

> *Il cherche à vous abuser* – He's trying to take advantage of you.

> *La ressemblance peut vous abuser* – The resemblance can fool you.

Similarly, *s'abuser* means to <u>be mistaken</u> (or to misunderstand).

> *Si je ne m'abuse, c'était l'année dernière* – If I'm not mistaken, it was last year.

These usages can obviously confuse you if you are not aware of them.

éventuel – eventual
éventuellement – eventually

The French word *éventuel* is often misused and often misunderstood by English speakers.

In English, eventual means ultimate, final, concluding, as in:

> It's impossible to predict the eventual outcome.

In French, *éventuel* doesn't mean that at all. It means possible in the sense that something may occur or ensue, depending on circumstances. For example:

> *Sa visite éventuelle* – His possible visit.

> *Une perte éventuelle* – A possible loss.

Similarly, *éventuellement* doesn't mean eventually, it means possibly in the sense of something which may occur depending on circumstances.

It's important to note that the French word ***possible*** also means possible and it can be a synonym for *éventuel*, but it is usually used in a different sense. *Possible* means possible in the sense of something that can be done, something that is feasible:

> *si c'est possible* – if it's possible / if you can do it

> *C'est pas possible !* – It can't be done. I can't do it. *(langue familière)*

> *C'est possible de rouler à cent cinquante ici* – It's possible to drive at a hundred and fifty here.

Éventuel, on the other hand, is restricted to possible

in the sense of things which may occur. In English, we use the same word, possible, for both of these meanings which are usually represented by two different words in French, *possible* and *éventuel*. And we have given the word eventual an entirely different meaning:

To translate the English word eventual into French, say *final* or *définitif*.

To translate the English word eventually into French, say *finalement, enfin, en fin de compte,* or *par la suite.*

For example, to translate "They eventually arrived," you can use one of the following:

> *Ils sont finalement arrivés.*

> *Ils sont enfin arrivés.*

> *Ils ont fini par arriver.*

Side Note: Although eventual means ultimate or final in English, and eventually means ultimately or finally, it's interesting to note that the English noun **an eventuality** provides a link to the French word *éventuel* and it's meaning of possible to occur. An eventuality is a possibility, a possible occurrence, or something which may occur, as in:

> It's important to be prepared for all eventualities.

> In the unlikely eventuality that...

As with so many other of our faux amis, this indicates that *éventuel* and eventual very likely came from the same source.

caution – caution
cautionner – to caution

The French word *caution* has nothing to do with the English word. It refers to a <u>guarantee</u>, a <u>security amount</u>, a <u>deposit</u>, or <u>bail</u>.

Similarly, *cautionner* means to <u>guarantee</u>, to <u>vouch for</u>, or to <u>bail out</u>.

To translate "He acted with caution" into French, use *avec prudence* or *avec précautions*.

To translate "We cautioned him (not to do it)", use *"Nous l'avons mis en garde."*

un car – a car

This one is very simple: *Un car* is a <u>bus</u> or <u>coach</u> in French.

If you want to refer to an automobile in French, say *une voiture*.

ignorer – to ignore

Ignorer in French **usually** means to <u>not know</u>, to <u>be unaware</u> of. Only **infrequently** will *ignorer* mean to <u>ignore</u>.

J'ignore qui elle est. – I don't know who she is.

Il ignore tout ça. – He doesn't know anything about that.

Je n'ignore pas les problèmes. – I'm not unaware of the problems (or: I'm not ignoring the problems).

On the other hand, in English, to ignore **never** means "to not know".

To translate the English verb to ignore into French without risk of ambivalence, you can use *ne pas faire attention à* (advice, a red light or a person), or *ne pas répondre à* (a summons, a request, or an invitation).

He ignored what she said – *Il n'a pas fait attention à ce qu'elle a dit.*

He ignored my invitation – *Il n'a pas répondu à mon invitation.*

l'évidence – the evidence

In English, evidence usually means proof, or has to do with facts or observations leading to a proof. For example: "The police have gathered a lot of evidence".

In French, *l'évidence* usually means <u>obviousness</u>, or <u>what is so obvious that it needs no proof</u>. It comes from the word *évident* (evident). Thus:

> *C'est une évidence !* – It's obvious.

> *nier l'évidence* – This doesn't mean "to deny the evidence", it means "to deny the obvious", which is not the same thing.

In both French and English *"en évidence"* and "in evidence" mean out in the open, or prominently displayed, although the nuance of meaning may be slightly different. For example:

> *On a laissé les livres bien en évidence sur la table.*

> Her artistic skill was much in evidence even though we only saw a few of her works.

To translate the English word "evidence" into French, use *preuve*.

évidemment – evidently

In English, evidently means plainly or obviously.

In French *évidemment* used to have the same meaning, but that usage is now archaic or obsolete.

In current usage, *évidemment* is used as a positive exclamation meaning: <u>Of course!</u> or Certainly! or Naturally! It is a synonym for *Bien sûr !* or *Bien entendu !*

> *Est-ce que vouz pouvez être là ? Évidemment !*

It can also mean <u>incontestably</u> or <u>without question</u>, especially when it starts a sentence. For example:

> *Évidemment, elle a fait une erreur !*

s'évader – to evade

In English, to evade means to <u>avoid</u> (responsibility, obligations, capture, responding to a question, etc.). It can also be used figuratively as in "Sleep continued to evade me".

In French, on the other hand, *s'évader*, means to <u>escape</u> (from prison, etc).

> *Il s'est évadé par la porte derrière le bar.*

It can be used, by extension, to mean to <u>slip away</u> (furtively), as a synonym of *s'éclipser*, or of *quitter à la dérobée* or *partir à la dérobée*.

> *Il s'est évadé du salon pour éviter de rencontre sa soeur.*

Finally, it can mean to escape figuratively as in:

> *Il essaie de s'évader de la réalité de sa condition.*

To translate the English verb to evade into French use *éviter, esquiver* or *éluder*.

évasion – evasion

Similarly, **in English,** evasion means <u>avoidance</u>, <u>dodging</u>, sidestepping, or giving indirect answers meant to avoid the question.

In French, on the other hand, *une évasion* is an <u>escape</u> (either literally as in an escape from prison, or figuratively as in an escape from monotony, reality, or everyday life).

To translate the English word evasion into French, use *une dérobade* (for a responsibility or commitment), or *un subterfuge* (when it is a subterfuge).

la cure – the cure

In English, a cure refers first to a treatment which can successfully bring an end to a disease condition and bring the restoration of good health, such as:

That may be a cure for cancer.

Second, it refers to the state of having good health restored.

She experienced a cure.

He was beyond cure.

In French, on the other hand, *une cure*, simply refers to a <u>course of treatment.</u>

une cure thermale

Il a fait une cure à Vichy.

Une cure is a course of treatment which has a certain length of duration. It doesn't mean that you are "cured" when you finish it. You can take it again next year.

To translate the English noun cure into French, *le remède* comes pretty close.

Side Note: As a curious aside, the idiom *n'avoir cure de quelque chose* means to not care about something. It has nothing to do with the usual meaning of *cure.*

> *Je n'ai cure de sa réputation.* – I don't care about his reputation

> *Je n'en ai cure.* – I don't care about it.

l'envie – the envy

The French word *envie* does mean <u>envy</u>, but that is just a small part of it's usage.

By far, the most common usage for *une envie* is a <u>desire</u> (or even a <u>craving</u>), as in:

> *J'ai envie de chocolat.*

> *J'ai envie de lire ce livre.*

> *Nous avons envie de manger dans ce restaurant.*

J'ai très envie de manger des myrtilles ! –
I have a real craving for blueberries.

*J'ai une folle envie de manger des myr-
tilles !* – I have a wild craving for blueberries.

As you can see, this has nothing at all to do with the
English word envy.

Side Note: Oddly, *une envie* can also mean a hang-
nail or a birthmark. You can tell, of course, from context.

s'amuser – to amuse yourself

Amuser does mean to amuse or entertain, as in:

Il a été très amusé par la blague

However the English expression "to amuse yourself" means to pass the time or occupy your time,
rather than meaning to have a good time and to be
amused.

I amused myself in reading the train
schedules during the long wait at the sta-
tion.

On the other hand, *s'amuser* has kept the meaning
of having fun, enjoying yourself, or having a good
time.

Je me suis bien amusé hier soir – I really
had a good time last night.

If you're trying **to translate** "I amused myself by…" in the sense of occupying your time doing something, try one of the following:

J'ai passé le temps à…

Je me suis occupé à …

herbe – herb

In French, the most common meaning of *l'herbe* is plain old <u>grass</u>.

> *tondre l'herbe, couper l'herbe* – to cut the grass
>
> *un brin d'herbe* – a blade of grass
>
> *les mauvaises herbes* – weeds

Une herbe can also mean an <u>aromatic herb</u> used for cooking, or a <u>medicinal herb</u>, as in English.

The expression *les aromates* can also denote aromatic herbes and spices.

Finally, just like "grass" in English slang, *herbe* in French slang can denote <u>marijuana</u>.

parasol – parasol
ombrelle – umbrella

In French:

Un parapluie is an <u>umbrella</u>.

Une ombrelle is a little hand-held <u>parasol</u>.

Un parasol usually refers in modern speech to a large, semi-fixed, or fixed, <u>sun shade</u>, in an outdoor café, for instance. (*Un parasol* used to refer to a small hand held parasol as well, but that meaning has become obsolete.)

Thus to summarize:

> A large fixed sunshade is *un parasol*
>
> What we would call a parasol is *une ombrelle*.
>
> What we would call an umbrella is *un parapluie*.

un physicien – a physician

In English, a physician is a doctor.

In French, *un physicien* is a <u>physicist</u>.

To translate physician into French, use *médecin*.

une phrase – a phrase

While in English a phrase is a small group of words or an expression, in French, *une phrase* is a <u>sentence</u>.

To translate the English word phrase into French, there is no good exact translation, but *une expression* or *quelques mots* come close.

It was just a phrase – *Ce n'était que quelques mots.*

une sentence – a sentence

In French, <u>in a grammatical sense</u>, *une sentence* is not a sentence but a maxim or adage. (You can also say *une maxime* or *un adage).*

To translate the English word, a sentence, into French in the <u>grammatical</u> sense, the correct translation is *une phrase.*

To summarize:

- *quelques mots* = a phrase

- *une phrase* = a sentence

- *une sentence* = a maxim or adage

- *une maxime* = a maxim

- *un adage* = an adage

<u>In a judicial context</u>, *une sentence* and a sentence mean almost the same thing but not exactly: In French *une sentence* usually refers to the decision rendered by the judge, while in English, as you know, the sentence usually refers to the punishment handed down.

To translate the English word sentence (in the <u>judicial</u> sense) into French use *la condamnation* or *la peine.*

He received a sentence of twenty years in prison – *Il a été condamné à vingt ans de prison.*

a death sentence / a life sentence – *une condamnation à mort / une condamnation à perpétuité*

He served his sentence at the prison in Marseille – *Il a purgé sa peine à la prison de Marseille.*

user – to use
usé – used

In French, the verb *user* has two meanings. The first is to <u>use</u>, as in English. In this sense it's a synonym for *utiliser*, but it seems to be restricted to abstract things, and it's written as *user de*, as in the examples below:

Il a usé de son influence.

Elle a usé de tendresse.

Il a usé d'un stratagème malin.

The second meaning of *user*, which is definitely **more common**, is to use something until it is worn out, or more simply, to <u>wear something out</u>.

Elle porte une robe très usée – She's wearing a dress that has seen better days.

The adjective *usé* almost always means <u>worn out</u> rather than just used.

assimiler à – assimilate

In French, the verb *assimiler* does mean to <u>assimilate</u> but it has another completely different meaning as well.

I first encountered this second meaning while reading a political column in a French newspaper. I read something like:

> *Le parti Républicain peut être assimilé à un parti conservateur européen, mais il y a quelques différences.*

Clearly *"assimilé à"* didn't mean "assimilated to". I looked in my dictionary and found out that *assimiler à* can also mean <u>liken to</u>, <u>present as similar to</u>, or <u>compare to</u>.

Thus the above sentence translates as:

> The Republican Party could be likened to, or compared to, a conservative party in Europe, but there are some differences.

More recently, in reading a *policier* translated into English from French, I came across something like the following:

> The attack on M. Blanc, which had al-

ready been assimilated to the provocations of the extreme right wing...

I thought: That doesn't make sense --- Oh! I see! The original French author must have written *"qui avait déjà été assimilé à des provocations de,* and the translator messed up the translation!!!

It meant "which had already been likened to the provocations of..." but the English translator totally missed it. He or she didn't know the French word *assimiler,* and translated it as if it was the English word assimilate!

That's why you are learning *faux amis.* So you don't make the same kind of mistake!

la cave – the cave
le cellier – the cellar

These are close enough to be recognizable, but they don't translate as you would expect.

A French *cave* is an English <u>cellar</u>.

> *la cave* or *la cave à vin* – the wine cellar

> *la cave à charbon* – the coal cellar

On the other hand a French *cellier* is an English <u>storeroom</u> (which can be in the cellar, but usually isn't).

If you want **to translate** the English word cave into

French, you can't use *la cave*. It simply doesn't mean the same thing. Use *la grotte*.

le tourniquet – the tourniquet

This one really surprised me. After all, what else could *un tourniquet* be, except a tourniquet. Well, a lot of things, apparently.

Un tourniquet can indeed be a <u>tourniquet</u> when used in a medical context. However, *un tourniquet* is also used for <u>a multitude of things that turn</u>, including a <u>turnstile</u>, a garden <u>sprinkler</u>, and a <u>revolving display table</u>, among others.

I discovered this while reading a Maigret mystery when *le commissaire* entered a bookstore and looked at books displayed on *le tourniquet*. That really had me stumped until I discovered it was a revolving table.

un parent – a parent

The first couple of times I heard someone refer to *mon parent* when he obviously wasn't referring to his parent, were puzzling. I learned that in French *un parent* has two meanings.

First *un parent* can mean a <u>parent</u> as in English: a mother or a father.

The second meaning of *un parent* is a relative, usually a <u>blood relative</u>, even if distant.

You can almost always tell the difference by context, as in:

> *Mes parents sont sortis ce soir* – My parents went out tonight.

> *Je n'ai que trois parents vivants* – I have only three living relatives.

> *C'est une parente éloignée* – She's a distant relative.

> *Jean est un parent de ma femme* – Jean is a relative of my wife.

évoluer – evolve

Évoluer is another word that has more meanings in French than it does in English. It does mean to <u>evolve</u>, change, or progress by small transformations as in English.

> *La technologie a beaucoup évolué depuis...*

However it has another meaning which is fairly unrelated. *Évoluer* also means to <u>maneuver</u> in the military sense, and can be used figuratively as in:

> *Beaucoup de couples évoluaient dans la salle de danse.*

> *Les gens évoluaient autour la cheminée pour se réchauffer.*

In this sense it sort of means to <u>move around among other people</u>.

impotent – impotent

In French, the adjective *impotent* means crippled, <u>unable to move</u>, having much difficulty in moving. Some French synonyms would be *infirme, invalide, paralytique*. It can refer to a person or to a body part. For example, one can speak of:

un bras impotent – a paralyzed arm

In English, the adjective impotent means powerless, or, when used in a sexual sense, unable to function.

If you want **to translate** impotent in the sense of powerless ("He felt impotent to do anything about it"), use *impuissant*.

If you want **to translate** impotent in the sexual sense, you use *impuissant* as well.

In French, the noun *un impotent* (or *une impotente* if you are talking aobut a woman), means <u>someone who is disabled</u> or crippled, unable to move about, or able to move about only with much difficulty.

impotence – impotence

The French noun *impotence* refers to the state of a person who is disabled or the state of a body part

74

which is disabled or unable to function. It can be translated as <u>disability</u> or <u>infirmity</u>.

If you want **to translate** the English noun impotence into French in the sense of powerlessness, use *impuissance*.

If you wish **to translate** impotence in the sexual sense, you use *impuissance* as well.

un palace – a palace

This one may surprise you: *un palace* in French is a <u>luxury hotel</u>.

To translate the English word palace into French, use *un palais*.

onéreux – onerous

In English, the adjective onerous refers to a duty, responsibility or task, and means that it is burdensome or heavy.

> Having to make three long trips in a week seemed like an onerous task.

It used to have this meaning in French as well but this sense of the word has become obsolete and is no longer used.

In modern French, the adjective *onéreux* refers to an expense and means <u>costly</u>. Some synonyms in French would be *cher, coûteux* and *dispendieux*.

Le loyer était trop onéreux.

To translate the English word onerous into French, some choices would be to use *pénible* if you are talking about a task or duty, and *lourd* if you are talking about a responsibility.

Side Note: The French idiom *"à titre onéreux"* means "on condition of payment being made".

un hasard – a hazard

In English a hazard is a danger, a peril, or a risk. For example:

a fire hazard

a health hazard

Ice is a hazard in this weather.

This article is about the hazards of smoking.

In French, on the other hand, *hasard* means <u>luck</u>, <u>chance</u> or <u>fate</u>, but **does not** mean danger.

C'est un coup de hasard – a stroke of luck

par un coup de hasard – by mere chance, by coincidence

par un heureux hasard – by a lucky chance

Je suis arrivé ici par hasard – I arrived here by accident, by chance.

J'ai pris un chemin au hasard – I took a path at random.

Remember that the French word hasard **does not** mean danger or risk. If you want to say danger or risk in French, say *danger, péril,* or *risque.*

Historical Note: The English word hazard comes, of course, from the French word *hasard,* which comes from Turkish and Persian words meaning dice (hence, chance). You can see that both the English meaning of danger, peril or risk, and the French meaning of chance or luck came from the same original meaning but have drifted apart slightly over the centuries.

While the French and English nouns "hazard" and "*hasard*" now have different meanings, the verbs "to hazard" and **hasarder** have kept pretty much the same meanings.

Je vais hasarder une opinion – I'm going to hasard an opinion. (to venture, to risk)

Je ne veux pas hasarder beaucoup d'argent – I don't want to hasard much money. (to risk)

un chandelier – a chandelier

In English, a chandelier is a decorative hanging ceiling light with multiple branches for bulbs.

In French, on the other hand, *un chandelier* is a candlestick holder (usually also with multiple branches), that we would call a candelabra.

If you want to refer to a ceiling light in French, say *un lustre.*

une casserole – a casserole

In English a casserole is a (slowly cooked) stew, or a casserole can refer to a container that the stew may be cooked in (usually made of glass or earthenware).

a beef casserole

It was cooked in a casserole.

In French, however, *une casserole* has an entirely different meaning. *Une casserole* is a saucepan, that is used for cooking on the stovetop.

To translate:

If you want to say a casserole referring to a stew, use *un ragoût* or *une daube.*

If you want to say a casserole referring to the container that the stew is cooked in, use *une cocotte.*

un pot – a pot

Here's another kitchen *faux ami*. Pot can have many meanings, both in English (belly, marijuana, etc.), and in French, but I am going to restrict my comments to the kitchen.

In English a pot can refer to a large round cylindrical (metal) pot for cooking, in which case it's *une marmite* in French.

On the other hand, a pot can also refer to a simple saucepan:

> It's in a pot on the stove.

> I just put it in a pot to warm it up.

In this case it's *une casserole* in French, as we have just learned.

The French word *un pot*, (the "t" is not pronounced by the way), usually means a <u>jar</u> (for jam, for example), or some other kitchen <u>container </u>for liquids or foods. (*Un bocal* is another word for a jar).

Un pot can also refer to an (earthenware) <u>jug</u> containing milk or water. To give someone *un pot-de-vin* is to give them a bribe.

Finally, *un pot* can mean a <u>flowerpot</u>, which I guess could also be in the kitchen.

Un pot may rarely mean *une marmite* or cooking pot, as in English:

un pot-au-feu

le plateau – the plateau

In French, *un plateau* can mean a (geologic) <u>plateau</u>, as in English.

However, the most common meaning of *un plateau* is a <u>(kitchen) tray</u>. (So we are still in the kitchen).

l'entrée – the entrée

To continue in the kitchen, **in American English** the entrée has come to mean the main course.

In French, *l'entrée* **does not** mean the main course. In normal French usage *l'entrée* is the "entrance" into the meal --- the small plate that we would call the <u>appetizer</u>.

It is really peculiar that this French word, which so obviously means the beginning of the meal, has taken such a different sense in American English.

Entrée, both in French and English has other meanings outside the kitchen, which meanings coincide for the most part. For example:

> He had entrée into the highest offices of the government

> *Il a ses entrées dans les bureaux les plus hauts...*

We are restricting ourselves, however, to the *faux ami* having to do with the kitchen.

le lard – the lard
le bacon – the bacon

Let's continue with faux amis from cooking:

In English, lard refers to the fat from the abdomen of a pig that has been rendered and clarified and which is used in cooking. In slang lard can also refer to unattractive excess fat on a person, as in:

> He's a ball of lard.

On the other hand, bacon in English refers to cured meat from the back or sides of a pig.

In French, the word *lard* means bacon. *Lard* **does not** mean lard. It refers to a layer of meat and fat rather than to rendered fat.

> *lard gras* – fatty bacon, mostly or almost entirely fat

> *lard maigre* – lean bacon, meat mixed with fat

> *une omelette au lard* – a bacon omelette

However, while we usually think of bacon in thinly sliced strips, in France *lard* is often in chunks. Small diced *lard gras*, or bacon fat, is called **lardon.**

The French noun **le bacon** refers to what we would

call Canadian bacon: smoked lean salted pork (or *lard maigre fumé*), cut in slices.

And finally, **la poitrine fumée** is another synonym for *le lard*, or the bacon.

Now let's turn it around to what you'd say **if you want to translate** the English word into a French word:

- If you want to translate the English word lard into French use *le saindoux.*

- If you want to translate the English word bacon into French use *le lard*, but expect it in diced cubes, rather than slices.

- If you want to translate Canadian bacon into French use *le bacon*.

And remember that none of these will turn out to be <u>exactly</u> what you expect, simply because the terms don't exactly coincide.

le change – the change

In English, ordinarily the noun change means alteration or the act of becoming different.

To translate the English noun change into French in the sense of <u>alteration</u>, you have to use **le change-ment**.

It's important to remember that you can't use the French noun *le change* to mean change!

In English again, when you are talking about money, the word change can refer to small coins:

I have a pocket full of change.

To translate small change into French, use *la petite monnaie*.

j'ai trop de petite monnaie dans la poche.

When you ask for change for a large bill, it's *la monnaie*.

Est-ce que vous avez la monnaie sur un billet de cinquante euros ?

Pouvez-vous me faire la monnaie de cinquante euros?

After a purchase, in English, the change refers to the difference between the money you tendered and the actual cost, in other words, what you will receive back.

She gave me three dollars in change.

To use change to mean what you get back after a purchase, use *la monnaie* as well.

Gardez la monnaie ! – Keep the change

In French, when talking about money, the noun *change* means exchange, as in foreign exchange.

un bureau de change – where you can exchange your money

Le change est avantageux aujourd'hui – The rate of exchange is good today.

Le change du dollar est... – The dollar exchange rate is...

Side Note: While you have to be careful with the French noun *le change,* the French verb *changer* usually can be used interchangeably with the English verb to change.

disposer de – to dispose of

To dispose has three possible meanings:

1. In English, "to dispose of" usually means to get rid of.

He disposed of the garbage.

It can also mean to get rid of by handling decisively as in:

He disposed of the problem.

In French, *disposer de* **never** means to get rid of. *Disposer de* **always** means to have at one's disposal.

Il peut disposer de cinq voitures – He can have five vehicles at his disposal.

> *les hommes dont je dispose* – the men at
> my disposal

As you can see, this is a true *faux ami.*

2. The French verb *disposer* (by itself, without the
de), means to <u>arrange</u> or set out. The English verb
to dispose may also be used in the same way, although it's a rare usage,:

> *Il faut disposer la chambre avec le lit à
> gauche* – It's necessary to arrange the
> bedroom with the bed on the left.

> *Comment est-ce que vous allez disposer
> les invités à la table ?* – How are you go-
> ing to arrange the guests at the table /
> seat the guests at the table?

> They disposed themselves around his
> office. (rare usage in English)

3. Finally, in English, "to dispose someone <u>towards</u>"
means to make someone willing.

Similarly, "to be disposed <u>towards</u>" something means
to be in the frame of mind to do something, as in:

> After what has happened she is not dis-
> posed to help him.

> He was disposed to agree.

In French *disposer* can have substantially the same
sense. It can mean to <u>put someone in the frame of</u>

<u>mind</u> to do something or to prepare someone psychologically for something, but it is used sometimes in nuanced ways in which it would not be used in English. For example:

> *Nous l'avons disposé à vous aider.* – We got him in a frame of mind to help you.

That pretty much corresponds with English usage. But consider, on the other hand,

> *Le médecin a disposé le malade à mourir* – The doctor has prepared the sick person for death.

This is not a usage for dispose that one would likely see in English.

marcher – to march

In French, the verb *marcher* has two general meanings, of which, to <u>march</u> in the military sense is only a very minor one.

First of all, *marcher* is the <u>general word for to walk</u>.

> *L'enfant a commencé à marcher tôt* – The child began walking early.

> *Il marche en boitant* – He limps when he walks.

> *Nous marchons à reculons* – We are walking backwards.

Les chats marchent à quatre pattes – Cats walk on four legs.

Les soldats marchent à travers les champs – The soldiers are walking across the fields.

Secondly, *marcher* means to <u>function</u> or to <u>work</u>, and can be used in a figurative sense as well, for instance referring to a plan.

Cette machine marche automatiquement – That machine works automatically.

Le moteur ne marche pas – The motor doesn't work.

Comment ça marche ? – How does that work?

Est-ce que les affaires marchent bien ? – How is business?

Est-ce que ça va marcher ? – Will that (plan, idea) work?

Qu'est-ce que vous pensez du plan ? --- *Ça marche !* – What do you think of the plan? --- It'll work!

Est-ce que ca marche ? – Do you agree? *(Vous êtes d'accord ?)* / Will that work?

Remember, in French, *marcher* means to walk in general on the one hand, or to function or work on the other. In English, to march does not have either of these meanings.

mystifier – to mystify

The dictionary says that mystify came from the French *mystifier* in the early 19th century. However, in that relatively short time of just two hundred years, the two words have slipped apart in their meanings, although they remain almost identical in appearance.

In English, the most common use of "to mystify someone" means to perplexe someone, to puzzle them, to bewilder them, to baffle them.

> The disappearance of his wallet from the locked drawer mystified him.

In French, on the other hand, *"mystifier quelqu'un"* means to <u>fool somebody</u>, to <u>take them in</u>, to trick them or to "pull their leg". It can be either to laugh at their expense, or simply to fool them.

To mystify used to have this meaning as well in English but that usage has become obsolete and dated.

Note that the English and French meanings are definitely **not** the same. Consider:

> How I could lose that mystifies me.

That is a standard English usage of mystify. There is

no implication of trickery, being taken in, or of being fooled by someone.

A good French synonym for *mystifier quelqu'un* is *faire marcher quelqu'un.*

balancer – to balance

In English, to balance something means to put or keep something steady and in equilibrium so that it won't fall.

> He balanced the stone on top of the post.

It can also mean to compare or offset as in:

> The costs are balanced against the benefits.

In French, *balancer* does not mean the same things at all. In fact it comes close to being an opposite.

Instead of meaning keeping something steady, *balancer* means to <u>swing</u> (your arms or legs), to <u>sway</u> (your hips), to <u>rock from side to side</u>, or to <u>oscillate</u>.

> *Arrête de balancer les bras !* – Stop swinging your arms!

> *Il balance le bébé pour l'endormir* – He is rocking the baby to sleep.

> *Elle balance les hanches en marchant* – She sways her hips while walking.

> *Les vagues balancent les bateaux à l'ancre* – The waves rock the boats at anchor.

In slang *balancer* can also mean to <u>toss</u> or throw. For example:

> *Balance-moi un coussin, s'il te plaît* – Toss me a cushion, if you would.

Similarly *balancer* can mean to <u>toss out</u>, to throw out, or to get rid of.

> *Il a balancé le noyau de la pêche par la fenêtre* – He threw the peach pit out the window.

> *Elle a décidé de balancer ses vieux vête-ments* – She decided to throw away her old clothes.

> *Il s'est balancé d'une fenêtre du qua-trième étage* – He threw himself out of a fourth floor window.

Balancer un compte means to <u>balance an account</u>, just like in English.

dresser – to dress

In English, to dress usually means to put clothes on oneself or someone else:

> She was dressed in a summer frock.

She dressed her daughter for the party.

To "dress a wound" can mean to treat and bandage the wound.

Less commonly, to dress a fowl can mean to clean and eviscerate it, which makes some sense as the dictionary points out that to dress comes from the Old French *dresser* meaning to arrange or prepare.

However, the modern French verb *dresser* doesn't have the same meanings as the English verb to dress. Not at all!

In French, *dresser* means to erect, put in a vertical position, and, by extending the meaning, to construct, or put up.

> *Ils ont dressé le mât* – They put up the mast.

> *Ils ont dressé le monument* – They raised the monument.

> *Elle a dressé la tête* – She raised her head.

> *Il s'est dressé* – He stood up.

> *Le chien a dressé les oreilles* – The dog pricked up it's ears.

Dresser can also mean to prepare or draw up a list or an inventory.

Dressez une liste pour moi, s'il vous plaît.

To translate, if you want to say something about getting dressed in French, use *s'habiller*.

confiner – to confine

As you might expect, *confiner* can mean **to confine**, and *se confiner* is used in pretty much the same way as "to confine oneself" in English.

> *L'enfant était confiné dans une petite chambre* – The child was confined to a small room.

> *Il se confine chez soi* – He confines himself to his home.

> *Elle se confine à parler des sujets quotidiens* – She limits herself to speaking of day-to-day subjects.

However *confiner* is very often used in another sense entirely, one which is not at all intuitive to an English speaker. In this sense *confiner* means to <u>verge on</u> or <u>border on</u>. For example:

> *Ses mots confinaient à la tendresse* – Her words were approaching tenderness.

> *Ses actes confinent à la folie* – His acts bordered on folly (or madness).

You may ask yourself, how did we go from "to confine" to 'to verge on". It's not as illogical as it may appear. *Confiner* is used geographically to say that one country <u>borders</u> on another:

L'Italie confine à La France.

One can see that, by bordering on France, Italy theoretically confines France in that direction.

The figurative sense (*confiner à la folie,* etc.) is an extension of this geographic usage of bordering on, but the figurative sense is used much more frequently than the original geographic one.

errer – to err
errant – errant

In English, to err means to make a mistake.

In French, the verb *errer* means simply to <u>wander</u> or rove as in:

Il errait dans les rues de Paris – He was wandering through the streets of Paris.

Errer itself has none of the negative conotation of to err. However, it is presumably by "wandering" off course that one makes *une erreur,* which does mean an error.

Errant also has a negative connotation in English as it means erring or straying from the proper course. An errant husband is an unfaithful one.

In French, again, *errant* simply means <u>wandering</u> as in:

> *des pensées errantes* – wandering thoughts
>
> *un chevalier errant* – a wandering knight
>
> *un chien errant* – a stray dog
>
> *la vie errante des nomades* – the wandering life of nomads

Side Note: From what I can glean from my dictionaries, both the English verb "to err", and the French verb *"errer"*, once had both meanings (to make a mistake and to wander).

However, to make a mistake is now listed as an obsolete usage of *errer* in French, and is no longer used. Similarly, to wander in search of adventure is now listed as an obsolete usage of to err in English. Thus the two languages have gone off in different directions.

compulser – to be compulsive, to compel

When you first see the French verb *compulser* you are likely to be sure that it must have something to do with English words of the same general appearance. Well it doesn't!

The French *compulser* means to attentively <u>examine</u> or <u>consult</u> notes, documents or books.

Il a compulsé ses notes avant d'entrer.

Side Note: The French words *compulsif* and *compulsion* are just alongside *compulser* in the *dictionnaire* and do mean compulsive and compulsion. *Compulser*, though, coming from the same word stem, dances to its own tune.

le starter – the starter

In speaking about automobiles, the French noun *le starter* means the <u>choke</u>.

To translate the English word starter into French, use *le démarreur*.

un stage – a stage

In English, the noun "a stage" can have several meanings. First, it can refer to a period of development of a plan, a process, or a person. For example:

at that stage in my life

The process was in an early stage.

She's in a late stage of pregnancy.

A stage is also a raised platform used for performances or plays, and there are other minor meanings for a stage as well (stage of a rocket, stage of a microscope, the stage referring to a career in the theatre, etc).

In French, *un stage* **does not** have any of these meanings. *Un stage* means a <u>training period</u>:

> *Ma fille est partie pour un stage de trois semaines à Lyon.*

> *Cet été elle va faire un stage de poterie.*

> *Il faut faire un stage de formation.*

Note that while the French meaning of *un stage* also refers to a period of time, it is not at all the same meaning as in English. In English a stage can refer to any period of time during a development or process, while in French *un stage* is specifically a training period undergone by a person.

To translate:

If you wish to refer in French to a stage in the sense of a period of time in a process, use *un stade* :

> *à ce stade de ma vie*

> *à ce stade du projet*

> *The processus était à un stade peu avancé.*

You can also use *point* or *moment* :

> *à ce point de ma vie*

> *à ce moment de ma vie*

If you want to refer to the kind of stage which is a raised platform use *une estrade.*

If you're talking about being "on stage" use *en scène.*

If you are talking about a stage of a journey, use *une étape.*

un toboggan – a toboggan

In French, the most common use for *un toboggan* is to denote a <u>slide for children</u> in a playground. In commerce it can also be a <u>slide for merchandise</u>.

In Canadian French *un toboggan* is a platform for carrying goods usually dragged along behind a horse. The word comes from the Algonquin language.

In English, a toboggan is a long thin sled for use in the snow.

To translate the English word toboggan, meaning a sled, into French, use *une luge.*

un tissu – a tissue

Both the English and French words come from the French verb *tisser*, to weave. In both languages *un tissu* or a tissue can refer to an <u>intricate structure</u>, "woven together", which can also be figurative, such as:

a tissue of lies

un tissu de mensonges

un tissu de bétises – a lot of nonsense

Le tissu urbain est plus dense dans les grandes villes.

In both languages *un tissu* or a tissue also may refer to <u>body tissue</u>. For example:

epithelial tissue

tissu musculaire

tissu nerveux

In French, however, the most common usage for the noun *tissu* is for <u>textiles, fabrics and cloths</u>, often woven, of course.

tissus de laine, de soie, de coton

tissus de fibres synthétiques

In English, on the other hand, a tissue **never** means a textile or a fabric. Probably the most common meaning for "a tissue" in English is a piece of facial tissue or a paper handkerchief, or, to use a brand name: a Kleenex.

Conversely, *un tissu* **never** means a facial tissue or a paper handkerchief in French.

To translate the English word tissue into French in the sense of a facial tissue or a paper handkerchief, say *un mouchoir en papier* or *un kleenex*.

blesser – to bless

The verb *blesser* in French has nothing to do with the English verb to bless.

In French, *blesser* means to <u>wound</u>. It can be used literally or figuratively:

> *Quand il est tombé il a été grièvement blessé.*

> *Est-ce que vous êtes blessé ?* – Are you hurt?

> *Ta suspicion m'a blessé* – Your suspicion wounded me (or hurt me).

> *Il m'a blessé au vif* – He cut me to the quick.

Remember that *"Il m'a blessé"* **does not** mean "He blessed me." It means "He wounded me." either literally or figuratively.

To translate the English verb bless into French, use *consacrer* or *bénir*.

blêmir – to blemish

Historical Note: The English verb, "to blemish" is listed in my dictionary as coming from the Old French verb *"ble(s)mir"*, meaning to injure, or to cause to turn pale. However, the two words "to blemish" and *"blêmir"* have drifted apart over the centuries.

By the way, the circumflex over the "ê", as in *blêmir*, often means that an "s" has been dropped over the years, as the dictionary indicates one was dropped from *blesmir* to produce *blêmir*. For example consider *forêt* and forest and *hôpital* and hospital).

In English, to blemish means to mar, to stain, or to spoil the appearance of something which would otherwise be spotless. It can be used figuratively as well:

> There was only a small blemish on her complexion.

> His reputation was blemished by the accusation.

In French, on the other hand, the verb *blêmir* means to <u>turn pale</u> and it refers to a person.

> *Il a blêmi de peur.*

> *Elle a blêmi de rage.*

Blêmir can occasionally be used poetically referring to a light which is fading or growing pale, as in:

> *Le jour blêmit* – The daylight faded.

The English verb "to blemish" **does not** mean to grow pale.

The French verb *"blêmir"* **does not** mean to stain or tarnish.

To translate the English verb to blemish into French,

use *tacher*, (or *entacher* if you are talking about honor or reputation). *Abîmer* or *gâcher* may also be suitable depending on what you are trying to say.

To translate the English adjective blemished, you can say something is *taché* or that it has *une tache* or *des taches*.

You'll remember that the dictionary said that the Old French verb *ble(s)mir* had two related meanings: to injure and to cause to grow pale. It's interesting to note that the English verb, to blemish, seems to have retained somewhat of a sense of "to injure" and has lost the sense of "to cause to grow pale". On the other hand, the French verb, *blêmir*, seems to have done the opposite, holding on to "become pale" without any necessary implication of injury.

lunatique – lunatic

In English, the adjective lunatic means crazy, foolish or absurd, as in:

>   a lunatic scheme, a lunatic idea

In French, on the other hand, the adjective *lunatique* means <u>moody</u> or <u>temperamental</u>, with changeable, unpredictable moods. It refers to a person:

>   *Il est extravagant et un peu lunatique*
>   – He's an immoderate person and also moody and unpredictable.

To translate the English word lunatic into French,

use *fou*. This works for the noun, a lunatic as well. It can be translated as *un fou*.

> He's behaving like a lunatic – *Il se comporte comme un fou.*

Historical Note: Both lunatic and *lunatique* come from the Old French *lunatique* and derive from the superstition that the moon *(lune)* made people moody and temporarily crazy. However, the meanings of the two words, as we have so often seen, have slipped a bit apart.

extravagant – **extravagant**

In English, the adjective extravagant has two meanings. The first meaning is immoderate, exceeding what is reasonable, going beyond reasonable limits, absurd, overly ornate. For example:

- extravagant remarks

- extravagant dress

- extravagant claims

- extravagant demands

- an extravagant price

In French, the adjective *extravagant* has this same first meaning and can be used interchangeably in this sense.

des prix extravagants – unreasonable, immoderate

une tenue extravagante – clothing (or behavior, depending on context), which is bizarre or beyond normal limits

des déclarations extravagantes – extravagant claims

However, **in English**, extravagant also means spending too much money, wasteful, lacking restraint in spending.

He is very extravagant and wastes a lot of money.

In French, *extravagant* **does not** mean wasteful and spending too much money.

To translate the English word extravagant into French in the sense of wasteful and spending too much money, use the adjective *dépensier / dépensière* instead.

supplier – to supply

This one is very simple. The French verb *supplier* means to beseech, beg, implore, entreat. It has nothing to do with to supply. it's more related to the English noun supplicant.

Il m'a supplié de venir – He begged me to come.

Écrivez-moi ! Je vous en supplie ! – Write
to me! I beg you!

To translate the English verb supply, into French,
use *fournir.*

ostensible – ostensible
ostensiblement – ostensibly

Ostensible is another very nice *faux ami.* Ostensible
and *ostensible* are two words with identical spelling,
which came from the same French word, but which
have drifted apart in meaning to the extent that they
verge on being opposites.

In English, ostensible is usually used as "the ostensible reason", or some similar wording, and it means
the reason which is given as true, but is <u>not necessarily true</u>. There is an implication that the real reason may be being concealed.

> The ostensible reason for his visit to Par-
> is was to visit his sister.

In French, the adjective *ostensible* means <u>not hid-
den</u>, <u>out in the open</u>, overt, done with the intention
of being seen openly. You can see that this is very
different than the English meaning.

> *Ce sont des faits publics et ostensibles* –
> They are facts which are public and out
> in the open.

> *son mépris ostensible* – his open scorn

In English, similarly, the adverb ostensibly means <u>apparently but not really</u> or actually. At least not necessarily really or actually. The speaker doubts the truth of the facts.

> He's ostensibly in Paris to visit his sister.

> It seems he works for the government, ostensibly as some kind of lower level bureaucrat, but he may have some other job we don't know about.

And again, ***ostensiblement***, in French means <u>openly</u>, <u>overtly</u>, out in the open.

> *Elle a même bâillé assez ostensiblement* – She even yawned fairly openly.

> *Il a ostensiblement montré son mépris* – He showed his scorn openly.

To translate the English adjective ostensible into French, use *prétendu* or *apparent*.

To translate the English adverb ostensibly into French, use *prétendument, apparemment, en apparence,* or *il paraît que.*

> *Il paraît qu'il est à Paris pour voir sa soeur.*

> *Il est à Paris apparemment pour voir sa soeur.*

organique – organic

The French adjective *organique* means organic in most usages of the word, but it **does not** apply to "organic farming" or "organic foods." The French say *"biologique."*

> *l'agriculture biologique* – organic farming
>
> *Je cherche des pommes biologiques* – I'm looking for organic apples.

Remember, don't say *"organique"* when you are looking for organic foods. Say *"biologique."*

un bigot – a bigot

In English, while a fanatic or a zealot exhibits extreme enthusiasm and devotion to a belief or cause, a bigot is someone who not only is devoted to the cause or belief but shows contempt, intolerance and prejudice against those who are of other beliefs, or who belong to other groups. A bigot can have prejudices having to do with race, class, or whatever, and not necessarily religion.

In French, on the other hand *un bigot* is specifically someone who is <u>excessively religious</u> and who has narrow religious beliefs. However, *un bigot* **does not** necessarily imply the same prejudice against other groups that it does in English.

Bigot can also be used as an adjective in French as in:

> *un homme bigot*

> *une éducation bigote*

but it doesn't mean bigoted, it means excessively religious.

To translate the English word bigoted into French, use *sectaire* or *intolérant*.

To translate "He is a bigot" into French, say *"C'est un homme sectaire et intolérant."*

une apologie – an apology

The English noun, an apology, came in into the language in the 16th century from the French *apologie*, and originally had the meaning of a formal defense against an accusation.

In English, the primary meaning of "make an apology" has evolved to mean to say you are sorry, to say that you regret what you have done, to excuse yourself, to present excuses.

An apology can also mean a sorry example of something as in:

> He's a poor apology for a man.

And finally, in literary speech, an apology can still

mean a defense as in "an exaggerated apology for rationalism".

In French, *une apologie* is still a speech or a piece of writing destined <u>to defend something</u> or to convince people of the correctness of something.

Faire une apologie **does not** at all imply making excuses or saying you are sorry.

> *Il a fait l'apologie du communisme* – He made a defense of communism.

To translate the English word apology, in the sense of excuses, into French, **dont** use *une apologie.* *Une apologie* just doesn't mean the same thing! Say *les excuses.*

To translate the English expression "to make an apology" into French use *"faire des excuses"* or *"présenter des excuses".*

une robe – a robe

In French, the most common meaning for *une robe* is a <u>woman's dress.</u>

Une robe can also mean a <u>robe</u>, like a judge's robe, a priest's robe, or a bathrobe or dressing gown *(une robe de chambre).*

In English, on the other hand, a robe **never** means a woman's dress.

roman – Roman
romanesque – Romanesque
un romancier – a romancer
une romance – a romance

This is kind of complicated, so bear with me. We'll start with:

1. *roman* and Roman.

In English, the adjective Roman means pertaining to or coming from Rome, either the current city of Rome or the ancient Roman Empire.

a Roman holiday

a Roman road, a Roman arch

In French, the adjective *roman* usually refers to the medieval architectural style that we call Romanesque in English.

une église romane

There is also a French noun, *un roman*, which used to refer to an old French type of literature, written in prose or verse, and involving romantic heroes, beautiful princesses, romantic love, and improbable, fabulous adventures. However, currently, *un roman* usually simply means a novel.

un roman policier – a detective novel

To translate the English word Roman into French, use *romain*.

a Roman arch – *une arche romaine*

Let's go on now to:

2. *romanesque* and Romanesque

In English, Romanesque, as we have just mentioned, refers to a medieval architectural syle.

In French, however, *romanesque* refers back to the traditional *roman*. In other words, it implies <u>sentimentality, heroes, improbability and romance</u>.

> *Il y a quelque chose de romanesque dans cette aventure.*

> *Elle a une imagination romanesque.*

> *un comportement romanesque* – romantic and unrealistic behavior

If you are talking about books, *romanesque* can refer to the current day *roman*, or <u>novel</u>, as in:

> *l'oeuvre romanesque de Sartre* – Sartre's novels (as opposed to his plays, poetry, essays, and other writing)

Remember that the French word *romanesque* has nothing to do with the medieval architectural style that we call Romanesque.

3. *un romancier* and a romancer

In English, a romancer is a rather dated and uncommon word but can refer to someone prone to exaggeration and embellishment, or a man who romances women.

In French, *un romancier* or *une romancière* is a <u>novelist</u>:

> *Simenon était un romancier très rénommé.*

This now brings us to:

4. *romantique* and romantic

Although **not** *faux amis*, these two words are discussed here because of their close relationship to the other words we have just been talking about, and because of the possibility of confusing them with these other words.

Romantic and *romantique* both refer to something <u>arousing sentimentality</u>, dealing with feelings of love, and moving the emotions in a somewhat idealized way.

> *le vieux quartier avec ses ruines, un endroit romantique*

You can see that *romanesque* and *romantique* may overlap a little, but they don't really mean the same thing. A James Bond movie is *romanesque*. The play Romeo and Juliet is *romantique*.

Both *romantique* and Romantic (usually capitalized in English), may also refer to the movement of Romanticism at the end of the 18th and beginning of the 19th centuries.

les poètes romantiques

the Romantic poets

Finally we have:

5. *une romance* and a romance

In English, a romance is a story, film, or novel about love. In referring to a relationship, it is a love relationship, often emotional and also often passing.

a summer romance

It can also refer to the simple charm of a place or situation.

In the old town there was romance all around us.

In French, on the other hand, *une romance* is a <u>sentimental ballad</u>, of a type in vogue in the 18th and 19th centuries in France. It's a historical word, but **not** a current word at all.

Romance seems like such a French concept that it is hard to believe that *"romance,"* in the sense we use it in English, is **not** a French word, but it's not!

To translate:

If you want to refer to a romance (book, etc) in French, use *un roman d'amour* or *une histoire d'amour*.

If it's between people it's *une idylle d'amour, une aventure amoureuse,* or just *l'amour.*

If you are referring to ambiance, *poésie,* which can mean poetic charm, comes pretty close.

propre – proper

I'm sorry but this is another rather complicated *faux ami.* **In English**, the adjective "proper" has at least a half dozen usages:

> the proper tools for the job – suitable, correct
>
> give it to the proper person, the proper thing to say – correct
>
> proper behavior, proper dress – according to, or following, social standards and conventions.
>
> in Asia proper – as strictly defined
>
> He never went to a proper school – genuine
>
> a proper night's sleep – good
>
> a proper lady – real
>
> and more.

In French, on the other hand, the two primary meanings of *"propre"* are <u>clean</u> and <u>personal, or one's own</u>:

> *Utilise ta serviette propre* – Use your clean towel.

> *Utilise ta propre serviette* – Use your own towel.

> *Sa réputation n'est pas propre* – clean or spotless (figuratively)

> *mon propre vélo* – my own bike, my personal bike

Note that, in general, *propre* comes after the noun when it means clean, and before the noun when it means personal.

L'amour-propre is a separate compound word meaning self-esteem (literally "love of oneself").

The English word proper **does not** mean either clean, or personal or one's own.

Let's continue now to try to match other secondary meanings of the French word *propre* to the meanings of the English word proper that we listed above.

First, **the French** word *propre* can mean <u>suitable</u> or <u>proper</u>, as in English:

> *Les conditions maintenant sont propres pour une discussion* – suitable, proper

C'est le terme propre – most suitable term to use

This is pretty much the only area where proper and *propre* have the same meaning. If we look at the other meanings of the English word proper, we find:

- "Proper dress" in English means according to social standards. *Propre* does **not** mean according to social standards in French.

- "a proper lady" (a real lady), "a proper school" (genuine), "a proper night's sleep" (good), "the proper person" (correct); all these usages in English would **not** be used in French!

- "in the village proper" (in the village itself), can be expressed in French by *"dans le village, proprement dit"* (thus using a derivative of *propre,* at least).

Is there an overlap in meanings between proper and *propre* ? Yes, but really just for the meaning "suitable". Proper and *propre* have slipped apart for other meanings so that now they barely touch.

propriété – propriety

In English, the noun propriety refers to the state of behaving properly and conforming to conventionally accepted standards.

In French, on the other hand, the noun *propriété* can mean either <u>ownership</u> or <u>property</u>.

propriété collective – collective owner-
ship

propriété de l'État – property of the
State

Thus this is a very simple *faux ami*.

To translate the English word propriety into French,
use *bienséance*.

comédien – comedian

In French *un comédien* or *une comédienne* is **not** a
comedian. He or she is an <u>actor</u> or an <u>actress</u> in the
theater.

Somewhat confusingly, *un acteur* or *une actrice* also
can be an actor or an actress. But while *un comédi-
en* is specifically an actor in the theater, *un acteur* or
une actrice refers to an actor or actress in general,
either in the theater or in the movies.

To translate the English word comedian into French
say *un comique* or *une comique*.

normalement – normally

In French, *normalement* has three different possible
senses.

First of all it can mean <u>in a normal fashion</u> (or "like a
normal person"), as in English:

Hier soir, elle semblait un peu bizarre. Elle ne se comportait pas normalement – Last evening she seemed a bit bizarre. She didn't behave normally.

Hier, tout s'est passé normalement – Everything went in a normal fashion yesterday.

Secondly, *normalement* can mean <u>usually</u>, or <u>ordinarily</u>, again as in English:

Normalement elle travaille le samedi à la boulangerie – Normally (ordinarily) she works Saturdays at the bakery.

However, *normalement* has a third meaning in French. *Normalement* often means <u>provided everything goes well</u> or <u>if all goes as expected</u>.

Normalement, nous arriverons vendredi – If all goes as planned we will arrive Friday.

Normalement je serai là – I expect to be there if all goes well.

Some possible synonyms in French would be *"Si tout va bien nous arriverons vendredi"* and *"En principe nous arriverons vendredi"*.

This third meaning is **very common** in French, and totally foreign in English. "The English word "normally" does not mean "provided everything goes well". It's a true *faux ami.*

un mécréant – a miscreant

Un mécréant and a miscreant both come from the Old French *mescreant*, meaning disbelieving or un-believing.

In French, *un mécréant* still means an <u>unbeliever</u> or a <u>heathen</u>. *(Mécréant,* used as an adjective is con-sidered obsolescent).

In English, a miscreant has changed to mean a lawbreaker. (The meaning heretic is now listed as obsolete).

misérable – miserable

These are two words which still resemble each other greatly in meaning but which have slipped apart in nuance.

In English, miserable has two meanings. It often means unhappy or sad.

> He has been miserable since the death of his daughter.

Secondly, it can refer to unpleasant conditions (which could make you feel unhappy or sad):

> It's a miserable day.

> My body feels miserable all over.

> He earns a miserable salary.

He has a miserable life.

Finally, it can refer to something very small and insignificant:

He got himself in trouble for a miserable little three dollars.

In French, *misérable* **never** means "unhappy or sad" as it does in English.

Misérable means <u>arousing pity</u>. This is not much different than the English meaning of being in unpleasant conditions:

Il vit dans des conditions misérables.

Il a une vie misérable.

Another related meaning for *misérable* is poor, <u>impoverished</u>, wretched, needy, or at the bottom of the social scale:

les populations misérables des pays du tiers-monde.

les vêtements misérables – shabby, worn, in rags, etc

Misérable can also mean insignificant, or <u>arousing scorn</u>. This also is little different than the English meaning:

un salaire misérable

pour une misérable somme de deux euros

Quel misérable !

To review the differences: in French, *misérable* **never** means unhappy. Also, while both miserable and *misérable* can both be used for someone in impoverished circumstances, the meanings differ in nuance:

If you refer to a miserable population, the English words "a miserable population" say that the circumstances are unpleasant and that the people are <u>unhappy</u>, while the French words *une population misérable* says that the people are <u>very poor</u>. In English, miserable **doesn't** specifically mean poor or impoverished.

la misère – the misery

In French, *la misère* has a number of meanings, but the primary meaning is <u>extreme poverty</u> or destitution.

Il est dans la misère – He's poverty stricken, destitute.

Il vit dans la misère – He's living in poverty.

un salaire de misère – starvation wages

La misère can also mean <u>troubles</u>.

Il m'a apporté la misère.

In English, misery does **not** mean poverty. The primary meaning of misery is sadness or suffering.

> The poor dog. We should put him out of his misery.

If you want **to translate** the English word misery into French in the sense of sadness, use *la tristesse*.

If you want **to translate** the English word misery into French in the sense of suffering, use *les souffrances* or *le supplice*.

truculent – truculent

In English, truculent refers to a person and means that he is argumentative and looking for a fight.

In French, the same word, *truculent*, has no such meaning. It also refers to a person or style of speech, but calling someone *truculent* means that he is <u>colorful</u>, <u>picturesque</u>, bigger than life, and usually <u>delightful</u>. When it refers to speech it means colorful and perhaps racy speech.

> *C'était un personnage truculent* – He was a colorful personality.

> *des plaisanteries truculentes et poivrées* – colorful and spicy remarks or jokes

Remember that the French word *truculent* does **not** mean argumentative.

To translate the English word truculent into French, use *agressif.*

Side Note: "having a fierce appearance" is given as an obsolete meaning for the French *truculent*, indicating that the words were once much closer.

trépasser – to trespass

These two words have nothing in common. The French word *trépasser* is a literary euphemistic word that means to <u>die</u>. *Un trépassé* is a <u>dead person</u>.

To translate the English verb "to trespass" into French, a good starting place would be *"entrer sans autorisation"*.

trivial – trivial

In English trivial means of little importance, of little value, banal, commonplace.

In French the meaning *"quelconque et insignifiant"* for *trivial* has become obsolescent. In current French, *trivial* has come to have a completely different meaning.

Trivial now means low, shocking, dirty, and <u>vulgar</u> and refers to speech or actions that are at the lowest levels and go against all societal norms. When referring to language *trivial* means <u>vulgar and obscene</u>.

This is rather important to remember. You can make

a real *faux pas* with this faux amis if you are not careful.

Consider, for example, what can happen if you call someones comment *trivial*, thinking you're just calling it unimportant, but you are actually calling it vulgar and obscene!

engin – engine

In French, *un engin* is a <u>machine</u>, a <u>device</u>, a tool, or a contrivance, but it is **not** an engine or motor:

> *des pinces, des ciseaux et d"autres engins*

The way you say engine or motor in French is *moteur*. If you are talking about a railroad engine or locomotive, the French word is also *la locomotive*.

à-propos – apropos

These words have similar meanings but are used differently.

In English, apropos is an adjective, meaning apt or appropriate:

> an apropos remark

> The remark was very apropos.

In French, *à-propos* is a noun and means <u>aptness</u> or <u>appropriateness</u>.

Il a repondu avec à-propos.

Remember that you can't say "an apropos remark" in French, because *à-propos* is **not** an adjective.

In English "apropos of" can also be a preposition meaning with reference to:

> He made remarks apropos of the new plan.

In French *"à propos de"* means the same thing. (Note that in this case, *à propos* is two words and is not hyphenated).

> *Il a constaté, à propos du plan, que...*

> *Il a constaté, à propos de rien, que ...* – He remarked, not in reference to anything, that ... or, He remarked, for no good reason, that ...

les appointements – the appointments

In French, *les appointements* is only seen in the plural and means the <u>salary</u>. It has nothing to do with the English word appointments

> *Il a réçu ses appointements* – He received his salary.

To translate an appointment into French in reference to a meeting, use *un rendez-vous*.

To translate an appointment into French in reference to being appointed to a position, use *une nomination*.

appointer – to appoint

In French, the verb *appointer* means to <u>pay a salary</u>.

> *Il est appointé au mois* – He is paid monthly.

Appointer can also mean to put a point on a pencil --- in other words, to <u>sharpen a pencil.</u>

To translate the English verb to appoint into French, use *nommer:*

> *Il m'a nommé directeur.*

l'application – the application

In French, *une application* **never** means an application for a job or a university. It also **never** means to ask for something, as it can in English.

In French, *application* **does** refer to the application of paint to a wall, energy to a job, money to a project, to the application of oneself to one's work, or to the application of a rule or a law. All of these usages are as in English.

> *Il a fait deux applications de peinture.*

Il travaille avec beaucoup de application.

C'est une bonne loi en théorie, mais il faut la mettre en application.

To translate:

- To say in French "to submit an application" for a job, use *présenter sa candidature.*

- To say in French "to submit an application" for admission to a university, use *un dossier d'inscription.*

- For an application for membership, *une demande d'inscription.*

- For an application for benefits or for money, use *un formulaire de demande.*

confus – confused

In French, the adjective *confus* can mean confused, as in English:

Il a des idées confuses.

However, **most often**, *confus* means embarrassed:

Je suis confus – I'm very embarrassed.

Elle était très confuse pour ce retard – She was very embarrassed because of the delay.

In English, confused **never** means embarrassed.

un bureau – a bureau

In both French and English a bureau can mean a <u>desk</u>.

In the United States, a bureau can be a government department, as in:

> The Federal Bureau of Investigation

> The Bureau of Indian Affairs

in French, *un bureau* **never** refers to a governmental department. *Un bureau,* in French, is the common name for an <u>office</u>.

> *Elle travaille dans son bureau* – She's working in her office.

A bureau is only **rarely** used for an office in English, and then just for the limited and impersonal case of the distant office of a firm:

> The London bureau of the news agency.

A bureau is **not** used in English for an individual person's office as it is in French.

fatal – fatal

In English, the adjective fatal means <u>causing death</u> or <u>producing failure</u>:

He had received a fatal wound.

There were fatal flaws in the plan.

In French, the adjective *fatal* has these same meanings:

Il a reçu un coup fatal.

un accident fatal

une blessure fatale

une erreur fatale

However, in French, a **very common** meaning for *fatal* is <u>inevitable</u>**:**

C'est presque fatal – It's almost inevitable.

C'est fatal que ça va tourner mal – It's inevitable that that will turn out badly.

In English, fatal **never** means inevitable. Fatal **always** means causing death or failure..

fatalement – fatally

In English, the meanings of the adverb fatally correspond to those of the adjective fatal:

He was fatally wounded.

The plan was fatally flawed.

In **French**, *fatalement* only means <u>inevitably</u> and thus is totally a *faux ami*.

> *Cela devait fatalement tourner mal.*

Synonyms in French are *forcément* and *inévitablement.*

To translate the English word fatally into French, use *mortellement* for a wound, and *irrémediablement* for a plan or project.

le sort – the sort

The French word, *le sort*, has nothing to do with the English word of the same spelling. *Le sort* means the <u>fate</u>, <u>destiny</u>.

> *Il était abandonné à son triste sort.*
>
> *Que sera son sort ?*
>
> *"Le sort fait les parents, le choix fait les amis".*
>
> *Une ironie du sort* – An irony of fate.

embrasser – to embrace

In **English**, to embrace means to hug, when it refers to people. In French this meaning is now obsolescent.

In **French**, *embrasser* used to mean to embrace, but

now usually means means <u>to kiss</u> when it refers to people.

> *Il l'a embrassé sur la joue/ sur la bouche* – He kissed her on the cheek, on the mouth.

> *Je t'embrasse* – In ending a letter or phone call this is a sign of affection.

In both languages the word can be used figuratively in the sense of embracing a philosophy, an idea, or another paradigm.

> *Il a embrassé sa nouvelle carrière.*

To say "to hug someone" or "to give someone a hug" in French, use *enlacer quelqu'un, prendre quelqu'un dans ses bras, serrer quelqu'un dans ses bras*, or, more literary, *étreindre quelqu'un*.

> *Il m'a serrée dans ses bras.*

> *Il m'a enlacée.*

> *Prends-moi dans tes bras* – Embrace me. Give me a hug. Take me in your arms.

fastidieux – fastidious

In English, the adjective fastidious usually refers to a person. It means the person is <u>very concerned with accuracy, detail or cleanliness</u>.

In French, the adjective *fastidieux* refers to a task.

It and implies that the task is <u>boring and tedious</u> because it's dull, monotonous and long.

To translate the English word fastidious into French, use *pointilleux* or *méticuleux*.

une idylle – an idyll

In English, an idyll is a very picturesque, peaceful and happy scene or episode, often in a pastoral setting.

In French, *une idylle* is usually a romance, a little amorous adventure, which is often naïve and innocent.

In literary French, *une idylle* can be a little poem on a pastoral and amorous subject.

l'issue – the issue

In French, *l'issue* is the way out, the <u>exit</u>, and figuratively, the <u>way to get out of a difficulty</u>.

>*route sans issue* – dead end street

>*issue de secours* – emergency exit

>*La situation paraissait sans issue.*

In ordinary English, an issue **does not** have these meanings.

In English, an issue can be a <u>subject for discussion</u> or debate, or a <u>particular date of a periodical</u>:

131

the issue of global warming

the December issue of the magazine

In French, *une issue* is **not** a subject for discussion, **neither** is it an issue of a magazine, and you **can't** use it in those ways.

Side Note: In rare instances one can use "issue out" as a verb in English to mean to exit.

le pétrole – the petrol

In British English, petrol is gasoline.

In French, *le pétrole* is **petroleum**.

pétrole brut – crude oil,

un puits de pétrole – an oil well

To say gasoline in French, use the word *essence*.

un photographe – a photograph

In French, *un photographe* is a photographer.

To translate the English word photograph into French, use *une photo* or *une photographie*.

un hôtel – an hotel

In French, *un hôtel* can mean a <u>hotel</u>.

Je vais rester à un hôtel ce soir.

It can also mean a <u>government building</u>.

L'Hôtel de ville – the Town Hall

Finally, *un hôtel* can mean a <u>private mansion</u> in the city.

In English, hotel has only the first of these meanings, which can be somewhat confusing when you are in Paris and find *"Hôtels"* all around you, which are obviously not hotels.

un récipient – a recipient

In English, a recipient is someone who receives something.

In French, *un récipient* is a <u>container</u>.

To translate the English word recipient into French, use *bénéficiaire* (for the recipient of a grant, etc), or *destinataire* (for the recipient of a letter or package).

l'expérience – the experience

In French, *l'expérience* can mean the <u>experience</u>, as in English.

Elle a trois années d'expérience.

L'expérience lui a montré que – Experience has shown him that

C'était une mauvaise expérience.

However in French, *l'expérience* has a second meaning which it **does not** have in English. *Une expérience* is an <u>experiment</u> or a trial, or a trying out.

> *faire une expérience* – to do an experiment

> *une expérience de chimie* – a chemistry experiment

> *Nous allons faire l'expérience de vivre ensemble* – We are going to experiment with living together, to try out living together.

Side Note: Interestingly, there is a French verb, *expérimenter*, which also means to experiment, to try out, or to test.

> *Il faut expérimenter ce médicament sur les animaux.*

expérimenté – experimented

While *une experience* in French can mean an experiment in English, the meanings are exchanged in the opposite direction with *expérimenté*.

Expérimenté in French means experienced in English.

> *Ce n'est pas une jeune fille, c'est une femme expérimentée* – She's not a young girl, she's an experienced woman.

rester – to rest

In English, to rest means to take a break from activity or work, to allow recuperation.

> He rested after his long run.

To rest something, can also mean to place it or to lean it.

> He rested the ladder against the wall.

> His arm was resting on her shoulder.

> Her hopes rested on the new doctor.

In French, on the other hand, *rester* means to remain.

> *Il y a que trois jours qui reste avant...* – There are only three days remaining before...

> *Restez ici !* – Stay here!

> *Qu'est-ce qui reste à faire ?* – What remains to be done?

To translate the English verb "to rest" into French, use *reposer* or *appuyer*, depending on the sense of the word.

> I need to rest – *Il faut me reposer.*

> Her hopes rest on the doctor – *Ses espoirs reposent sur le médecin.*

He rested the ladder against the wall – *Il a appuyé l'échelle contre le mur.*

la réalisation – the realization

In English, realization has two meanings, a minor one and a common one. The minor, less common meaning is the fulfillment or the achievement of something.

It was the realization of her dreams.

However, by far the **most common** usage of a realization is the act of becoming aware of something as a fact. It's often seen in the form "to have a realization" which means to become aware of something (as true, as fact), to realize.

He had the realization that he had made a mistake.

In French, le réalisation has only one of these meanings, and only the one which is least common in English.

Le *réalisation* **does not** mean the act of becoming aware. It **only** means the turning of something into reality, the fulfillment, the achievement, the carrying out, the production (of a piece of work, a television show, etc), the creation (of a piece of art).

On the other hand, as you will see in the examples below, *réalisation* is used much more broadly and commonly in these senses than realization is in English:

> la dernière réalisation de Cézanne – Cezannes last work of art

> La réalisation de la coupure de bois va être en novembre – The cutting of the wood will be in November.

> Ce projet est en cours de réalisation.

> Le pont de Millau est une belle réalisation.

> Jean est le responsable de la réalisation du film – Jean is in charge of the production of the film.

To translate the English expression "to have a realization", into French, you **can't** say *avoir une réalisation*. It doesn't work. Use *se rendre compte,* or *réaliser*.

> Il s'est rendu compte qu'il a fait une erreur.

> Il a réalisé qu'il a fait une erreur.

réaliser – to realize

The verbs to realize and *réaliser* aren't true faux amis, but I'm discussing them because of their relationship to realization and *réalisation*.

In English, as with realization, the verb to realize has two different meanings, a common one and an uncommon one. It usually means to <u>become aware of</u> a truth. You are quite familiar with this sense.

He realized he had made an error.

However, in a less common usage, to realize can also mean to <u>make something happen</u>:

They will be able to realize their dream.

They realized a good profit from their investment.

In French, the verb *réaliser* **usually** has this second meaning: to <u>make something happen or to fulfill</u>. However, *réaliser* is used much more broadly in this sense than it's English counterpart is, as you will see from the examples below. Most can't be translated into English with the English word realise.

Il a réalisé son rêve – He realised his dream.

Il a réalisé son désir – He achieved his desire.

Il a réalisé des projets – He accomplished several projects.

Il a réalisé un contrat – He made a contract.

Il a réalisé un achat – He completed a purchase.

Il a réalisé des économies – He has succeeded in saving some money.

Il a réalisé le film – He created the film.

Il a réalisé la sculpture – He created the sculpture.

However, *réaliser* can also mean to <u>realize</u>, to <u>become aware</u>, in the English sense. This used to be considered an anglicism and it is still listed in my Petit Robert as as an *anglicisme* with *emploi critiqué*. However my French friends say that it has come into common usage now and is just as acceptable to their ears as *se rendre compte*.

I think what all this means when you put it together is that if you use *réaliser* to mean to become aware, you will definitely be understood, but in rarified circles it might not be considered the best French.

Il a réalisé qu'il avait fait une erreur – He realized that he had made an error.

To summarize:

- **In English**, the primary meaning for realize is to become aware, but in limited circumstances it can mean to make something happen.

- **In French**, the primary meaning for *réaliser* is to make something happen or to fulfill, which is used much more broadly than in English. *Réaliser* can also mean realize in the sense of to become aware. This latter sense used to be considered an anglicism.

apostropher – apostrophe

In English, an apostrophe is a punctuation mark. There is another rare and very literary meaning which is an exclamatory passage in a speech or poem, addressed to someone who is not present.

In French, on the other hand, the verb *apostropher quelqu'un* means to <u>shout at someone to get their attention</u>, or to <u>address someone sharply and rudely</u>. It has nothing to do with the English meanings and it sounds very strange when you hear it. I'm sure that both words came from the same Latin stem and I wonder how they got so far apart in meaning.

Similarly, the French noun *une apostrophe* can be a <u>rude shout</u> in addition being an <u>apostrophe</u>.

> *Les supporters de l'autre équipe nous ont apostrophés* – The fans of the other team shouted rudely at us.

> *On pouvait entendre les apostrophes des automobilistes frustrés* – One could hear the shouts of the frustrated motorists.

l'allure – the allure

In English, allure is the quality of being enticing, attractive, or fascinating.

In French, *l'allure* doesn't mean that at all. *L'allure* means the speed, or pace, and can also mean the bearing or style.

> *Il roule à toute allure* – He's driving at full speed.

> *Les allures naturelles du cheval sont le pas, le trot, et le galop* – The natural paces of a horse are walk, trot and gallop.

> *Il a fière allure* – He holds himself proudly / He has a proud manner about him.

> *Il a de l'allure* – He has style, He has a certain elegance.

To translate the English expression "she has allure" into French, say *elle est attirante, séduisante,* or *attrayante.*

dissimuler – to dissimulate

In English to dissimulate means to conceal and applies to feelings or thoughts.

> He dissimulated his true feelings.

In French, *dissimuler* also means to conceal, but applies to the real world as well as the internal world.

This causes it to sometimes have a very foreign sound to us.

> *Quelque chose était dissimulé sous la couverture* – Something was concealed under the covers.

To dissimulate is simply **not** used this way in English.

subtiliser – subtle, to subtilise

In English, subtle means making use of fine distinctions or nuances. To subtilise is an obsolete English word meaning to make more subtle or refined.

In French, the verb *subtiliser* is similarly related to the French word *subtil* (subtle). Interestingly, *subtiliser* also has the same obsolete meaning as the English word to subtilise: to make more subtle. It can also mean to cut hairs or overdiscuss details.

However, in familiar French **current usage**, *subtiliser* means to <u>pinch or swipe</u> something adroitly on the sly.

> *Quelqu'un m'a subtilisé mon portefeuille dans le métro.*

This usage is common. Since it has nothing obvious to do with subtle, (except, perhaps, that someone had been subtle about swiping it), it may well cause confusion when you see or hear it.

un profane – the profane
profane – profane

In French, *un* or *une profane* is <u>a person who is not initiated</u> into an art, a science or a technique. For example:

> *Je n'ai jamais fait de ski. Je suis un profane* – I've never skied. I'm a beginner (or novice).

> *En peinture, c'est facile d'abuser le profane. Il est beaucoup plus difficile de fabriquer une pièce qui trompera un spécialiste* – In painting, it's easy to take advantage of the uninitiated. It's much harder to make a piece which will fool a specialist.

> *Il y a les choses que les profanes ne voient pas* – There are the things that the uninitiated don't see.

In English, profane is **never** used in this sense. You can't even say "a profane" as a noun. In fact profane is rarely used as a noun at all. Only in an expression contrasting the religious and the secular, as in "the sacred and the profane".

In French, *profane* as an adjective means <u>uninitiated</u> to a religion, and by extension, <u>secular</u>.

However, figuratively, and **most commonly** in current usage in French, *profane* means <u>uninitiated to an art, science, sport, technique</u>, etc.

> *musique profane* – secular music

> *le monde profane* – the secular world

> *Il est profane en ce sujet* – He doesn't know anything about the subject.

In English, profane as an adjective means either <u>secular</u> or <u>irreverent</u>. It does not mean uninitiated.

Historical Note: I even found a citation in one English dictionary indicating that in the past profane did have a meaning of uninitiated into the mysteries of something. This sense was indicated as obsolete. It shows the meanings of profane in the two languages were once closer, but this meaning is not used in current day English.

The verbs to profane and *profaner* both mean to treat something of a sacred character without respect and with scorn, and thus are **not** faux amis.

opiner – to opine

In English, to opine is a somewhat formal way of saying "to give an opinion."

In French, on the other hand, *opiner* means to <u>agree</u>, and *opiner de la tête* means to <u>nod in agreement</u>. Often one shortens *opiner de la tête* to just *opiner*.

Remember, *"Il a opiné"* doesn't mean he gave his opinion. It means he nodded in agreement.

To translate the English expression "to give an opinion" into French, use *exprimer l'avis* or *donner l'avis*.

un slip – a slip

Un slip is not a slip, not at all. *Un slip* is a pair of bikini type <u>underpants</u>, for either men or women, or the <u>bikini bottom</u> of a woman's two piece bathing suit.

> *Quand je suis entré, elle était en soutien-gorge et en slip* – When I came in she was in bra and panties.

> *Il a fourré quelques chaussettes et quelques slips dans sa valise* – He stuffed some socks and underpants into his valise.

> *Elle portait le slip de son maillot de bain sans le haut* – She was wearing her bathing suit bottom but no top.

To translate the English word slip into French in the sense of a piece of women's clothing, it's *une combinaison*. A half slip is *un jupon*.

(As an interesting aside, note that a skirt is *une jupe* and *"–on"* is a diminutive ending in French, hence *un jupon* becomes a half slip.)

A slip can have other meanings **in English**, like

> a slip on ice – *une glissade)*
>
> a slip of the tongue – *un lapsus, une erreur, ma langue a fourché*
>
> a slip in prices – *une chute*
>
> a slip-up – *une erreur, un faux pas*
>
> it slipped my mind – *cela m'est sorti de la tête*
>
> a slip of paper – *une feuille de papier, un bordereau*

Note that, just as with a woman's slip, **none of these** is translated by the French word *slip* either.

You can use *le slip* for a boat slip, though. It is listed in the dictionary as *un anglicisme*.

Side Note: A man's looser underpants, that we would call boxer shorts, are called *un caleçon*.

la promiscuité – the promiscuity

It's easy to assume that two words which appear so identical mean the same thing, but they don't.

In English, promiscuity usually refers to licentiousness. Specifically to having many sexual relationships without discrimination, to having multiple sexual partners.

Her frequent changes of boyfriends is nothing but promiscuity in disguise.

In French, however, the usual meaning of *promiscuité* has nothing to do with multiple sexual partners. *Promiscuité* refers to an unpleasant state of having neighbors too close and too many, in other words: overcrowding.

> *Je n'aime pas la promiscuité de la côte pendant l'été* – I don't like the overcrowding at the coast during the summer.

> *Je ne supporte pas la promiscuité dans les magasins avant Noël* – I can't stand the overcrowding in the stores before Christmas.

Side Note: Interestingly, in the past, promiscuity and *promiscuité* both used to describe a mixture of different elements mingled together without discrimination. This second meaning is now obsolete in both languages, but it well illustrates the common origin of these two words which have drifted so far apart in current usage.

le procureur – procurer
la procuration

Le procureur and the procurer are two words you definitely don't want to confuse.

In English, a procurer is generally someone who procures women for prostitution.

In French, *le procureur* is the <u>public prosecutor</u>.

Another related French word, *la procuration*, has a meaning very different from what one would expect from the English stem, to procure. *La procuration* means the <u>proxy or the power of attorney</u> and has nothing to do with procuring. You might well hear someone say

> *Je vais voter par procuration* – I'm going to vote by proxy.

In legal English, the procuration can mean the same thing, but the word has become dated and is little used.

arcane – arcane

These two words still show their common origin but have slipped apart in how they are used.

In English, arcane is only an **adjective** and means mysterious and understood by few. One would thus say:

> He is trying to understand the arcane rules / the arcane mysteries of the game of go.

In French, on the other hand, arcane is only a **noun**, is used primarily in the plural (as *les arcanes)*, and means the mysteries or the mysterious secrets. Thus, in French one would say:

Il essaie de comprendre les arcanes du jeu de go – He is trying to understand the mysteries / the secrets of the game of go.

Les arcanes des humeurs d'une femme sont trop compliqués pour moi / m'embrouillent toujours – The mysteries of a woman's moods are too complicated for me / always confuse me.

When one says *les arcanes de go*, for instance, to an English speaker's ear it's as if one has left off the noun that arcane is supposed to be modifying --- but in French, *les arcanes* is the noun!

licencier – to license
le licenciement – the licensing

Licencier does not mean to license, or to grant a license to. It means to fire or lay off a worker.

Elle a été licenciée sans raison – She was fired for no reason.

Ils étaient licenciés et réduits au chômage – They were laid off and had to go on unemployment.

If you wish **to translate** the English verb to license into French, use *accorder une licence* or *autoriser*.

Similarly, *le licenciement* means the layoff or the firing. It doesn't mean the licensing.

C'était un licenciement d'une douzaine d'ouvriers – It was a layoff of a dozen workers.

While *licencier* and *le licenciement* are *faux amis*, **la licence** is **not** a *faux ami*. *La licence* has the same three meanings as the English word license:

> *Une licence* can be an official <u>authorisation</u> as in a teachers license, or the license to open a business.

> *La licence* also can mean a <u>liberty</u> that one grants oneself, as in "He takes license with correct grammar".

> And finally, *la licence* can mean license, meaning <u>loose behavior</u>, as in licentousness.

une patente – a patent
patenté – patented

For a related word, in French *une patente* is **not** a patent but was a license to practice a trade or profession in the sense of a receipt acknowledging that you had paid the tax required to allow you to practice your trade. Thus *patenté* means licensed and *patenté* is often used figuratively in slang to give emphasis, as in:

> *C'est un casse-pieds patenté* – He's a total peste (literally it means he acts as if he has a license to be a pest).

The French term for a patent is *un brevet d'invention*.

> He had his invention patented – *Il a fait breveter son invention*.

> He asked for a patent for his invention – *Il a demandé un brevet pour son invention*.

> The patent is pending – *La demande de brevet est déposée*.

un pupille – a pupil

In French, *un* or *une pupille* is a legal word meaning a <u>ward</u> (a minor under the legal care of someone other than his or her parents).

> *un pupille de l'État* – a ward of the State

In an anatomical context, *la pupille* is the <u>pupil of the eye</u>.

Un pupille **does not** mean a student. If you want **to translate** the English word pupil into French in the sense of a student, use *un élève* or *un étudiant*.

la trépidation – trepidation

In English, as you know, trepidation means apprehension, anxiety, and even agitation.

> He was filled with trepidation.

They set off on their trip with a certain amount of trepidation.

In French, on the other hand, the same word, *trépidation*, is related to movement. In talking about a machine or a motor *trépidation* means <u>vibration</u>. In medicine it can refer to <u>trembling</u>. And figuratively, *la trépidation de la vie* refers to the whirl or bustle of life.

Historical Note: You have probably guessed that two words with such similar spelling and appearance must have once been related. Indeed, one of my English dictionaries gives "a trembling motion" as an archaïc meaning for trepidation, showing that the two words used to be closer in meaning.

agoniser – to agonise
l'agonie – the agony

In English the usual meaning of agony is severe pain. It can be physical or mental, it's normally temporary, and one can expect to recover from it.

I was in agony when my appendix burst.

She was in agony over her daughter's illness.

In French, however, the usual meaning of *agonie* is a <u>terminal illness</u>, the <u>act of dying</u>, the <u>throes of death</u>. It's not something that one expects to recover from.

Elle est à l'agonie – She's dying / She's at death's door.

L'agonie de mon père a été très dure – My father's death was very painful / difficult.

To translate the English word agony into French in the mental sense, choose *l'angoisse.*

She was in agony over her daughter's illness – *Elle a été saisie d'angoisse quand sa fille a été malade.*

To translate the English word agony into French in the sense of severe physical pain, use *une douleur épouvantable* or *une douleur horrible.*

I was in agony when my appendix burst – *J'ai eu une douleur épouvantable quand mon appendice a éclaté.*

(Note that the specific English term "death agony" captures the French sense of the word.)

la chair – the chair

La chair has nothing to do with the chair, of course. *La chair* means the <u>flesh</u>.

Ce poulet est bien en chair – That chicken is nice and plump.

Ça me donne la chair de poule – That gives me goose bumps.

la confection – the confection

What comes to the mind of **English** speakers when they hear someone talk about a confection is a fancy **dessert**, usually put together by combining several ingredients. When a confection refers to clothing, it is used figuratively, and thus is a fancy, stylish article of womans clothing.

In French, on the other hand, *la confection* is the **clothing industry**, specifically the ready-to-wear industry.

> *Elle a un emploi dans la confection* – She works in the clothing industry.

> *Ce sont des vêtements de confection* – They are ready-made clothing.

In both languages, the confection or *la confection* can refer to the process of combining things together to make something, but it's a pretty fancy usage in English.

> *Elle est occupée à la confection d'un plat spécial pour ce soir* – She's engaged in the confection of a special dish for this evening.

Similarly, the verb *confectionner* means to make an article of clothing or to prepare a dish of food, etc.

le procès – the process

In French, *un procès* is not a process. It's a <u>trial</u> or other <u>legal proceeding</u>.

> *un procès criminel* – a criminal trial

> *Il va intenter un procès contre elle / Il va lui intenter un procès* – He's going to institute proceedings against her / He's going to sue her.

> *Elle a gagné son procès* – She won her trial.

To translate: If you want to use the English word process in the sense of a gradual series of changes, the usual translation is *un processus*. However, if you are talking about an industrial or chemical process, *un procédé* is better.

> It's an irreversible process – *C'est un processus irréversible.*

> The manufacturing process is... – *Le procédé de fabrication est...*

insulaire – insular

In French, *insulaire* means having to do with an island, or living on an island.

> *Les Irlandais sont un peuple insulaire* – The Irish are an island people.

In English, insular has been used figuratively to mean having the restricted and limited view of an island people, and from that it was generalized to mean having the restricted and limited view of people who lead an isolated life and who have limited exposure to the world. It could refer to someone in a small farming community in the middle of the continent, far from any island.

> They are an insular people – They are a people who have a restricted view of the world and are likely biased by it.

Insulaire doesn't necessarily have this meaning in French. **To translate** the English word insular into French, use *étriqué* or *borné*.

> He has an insular point of view – *Il a une perspective étriquée / un point de vue étriqué.*

l'assurance – assurance

In French, *l'assurance* does mean assurance in the sense of <u>confidence</u>, as in:

> *Il a beaucoup d' assurance* – He's very self-confident.

If you think that you could possibly be misunderstood, you can use *confiance* instead: *Il a une grande confiance en lui.*

L'assurance also means assurance in the sense of a promise or guarantee, as in

> *Il a donné son assurance que ce sera fait* – He has given his assurance that it will be done.

Both of these meanings are exactly as in English.

However, *assurance* doesn't only mean assurance in French. *Assurance* is also the word for insurance. On the other hand, assurance **never** means insurance in English.

> *J'ai une bonne assurance* – I am well insured / I have a good insurance.

And remember that there **is no** French word *"insurance"*. It's *assurance.*

un courtier – a courtier

You'd swear an English word like courtier must be a direct import from French, but the French translation of courtier is not *un courtier*. The French word *courtier* has nothing to do with medieval courts or knights. *Un courtier* is just a broker, someone who acts as a middleman in commercial transactions:

> *un courtier* – a stock broker

> *un courtier d'assurances* – an insurance broker

> *un courtier / négociant en vins* – a wine broker

To translate the English word courtier into French, in the sense of a court personage, the correct word is *un courtisan*.

le pendant – the pendant

In English, a pendant usually refers to a piece of jewelry hanging from a necklace chain. Since "pendant" sounds so French, it's tempting to try to use *un pendant* in French the same way.

In French, however, *un pendant* **never** refers to a necklace or the pendant hanging from it.

Un pendant d'oreille can refer to a drop earring, but you will usually see *le pendant* used as *le pendant de*, meaning the <u>counterpart of</u>, the <u>matching piece</u>, the <u>symmetrical piece</u>, or <u>either one of a pair</u>.

> *Ce tableau est le pendant de l'autre* – This painting is the pair of the other / goes with the other.

> *Ces deux lustres font pendant* – These two chandeliers make a pair.

To translate a necklace pendant into French, the correct word is *un pendentif.*

> C'est un joli pendentif.

Side Note: As an interesting aside, my English

dictionary gives a secondary meaning for pendant which matches the French meaning (a matching piece), but it is used only in specific artistic contexts (for parts of a triptych, for instance), and the average English speaker would not be familiar with it.

rentable – rentable

Rentable in French has nothing to do with rentable. *Rentable* means <u>profitable</u>, giving an income commensurate with the capital invested.

> *C'est une affaire rentable* – It's a profitable business / profitable deal.

> *Avec si peu de clients, ce magasin ne peut pas être rentable* – With so few customers, this store can't be profitable.

Figuratively, and in familiar language, *rentable* can mean something is <u>worth the trouble</u>, or will give results.

> *Je doute que ce voyage soit rentable* – I doubt that this voyage will be worth the trouble / will produce results.

To translate the English word rentable into French, try something like this:

> I think that that house will be rentable this summer – *Je crois que cette maison sera louable pour l'été / Je crois qu'on peut louer cette maison pour l'été / Je crois*

que c'est possible de louer cette maison cet été.

rentabilité – rentability

Similarly, *rentablilité* means <u>profitability</u>.

> *Il est évident que la rentabilité de celui-ci sera meilleure* – It's clear that the profitability of this one will be greater.

> *Ça n'a aucune rentabilité* – That has no profitability.

une rente – a rent

Une rente is not a rent but a <u>private income</u>, such as dividends from stocks, interest from bonds or from savings, proceeds from a pension, or yes, even rental income from property.

> *Il vit de ses rentes* – He lives off his private income.

> *Il a une rente viagère* – He has a lifetime annuity.

> *Elle touche une rente en supplément de son salaire* – She has some income beyond her salary.

To translate the English noun rent into French, use *le loyer.*

What is the rent for that apartment? – *C'est combien, le loyer de cet appartement ? / Quel est le loyer de cet appartement ?*

un rentier – a renter

Thus *un rentier* or *une rentière* isn't a renter, but <u>someone who lives off his or her income</u>, someone who is "a gentleman or a lady of leisure".

> *Un rentier est quelqu'un qui a des revenus suffisants pour vivre sans travailler.*

To translate the English word renter, in the sense of a person who rents, into French, try something like this:

> He's a renter – *Il loue sa maison.*

regretter – to regret

When talking about a thing that has been done, or not done, *regretter* means to <u>regret</u> or to be sorry, exactly as in English.

> *Tu le regretteras !* – You'll regret it! You'll be sorry!

> *Je regrette d'être arrivé en retard* – I'm sorry to have arrived late.

> *Je regrette qu'il ne soit pas ici* – I'm sorry that he's not here.

However, when talking of a person, thing or place, *regretter* means to <u>miss</u>. This meaning has become obsolete in English, and in English current usage to regret never means to miss.

Regretter has a slightly different nuance than *manquer*. If you say,

> *Ma soeur me manque* – I miss my sister.

it means that you miss your sister because she isn't here. But if you say

> *Je regrette mon ancienne maison* – I miss my old home.

it means that you miss something that you no longer have access to, and will no longer be able to have. In other words, something that you have lost for good. *Regretter* thus usually refers to a permanent loss. For example:

> *Je regrette ma jeunesse !* – I miss my youth!

Note that this means "I <u>miss</u> my youth!", and **does not** mean "I <u>regret</u> my youth!" in the sense of being sorry about it, as it would mean in English

> *J'avais de beaux rosiers. Je les regrette beaucoup* – I used to have beautiful rose bushes. I miss them very much.

Il est regretté de tous – He is missed / is mourned by everyone.

un bail – a bail

In English, a bail means the temporary release from jail of an accused person in exchange for a sum of money placed to guarantee his or her return for trial.

He was released on bail.

It can also refer to the money itself.

He put up bail to get his friend out of jail.

In French, *un bail* has neither of these meanings. *Un bail* is a <u>lease</u>, usually a commercial lease.

C'est un bail de sept années – It's a seven year lease.

And, as an extension, in French slang un bail can mean "ages". For example:

Ça fait un bail ! – It's been ages (since we've seen each other)!

To translate the English word bail into French, the correct word is *une caution.*

He was released on bail – *Il a été libéré sous caution.*

He put up bail for his friend — *Il a fourni une caution pour son ami.*

(The *faux amis caution* and *cautionner* were discussed earlier).

une veste – a vest
une jaquette – a jacket

Une veste has too many meanings to go into in this setting, but just let me say that in French, **une veste** is the generic name for what we would call a <u>jacket</u>. In other words, a long sleeved outer garment, coming to the waist or hips and opening in front.

What we would call a vest or a suit vest, with no sleeves, is **un gilet** in French.

And **une jaquette** is a women's tailored jacket, and is a word that is a bit outdated in French. It can also refer to a man's formal or ceremonial morning coat (down to the knees), as well as a book jacket.

Remember that *une jaquette* is not the generic term for a jacket. That term, as I stated above, is *une veste*. You will probably rarely have occasion to refer to *une jaquette* in talking about clothing.

négligé – negligee, negligée

The verb *négliger* in French means to neglect. Thus *elle était en tenue négligée* doesn't mean that she was in a negligee, but means that she was dressed sloppily, slovenly, without care, that her clothing was in a state of "neglect".

Un négligé in the sense we use it when we say a negligee: a light-weight attractive piece of clothing that a woman would wear in privacy or in an intimate setting, is a word that is now pretty much obsolete in French.

To translate the English word negligee into French, one would use *un déshabillé*. More everyday garments would be *un peignoir* or *une robe de chambre*.

> She was in her negligee – *Elle était vêtue en déshabillé.*

It's obvious that you should remain aware of this distinction as you could unintentionally offend if you used the English term, and improperly said that someone was dressed in *"une negligee",* as they might think you were saying that they were sloppily dressed *(en négligé).*

exonérer – to exonerate
exonéré – exonerated

In French, *exonérer* means to exempt from taxes or other fiscal responsibility. It **does not** mean to absolve from blame or to find innocent.

Similarly, *exonéré* means tax exempt. It does **not** mean cleared from blame.

Ces revenus sont exonérés de taxes – This income is tax exempt.

Le gouvernement a exceptionnellement exonéré ces employeurs des cotisations sociales – As an exception, the government has exempted those employers from paying their Social Security payments.

To translate the English word exonerate into French, you can use *disculper* or *innocenter*.

These depositions by witnesses definitely prove him innocent – *Ces dépositions des témoins l'innocentent définitvement.*

After the investigation, the judge exonerated him – *Après enquête le juge l'a disculpé.*

Historical Note: It's interesting to note that exonerate in English originally meant to relieve of a burden or obligation, and *exonérer* in French also originally meant to discharge from an obligation or a duty *(décharger quelqu'un d'une obligation ou d'un devoir),* thus showing the common origin of the two words.

grégaire – gregarious

In English, gregarious means sociable and liking to have company when it describes a person

He has a lot of friends and is very gregarious.

and it means preferring to herd together when describing an animal.

Sheep are a gregarious species.

In French, *grégaire* **only** means <u>following a herd instinct</u>. When used for a person it would imply the person tends to go along the group docilely. It **does not** mean that he or she is sociable.

To translate the English word gregarious in order to say that a person likes to socialize and to have company, use *sociable* or *aimable*. Neither is an exact translation, but they come reasonably close.

la rampe – the ramp

In French la rampe can have two different meanings. It can mean **either** an <u>inclined plane</u> joining two levels, or a <u>handrail</u> or banister.

In English a ramp **only** means an inclined plane joining two levels. A ramp **never** means a handrail or bannister.

> *Il montait l'escalier en tenant la rampe* – (It takes you aback at first, doesn't it!) He went up the stairs holding on to the banister.

In French, *une rampe* also can mean a simple slope

or incline, and it can have some specialized meanings such as, among others:

> *une rampe d'accès* – an access ramp

> *une rampe d'atterrissage* – a landing strip

un sot – a sot

In English, a sot is a chronic drunkard.

In French, *un sot* (or *une sotte* for a woman) is a <u>fool</u> or an idiotic person, lacking intelligence and judgement, but *un sot* says nothing about the person's drinking habits.

> *Qu'il est sot !* – He's really dumb! / He's really a fool!

Note that in the masculine form you don't pronounce the *"t"* in *sot*.

To say a drunkard in French, the correct word is *un* or *une ivrogne*. However, just as in English, there are plenty of slang words in French for drunkard, such as *un soûlard, un éponge,* and *un picoleur*. And of course you can also say *un alcoolique*.

malingre – to malinger, a malingerer

While in English, to malinger means to fake illness (usually to avoid some responsibility), the French meaning has nothing to do with faking. *Malingre* in

French is not a verb, but an adjective meaning <u>feeble, puny or frail</u>. It can even mean sickly, but that is not the primary thrust of the word.

> *C'est un garçon malingre* – He's a frail, puny kid.

Note that *C'est un garçon malingre* has no implication that he is faking anything, malingering in any way, or that he is a malingerer.

There isn't any simple, one word translation of to malinger into French. You'd have to say:

> *Il fait semblant d'être malade* – He's making believe he's sick.

or in slang:

> *Il tire au flanc* – He's malingering.

To say someone is a malingerer, you'd say:

> *C'est un faux malade / une fausse malade* or *C'est un tire-au-flanc.*

une courbature – a curvature

If you hear someone in French talking, for example, about having *une courbature dans le dos* it's easy to mistakenly think that they have a curvature of the back. However, *une courbature* is an <u>ache</u>, not a curvature, and thus *une courbature dans le dos* is not a curved spine but a backache.

If you want **to translate** the English word curvature into French, the closest word is *une courbure* if you are talking about a line, a surface, the spine or some other body part. If it's a curve in the road you could theoretically use *une courbure* here as well, but the common word is *un virage*.

une commodité – a commodity

In English, a commodity is a raw material or a substance which can be bought and sold.

In French, however, the noun *une commodité* comes from the adjective *commode* (convenient, suitable, comfortable, etc) and thus *une commodité* means a convenience.

> *Elle aime la commodité de sa chambre bien aménagée* – She likes the convenience of having her bedroom so nicely fixed up.

> *Il apprécie la commodité du logement si près de son travail* – He appreciates the convenience of a lodging so close to his work.

Unfortunately, **in translating** the English word commodity into French, there isn't a good synonym that works all the time. According to the context you might use *la marchandise* or *la denrée,* while in stock exchange language, a commodity market is *un marché des matières premières* (a market in basic materials).

une radio – a radio

The French word *radio* is an abbreviation for *radio-télégraphie sans fils.* Thus, *une radio* can mean a radio in the same sense as in English.

However, *une radio* is also an abbreviation for *une radiographie,* and thus *une radio* is also the standard word for an X-ray.

> *Heureusement ses radios sont normales.*
> *Elle ne s'est pas cassé la jambe* – Fortunately her X-rays are normal. She didn't break her leg.

Rayons X can be used to refer to the short electromagnetic waves that we call X-ray waves, but an X-ray is *une radiographie* or *une radio,* and X-ray therapy is *radiothérapie.*

If you say to someone in French that you are going to get an *X- ray* or *un rayon X,* they will look at you blankly. There is no word *X-ray* in French.

indemne – indemnified

In English, to indemnify someone means to compensate them for a loss.

In French, the verb *indemniser* means sustantially the same thing, to compensate someone so that they will come out of the situation without loss, unharmed. However, the adjective ***indemne*** has come to mean simply <u>unharmed</u> and has lost the sense of compensated for a loss. Thus:

Il est sorti de l'accident indemne.

means that he came out of the accident <u>unharmed</u>. It **does not** mean that he was compensated for the accident.

succéder à – to succeed

In French, the verb *succéder à* means to succeed in the sense of to follow after, to inherit, to take the place of, while *réussir* means to succeed in the sense of accomplishing.

In English, on the other hand, to succeed has both senses.

> *Elle a succédé à son père à la direction de l'entreprise* – She succeeded her father and took over the direction of the business.

> *Tous les gouvernements qui se sont succédés depuis quarante ans ont....* – All the governments who have succeeded each other for the past forty years have...

> *Enfin ! Il a réussi à arriver à l'heure !* – Finally! He has succeeded in arriving on time! / He has managed to arrive on time!

Il a réussi son examen – He succeeded in passing his exam / He passed his exam.

What is **important to remember** is that you can't use *succéder à* when you are talking about success in doing something.

l'étable – the stable

While the context is the same (keeping animals), the meaning is not.

In English, a stable is for horses.

In French, *une étable* is a cowshed or cowbarn, while *une écurie* is a stable (for horses).

le hangar – the hangar

While we are on the subject of farm buildings let's consider *un hangar*. Yes, *un hangar* on a farm!

In English, the word hangar is used almost exclusively for a large storage facility for airplanes (or helicopters).

In French, *un hangar* is a generic word for a large shelter, and unless you work at an airport you are more likely to hear *un hangar* used for a storage building for farm equipment on a farm, as a warehouse for material, or as a boathouse for storing boats, etc.

Il va garer son tracteur dans le hangar

– He's going to park his tractor in the barn.

Possible French near-synonyms are *une grange* for a barn, and *un entrepôt* for a warehouse.

le groin – the groin

Le groin in French is the <u>snout</u> of an animal and has nothing to do with the groin.

To translate the English word groin into French, the correct word is *l'aine.*

la combinaison – the combination

While the French word *combinaison* does mean the combination as in English (including even the combination of a safe), in French there are <u>a number of items of clothing</u> that are also referred to as *une combinaison*. These include:

a woman's full slip,

and various one piece suits such as:

a one piece ski suit,

a deep sea diver's suit, an aviator's suit, or an astronaut's suit,

a wet suit for a swimmer or snorkeler,

and finally, the one-piece mechanic's type work suit that is referred to as coveralls in the U.S., and as a boilersuit in the United Kingdom.

In addition, *une combinaison* can also refer to a plan devised to solve a problem:

> *Il faut trouver une combinaison pour en sortir* – We need to find a solution / a maneuver to get out of this fix.

le parfum – the perfume

Le parfum can mean the perfume or the scent, as in English, but it has another usage which sounds strange to our ears. *Le parfum* is used to designate the flavor when there is a choice of flavors, for example: with ice cream or yogurt.

> *Quel parfum de glace voulez-vous ?* – What flavor of ice cream do you want?

> *N'importe. J'aime tous les parfums* – It doesn't matter, I like all the flavors.

une grappe – a grape

Une grappe in French doesn't mean a grape. *Une grappe* means a bunch of grapes if you are talking about grapes, or a cluster or a bunch of flowers if you are discussing flowers.

If you want to say a grape in French, as we learned earlier in the book, it's *un raisin*.

La grappe is also used in the following slang expression:

> *Lâche-lui la grappe !* – Leave him alone!

> *Lâche-moi la grappe !* – Leave me in peace! / Get off my back! / Quit hassling me!

la période – the period

In English, the period can have a number of different meanings. But the French word, *une période* corresponds only to <u>a period of time</u>.

> They will be here for a period of two weeks – *Ils seront ici pendant une période de deux semaines.*

> Picasso's Blue Period – *la période bleue de Picasso*

> It's the second period of the game – *C'est la deuxième période du jeu.*

However, **in French** *une période* **doesn't** have the other English meanings, and if you use it as if it does, people won't understand you.

First of all, in casual English, a "period" can refer to <u>menstruation</u>. This doesn't work in French. In French, menstruation can be translated as *la menstruation* in a medical or physiologic context, or as *les règles* in an informal setting.

I have my period – *J'ai mes règles*.

Secondly, if you are referring to a "period" as the <u>puntuation mark</u> at the end of a sentence, you should translate it as *un point*. *Un point* can even be used figuratively for emphasis in the same way as "Period!" is used in English:

> You can't go to the party, period ! – *Tu ne peux pas sortir ce soir. Un point, c'est tout !*

Thirdly, if you are talking about a <u>historical</u> "period", the correct translation is *une époque* or *une ère*.

> The actors were dressed in costumes of the period– *Les comédiens étaient en costumes d'époque.*

Finally, in a school setting we refer to a "period" when we are talking about a <u>class time</u>.

> I have History in my fourth period today.

Une période is not used that way in French. You'd say: *J'ai histoire en quatrième heure aujourd'hui.*

contrôler – to control
le contrôle – the control

In French, the **verb** *contrôler* has two different meanings. The first meaning, as for its counterpart in English, is to <u>exert power over</u> or to direct the course of.

In the same way, the French **noun** *le contrôle* has two different meanings, of which the first is <u>the exertion of power</u> or influence.

> *Elle a contrôlé ses réactions à la mauvaise nouvelle* – She controlled her reactions to the bad news.

> *L'armée maintenant exerce son contrôle dans tout le pays* – The army is now in control of the entire country.

However the second meaning of *contrôler* in French is to <u>examine</u>, <u>check</u>, verify or test, and the second meaning of *un contrôle* is an <u>examination</u>, a <u>check</u>, a verification or a test.

> *Vitesse contrôlée par caméras* – Speed checked by cameras. (Note that this **doesn't** mean speed <u>controlled</u> by cameras, it means speed <u>checked</u> by cameras.)

> *J'ai un contrôle de maths aujourd'hui* – I have a math test today.

To control and a control don't have this meaning in English.

Finally, in English, "a control" has a specialized meaning in a scientific experiment. To translate a control in the scientific sense into French, use *un témoin*. A control group is *un groupe témoin*.

la morale – the morale

le moral – the morals (remember that these are *faux amis*)

These two words got switched around in making the voyage from French to English: *La morale* means the morals and *le moral* means the morale. That may sound a bit complicated so let me illustrate it with a few examples. First we'll look at *le moral :*

> *Comment va le moral ?* – How is your morale?
>
> *Il a le moral à zéro* – His morale is at zero / He's really down.
>
> *Ça lui a sapé le moral* – That undermined his morale.

Now we'll look at *la morale:*

> *La Morale est la science du bien et du mal* – Morals (Ethics) is the study of good and evil.
>
> *La morale chrétienne / hédoniste* – Christian / hedonistic morals
>
> *Elle se conforme à la morale* – She conforms to good morals.
>
> *C'est une morale sévère* – It's a severe moral code.

This is so unintuitive for an English speaker that it

will probably take some time before you can get it right without reflecting. Just remember that you have to reverse the meaning of the two words.

It is a bit complicated by the fact that both words are pronounced the same in French, (the way we pronounce "morale"). You can often tell the meaning by context, but what also tells them apart for a French person is whether he or she hears a *le* or a *la* with the word. So remember, if you want to say the English word morale, it's *le moral*, which is the masculine word in French. Say *le, mon, son* or *ton moral* and you'll have it right.

les boots – the boots

The noun *les boots* is a recent inport into French from English, and the use of *les boots* is restricted specifically to <u>dressy ankle-length city boots</u>. Thus we have:

> **Les boots**, which are ankle length city boots.

> **Les bottines**, which are fitted mid-calf boots.

> **Les bottes**, which is the general or generic word for boots, and which also refers to high boots such as riding boots *(bottes de cheval* or *bottes de cavalier).*

> **Les godillots**, which are military boots

and, in slang, big old country shoes, what we would call clodhoppers.

Les cuissardes, which are thigh boots (note the word *cuisse* which means thigh), which a fisherman might wear while wading, for instance.

On the other hand, some footwear which we refer to as boots, the French refer to as shoes *(chaussures).* For example,

Les chaussures de ski, which are ski boots.

Les chaussures de marche, which are hiking or walking boots.

To avoid confusion, the thing to remember is that if you refer to *les boots* and you are thinking of a large pair of outdoor boots, people are likely to misunderstand you, as *les boots* refer to specific short city boots.

Side Note: If you want to translate to "boot up" a computer, the French term is *initialiser l'ordinateur.*

le froc – the frock

We would most likely recognize a frock as a woman's or girl's dress. Historically a frock had several other meanings, most prominently a priest's or monk's habit, hence the expression "a defrocked priest" in

English and the corresponding verb *défroquer* (to defrock), in French.

In French, un froc also used to refer to a monk's habit, but now, in French slang, *un froc* refers to a pair of <u>pants</u> *(pantalons).*

> *Il a eu si peur qu'il a fait dans son froc* –
> He was so scared he went in his pants.

It's not a common word, but the thing to remember is that, rather than being a dress, *un froc* is a pair of pants.

une mitaine – a mitten

If you are looking for mittens, the correct word is *moufles. Mitaines* in French are gloves with sawed off fingers like bicycling gloves. *Mitaines* are **not** mittens.

> *Il faut porter les moufles* – You need to wear your mittens.

Side Note: My English dictionary shows mitten coming from the Old French *mitaine*. Mitten probably entered English from French many years ago, back when *mitaines* were some kind of mittens. Only in Quebec, which has retained a more ancient French, are *mitaines* currently mittens. In France if you say *mitaine* you will be misunderstood for sure.

les coordonnées – the coordinates

While in mathematics, *les coordonnées* refer to the coordinates of a point on a Cartesian plane, and in geography, to points of longitude and latitude, you are most likely by far to hear:

> *Donnez-moi vos coordonnées, s'il vous plaît.*

which means:

> Please tell me how to contact you / Please give me your <u>address and phone number</u> (and email address, perhaps).

This is a very common expression! On the other hand, you would never hear "Give me your coordinates" in English, unless you were doing some form of global positioning.

On the other hand *coordonner* (the verb) and *coordonné* (as an adjective), are **not** *faux amis* and do mean to coordinate and coordinated, as you would expect.

l'agrément – the agreement

In English, agreement can have several meanings.

First, it can mean the approval or <u>consent of an authority</u>.

> We will have to get the agreement of his boss before we can proceed.

Secondly, it can mean a harmony of opinions:

> There is wide agreement that…

> Are we in agreement that…?

> They nodded in agreement.

Thirdly, agreement can mean a formal accord.

> They signed a trade agreement / an arms control agreement.

Fourthly, agreement can refer to a compatibility or consistency between two ideas or observations:

> The testimony of all the witnesses was in agreement.

In French, *l'agrément* can have **only** the first of these meanings. It can refer to the permission or consent of an authority, the same as its English counterpart.

> *J'ai l'agrément du propriétaire pour le faire.*

On the other hand, in French, *l'agrément* **never** means a harmony of opinions, **nor** a formal accord, **nor** a compatibility between observations or ideas.

By far the **most common** meaning for *agrément* in French is attractiveness or charm, and in certain expressions, pleasure.

Agreement **never** means attractiveness, charm, or pleasure in English.

First let's look at how *agrément* is used in French to mean pleasure:

> *Ce sera un voyage d'agrément* – It will be a pleasure trip.

> *Ce sont des livres d'agrément* – They are light reading / I'm reading them just for pleasure.

Second, let's look at how it's used to mean charm and attractiveness.

> *C'est une maison sans agrément* – It's a house without any attractiveness or charm.

> *C'est une maison avec beaucoup d'agrément* – It's a house with a lot of charm.

> *J'ai trouvé la ville sans agrément* – I found the city to be without any charm.

To translate the English concept of an agreement in the sense of a harmony of opinions, or in the sense of a formal agreement, into French, use *un accord*.

> Are we in agreement?– *Est-ce que nous sommes d'accord ?*

a trade agreement – *un accord commercial*

To translate in agreement into French in the sense of being consistent with, try one of the following:

These results are in agreement with ... – *Ces résultats concordent avec... or Ces résultats sont en conformité avec...*

agrémenter – to agree

Since *agrément* means attractiveness and charm, *agrémenter* means to <u>add attractiveness and charm</u>, to <u>fix up</u>, to <u>adorn</u>. *Agrémenter* has nothing to do with to agree.

There is no single word in English which expresses *agrémenter* well but the following examples will make clear what it means:

Elle a agrémenté son ensemble avec un joli collier – She added to the attractiveness of her outfit with a pretty necklace.

Le salon a été agrémenté avec plusieurs tableaux – The living room had been decorated with several paintings.

To translate the English verb to agree into French, the best choices are *s'accorder* or *être d'accord*.

We agree – *Nous sommes d'accord.*

He agrees with you – *Il est d'accord avec toi.*

They agreed to live together – *Ils se sont mis d'accord pour vivre ensemble.*

désigner – to design
dessiner – to design

In French, the verb *désigner* does not mean to design. It means to <u>designate</u>, to <u>point out</u>, to indicate, or even, by extension, to <u>choose</u>.

For example:

Elle a été désignée par un vote des membres – She was designated by a vote of the members.

Leur entreprise a été designée pour commencer le travail – Their company was designated / was chosen to begin the job.

Il désigne du doigt un village sur la carte – He points out a village on the map with his finger.

Je lui ai désigné la bonne route – I indicated the correct route to him / I pointed out the best route to him.

Il faut désigner un jour pour le faire – It's

necessary to designate (or choose) a date to do it.

> *M. Dupont est son successeur désigné –* Mr. Dupont is his designated successor.

Similarly, the French verb **dessiner** usually doesn't mean to design, but rather, to <u>draw</u>.

> *Il a dessiné un paysage au crayon –* He drew a landscape in pencil.

> *Je ne sais pas dessiner –* I don't know how to draw.

> *Il l'a dessiné de mémoire –* He drew it from memory.

Dessiner, by extension, can mean to <u>make apparent</u>, to show off, as in:

> *Cette robe dessine très bien les formes de son corps –* That dress shows the curves of her body very well.

In a stretch, *dessiner* can be translated as <u>design</u>, as in

> *Elle a dessiné les costumes pour le film –* She sketched / designed the costumes for the film.

but even here the French meaning of *dessiné* is between drew up and designed. To design is **not** a primary meaning for *dessiner*.

To translate the English verb to design into French, the best choice is *concevoir* if you are talking about a plane, a car, a building, etc. If you are talking about an article of designer clothing, use *créer*.

> *Il a bien conçu cette maison* – He designed that house well.

> *Cette voiture a été conçue pour rouler vite* – That car was designed to go fast.

> *Cet outil était conçu pour cet usage / ce travail* – This tool was designed for this use / this job.

And finally, the words *le design* and *le designer* are nouns which were borrowed from English as recently as the 1960's. They have pretty much kept their English meanings. The *"er"* at the end of *designer* is pronounced roughly as in English, or as a light French *"eur"*.

> *design industriel* – industrial design

> *un designer graphiste* – a graphic designer

> *Leur salon est meublé en design* – Their living room is furnished in designer furniture.

> *L'immeuble a été refait par un designer* – The building was redone by a designer.

débonnaire – debonair

In English, debonair means suave, elegant, charming, self-assured, urbane and sophisticated.

In French, on the other hand, *débonnaire* means mild-mannered, easy-going and good natured, that is to say: affable and genial.

It's not the same thing! I discovered this *faux ami* while watching an American movie in France with French subtitles. One of the characters was described in English as "meek" and the subtitler translated meek as *"débonnaire"*.

As you might imagine, I was struck by this! It turns out that *débonnaire* is not such a good translation for meek. *Doux*, *docile* or *humble* would have been much better. But the very fact that the translator could even consider *débonnaire* as a translation for meek shows how different the meaning of *débonnaire* is from that of debonair.

To translate the English word debonair into French, try the following:

> He looks very debonair – *Il est vraiment élégant*.

> He is debonair – *Il est d'une élégance nonchalante*.

Historical Note: One source pointed out that the derivation of both of these words is from Old French in the expression *"de bon aire"* meaning of good disposition. Thus the current French meaning mild-mannered and easy-going fits the original meaning fairly well.

une décade – a decade

In English, a decade is a period of ten years.

In French, *une décade* is almost always a period of <u>ten days</u> (although as *un anglicisme*, the English meaning can occasionally be heard).

If you want to refer to a period of ten years in French, the correct word is *une décennie*.

une gratuité – a gratuity

A gratuity, **in English**, is a tip.

La gratuité **in French**, has nothing to do with a tip. It refers to the character of being <u>free, without charge</u>.

> *la gratuité de l'enseignement* – free education

It can also mean gratuitousness, the property of being without good cause.

> *la gratuité d'une insulte* – the gratuitousness of an insult

You probably won't have occasion to use *la gratuité* very often, but **what you need to remember** is that, even though a gratuity sounds like it came direct from French, you **can not** say *"Je vais lui donner une gratuité"* to mean you are giving him a tip. It's wrong. The correct word for a tip is *un pourboire.*

un cavaleur – a cavalier

Un cavalier in French does mean a horseman, a knight in chess, or a cavalryman.

However, be careful not to mistakenly call someone *un cavaleur*, which means a run-around, <u>woman-izer</u> and skirt-chaser.

capillaire – capillary

The adjective *capillaire* does mean capillary in an anatomical context, as you would expect.

> *les vaisseaux capillaires* – the capillary vessels

However *capillaire* has another very surprising meaning. It means having to do with hair styling:

> *une lotion capillaire* – a hair lotion

> *les soins capillaires* – hair care, hair treatment

ponctuel – punctual
ponctuellement – punctually

The French adjective ** *ponctuel*** can mean <u>on time</u>, similarly to the English word punctual.

However, while **the English** word punctual has only this meaning, **the French** word *ponctuel* has other meanings which can take you aback if you hear or read them without knowing what they mean.

First of all, by extension, *ponctuel* can mean <u>meticulous and punctilious</u> in one's work, always getting the job done correctly and on time. This meaning is a stretching of the usual meaning of punctual in English (but gives you an idea where the English word punctilious came from).

In science, *ponctuel* can mean related to <u>a point source</u>.

> *une source lumineuse ponctuelle* – a pinpoint light source

Finally, *ponctuel* can refer to something which happens <u>just once</u>, as an exception, or in a pin-point manner.

> *C'était une intervention ponctuelle des autorités* – It was a single / one-time intervention by the authorities.

> *C'est une grève ponctuelle. Ils vont travailler demain* – It's a one-day strike. They'll be working tomorrow.

Ce sont des changements ponctuels –
They are just pinpoint changes.

You can say the same thing for the adverbs **ponctuellement** and punctually. *Ponctuellement* can mean punctually in the sense of on time, but it can have other surprising meanings. For example, just last night I heard a restaurant owner say, in describing certain clients:

Ils viennent ponctuellement.

He didn't mean that they arrive punctually. He meant that they come now and then, sporadically, in a "point-like" fashion. This was made clear by his next sentence:

Ils ne sont pas les clients reguliers.

la vacation – the vacation

You can't say *la vacation* and expect it to mean the vacation. The French word for vacation is *les vacances*.

I'm going to take my vacation in July – *Je vais prendre mes vacances en juillet.*

Une vacation, in French, is a predetermined period of time set aside, for an attorney or for an expert, for example, to accomplish a specific task. It can also refer to the payment for the period of time. The closest word in English is probably a session, or the payment for a session.

le cargo – *the cargo*

In French, *un cargo* is a freighter.

in English, the cargo is what is carried in the freighter.

To translate the English word cargo into French, the correct word is *la cargaison.*

> *Il y avait une grande cargaison dans le cargo* – There was a lot of cargo in the freighter.

achever – **to achieve**

The verbs *achever* and to achieve have meanings close enough that they may be confused, but to achieve **never** means *achever*.

In English, to achieve means to succeed at, or to reach a desired goal.

In French, *achever* means to end, to finish, to terminate or to <u>conclude</u>.

Before you decide that there's almost no difference between the meanings in the two languages, let me give you some examples of the use of *achever* where you would never use achieve:

> *Il s'est dressé en achevant ses mots* – He stood up after finishing what he had to say. (literary usage)

Ses ennuis ne sont pas achevés / sont loin d'être achevés – His troubles aren't over / are far from being over.

Laissez-le achever / terminer ce qu'il veut dire – Let him finish what he wants to say.

Thus, you won't be fooled. If you see:

J'ai achevé d'arroser les jardins.

you will know that it doesn't mean "I succeeded in watering the gardens" or "I accomplished watering the gardens". You will know that it means "I <u>finished</u> watering the gardens".

Achever can be a bit formal or literary. A couple of more informal synonyms (or almost synonyms), in French, would be *finir* or *terminer*.

Achever has another meaning which is less commonly seen. It can mean to "finish off", to <u>annihilate</u> or to defeat. To achieve **never** means to annihilate or defeat in English.

Cette perte l'a achevé – That loss finished him off.

Ils ont achevé leur ennemis – They defeated their enemies / They annihilated their enemies.

To translate the English verb to achieve into French,

use *réussir, accomplir, réaliser, arriver à,* or *atteindre.*

> He will achieve his goal – *Il va atteindre son but / Il va réaliser son objectif / Il va atteindre son objectif.*

> He achieved a great deal – *Il a accompli beaucoup de choses.*

> They achieved the impossible – *Ils ont réussi l'impossible.*

l'achèvement – the achievement

This faux ami is exactly parallel to the one above.

In English, the achievement is a task successfully accomplished, or, more simply, a success.

In French, on the other hand, *l'achèvement* means the <u>completion</u>. Just as with to achieve and *achever*, superficially you might think that these two mean the same thing, but just as with achieve and *achever*, they **don't!** Consider:

> *La route va être fermée jusqu'à l'achèvement des travaux.*

This doesn't mean the road will be closed until the success of the work. It means the road will be closed until the <u>completion</u> of the work.

To translate the English word achievement into

French, use *un succès, une réussite, un exploit, un accomplissement.*

What an achievement! – *Quel exploit !*

That's only one of her many achievements – *Ce n'est qu'un de ses nombreux succès / ses nombreux exploits.* (*un de ses nombreux achèvements* obviously wouldn't work. It doesn't mean the same thing.)

l'action – the action

L'action does mean the <u>action</u> in most cases. Where it can confuse you though, is in a financial context, where ***une action*** means a <u>share of stock</u>.

Il a des actions de Microsoft – He has shares in Microsoft.

Il y a eu une hausse des actions à la Bourse hier – The stocks rose on the Stock Exchange yesterday.

Similarly, ***un actionnaire*** is a <u>stockholder</u>.

Il est l'actionnaire majoritaire – He is the majority stockholder.

l'adresse – the address

L'adresse in French overlaps with the English word address in a couple of its meanings: It does mean address in the sense of the coordinates or <u>street address</u> of a building or home.

> *Ils ont échangé leur adresse* – They exchanged their addresses.

It also can refer to an <u>internet address</u>, just as in English.

So far so good. But now we come to a meaning for address in English which *l'adresse* doesn't have in French:

In English, an address can be a <u>major speech</u>, given at a conference for instance. This kind of address would not usually be translated as *une adresse* in French, but as *un discours, or une allocution.*

> He gave a major address at the conference – *Il a fait un discours important à la conférence / au congrès.*

Finally we come to meanings for *adresse* in French which address doesn't have in English.

In French, *une adresse* can refer to the <u>response from a parliament</u> to the wishes of a king in a constitutional monarchy. This is a dated usage which you'd probably only encounter in a history text. (However, the English meaning of a major speech may have come from this French usage.)

For a more important usage, restricted to French, *l'adresse* refers to <u>skill and dexterity</u>, either physical or mental. In English, this usage is now dated and just about obsolete.

> *Ce travail va exiger de l'adresse* – This work is going to require skill.

> *Son travail est dénué d'adresse* – His work is crummy.

> *Il lui faudra une sacrée adresse pour se tirer de / pour se sortir de cette situation délicate* – He'll need a lot of skill / diplomacy to get himself out of that ticklish situation.

une notice – a notice

In French, *une notice* has much fewer meanings than the English word notice.

The first meaning of *une notice* is a <u>little summary in the front of a book</u>, with a brief biographical sketch of the author and a summary of the contents. This is obviously a fairly resticted usage and you are unlikely to come across it very often.

On the other hand, *une notice* also is a <u>manufacturers instruction booklet</u> or insert. This is a very common usage and you will clearly encounter it frequently.

> *Avant de l'utiliser il vaut mieux lire la notice !* – Before using it you should read the instructions.

In English, the noun "a notice" has lots of meanings, and you **can't** translate any of them by *une notice*. I'll give you some examples with possible translations:

I gave him notice that I'd be late – *Je l'ai averti / Je l'ai prévenu que j'allais être en retard.*

Closed until further notice – *Fermé jusqu'à nouvel ordre / jusqu'à nouvel avis.*

If you want me to do it I will need a full week's notice in advance – *Si vous voulez que je le fasse je vais avoir besoin d'un délai d'une bonne semaine / de huit jours.*

There's a notice on the wall – *Il y a une affiche au mur.*

He left a notice on his door – *Il a laissé un écriteau / une pancarte sur la porte.*

Did anybody take notice of that? – *Est-ce que quelqu'un a fait attention à cela ? / Quelqu'un a-t-il prêté attention à cela ?*

Note that there is **NO** French **verb** *"noticer"* to correspond with the English verb to notice. **It doesn't exist.** Use *remarquer* or *apercevoir* to translate the verb notice.

I didn't notice anything – *Je n'ai rien*

remarqué / Je ne m'en suis pas rendu compte.

Nobody noticed him – *Personne ne l'a aperçu / Personne ne l'a remarqué.*

un dispositif – a disposal

Earlier we discussed the French verb *disposer de* which means to have at ones disposal, and *disposer* (by itself), which means to arrange.

We are now going to discuss the noun **un dispositif** which also has nothing to do with disposing or with a disposal. *Un dispositif* is usually a <u>device</u> of some kind.

> *un dispositif d'alimentation* – a power unit (for a computer, for instance)
>
> *un dispositif d'alimentation papier* – a paper feeder (on a printer)
>
> *un dispositif de visualisation* – a display device
>
> *un dispositif de stockage* – a storage device (computer)
>
> *un dispositif de préchauffage* – a preheating device (for a car)

Un dispositif has a second, somewhat related meaning. It can refer to a <u>total system</u> for getting something done, the total machinery for accomplishing it (speaking figuratively).

>*un dispositif de défense* – a defense system
>
>*le dispositif de manoeuvre* – the system or mechanism for steering a vehicle (a car, for example)
>
>*un dispositif gouvernemental pour la réduction du chômage* – a government system / program for reducing unemployment
>
>*Il y a un important dispositif policier devant le Sénat* – There is an important police presence in front of the Senate.

le découvert, la découverte – the discovery

La découverte does indeed mean the <u>discovery</u>. It comes from découvrir, to "un-cover". For example:

>*Cela a mené à la découverte d'un complot* – That led to the discovery of a plot.
>
>*Ils sont partis à la découverte de la ville* – They left to explore the city.

Le découvert, however, means the <u>overdraft</u>. It also comes from découvrir but it comes from a different direction: It comes from the idea of a check or a withdrawal being "un-covered" or "not-covered".

> *Vous avez mis votre compte à découvert*
> – You've overdrawn your account.

> *Vous avez un découvert autorisé de mille euros* – You are covered for an overdraft of up to a thousand euros. You are allowed up to a thousand euros overdraft without serious consequences / without us bouncing your check.

> *Votre compte est à découvert de 1435 euros* – Your account is overdrawn by 1435 euros.

Note from the two last examples that it is not always immediately obvious from the wording whether you are allowed an overdraft or whether you have overdrawn. You can almost always tell from context though.

Découvert is also an **adjective** meaning <u>bare</u> or uncovered (head, shoulders, etc), or open and <u>exposed</u> (for a place).

Finally, *à découvert* is an **adverb** meaning openly, without being covered, <u>while exposed</u>. For example:

> *Il faut avancer à découvert* – We have to advance without cover / We have to advance even though we'll be exposed.

une amende – amend

In English, to amend means to make small changes in a document. The noun, an amendment, refers to one of those changes.

In French, the words *amender* and *l'amendement* can have pretty much the same meanings. *Amender* can mean to make small changes in a document. *Un amendement* is one of those changes.

More generally, however, *amender* can mean to improve something by making changes in it, especially to improve farmland by fertilizing it.

> *Ce champ a été amendé avec du fumier* – This field was fertilized with manure / dung.

On the other hand, the French noun *l'amende* is a real *faux ami*. *L'amende* never refers to one of these changes and, more specifically, *l'amende* has nothing to do with a change in a document.

Une amende is a <u>fine</u> or <u>penalty</u>. You're most likely to run into *une amende* as a <u>parking fine</u> or as a fine for speeding.

> *La police m'a mis une amende pour stationnement interdit* – The police fined me for illegal parking.

> *C'était une amende de soixante euros* – It was a fine of sixty euros.

Side Note: While the English word amend has nothing to do with fines or penalties, the expression <u>to make amends</u> has a counterpart in French:

To make amends **in English** means to try to make up for a wrong you inflicted on somebody.

Faire amende honorable **in French** means to recognize that you've done wrong and ask for pardon. Thus *faire amende honorable* is not a *faux ami* but a true *ami*. It's basically the same meaning as to make amends. (It's plausible also that the French word *l'amende* comes from the idea of making up for a wrong by paying a fine).

> *Elle a fait amende honorable* – She made amends.

Finally, *s'amender* means to turn over a new leaf (to make changes in order to improve oneself).

gentil, gentille – **genteel**
gentil, gentille – **gentle**

The French adjective *gentil* **never** means genteel, and genteel never means *gentil*.

In English, genteel usually means respectable and proper, but genteel sometimes can have an ironic overtone, implying ostentation or an affected manner. Thus,

> His aunt and uncle are very genteel.

could mean that the couple is respectable, or it could mean that they are affected. You'd have to tell from context and tone of voice.

> They lived in genteel poverty – *Même pauvre / En dépit de leur pauvreté, ils ont gardé leur respectabilité / leurs prétentions de respectabilité.*

In French, on the other hand, *gentil* means <u>kind and nice</u>. It's a very commonly used word in conversation.

> *C'est très gentil de votre part de m'aider* – It's very nice / very kind of you to help me.

> *Il est très gentil* – He's very nice / very kind.

In talking to a child *gentil* can mean having good behavior.

> *Tu n'as pas été gentil. Pas de bonbon !* – You weren't good. No candy for you.

> *Sois gentil !* – Be a good boy!

To translate the English word genteel into French, use *respectable* or *comme il faut* if you mean respectable, and *maniéré* or *affecté* if you mean affected.

Note that *gentil* **doesn't** mean gentle either. While "kind and nice" and "gentle" can sometimes overlap in referring to the same action or person (one may often be gentle while being kind and nice), they are not the same. Consider the following sentences:

> Although he was brusque and rough in his manner, he kindly let me come in out of the snow. (Kind, but not gentle).

> *C'est bien gentil de m'aider à changer la roue.* (Kind, but no implication of gentle).

> Although hurried, the doctor's hands were gentle. (Gentle, yes, but kind or not kind isn't specified one way or the other).

To translate the English word gentle into French use *doux / douce*.

> She was very gentle with me – *Elle a été très douce avec moi.*

fortuné – **fortunate**

In French, the adjective *fortuné*, in current usage, doesn't mean fortunate, but means <u>wealthy</u> instead. In other words, *fortuné* means <u>having a fortune.</u>

> *C'est une famille fortunée* – It's a wealthy family.

Now you might think, "You are fortunate if you have a fortune," but it's not the same thing at all. Consider these two examples:

He was fortunate that the stone didn't fall on his head.

It's fortunate that she brought a bottle of water.

Neither has anything to do with wealth. You wouldn't translate them with *fortuné* but with *avoir de la chance* or *être chanceux*.

Il a de la chance que le caillou ne lui soit pas tombé sur la tête / Quelle chance qu'il n'ait pas reçu la pierre sur la tête.

Elle a de la chance d'avoir apporté une bouteille d'eau / Nous avons de la chance qu'elle ait apporté une bouteille d'eau.

And consider the inverse:

C'est une famille fortunée mais avec beaucoup de malchance / mais malchanceuse – It's a family that's wealthy but unfortunate / but that has had bad luck.

As you see, you can be *fortuné* but unfortunate!

Historical Note: It should be noted that in the past, *fortuné* did also have the meaning fortunate, just as it does in English. While you may come across this meaning in older literature, it is obsolete in current usage.

la denture – the dentures

In French, *la denture* doesn't refer to a denture but to a set of teeth.

> *Il a une mauvaise denture* – He has bad teeth.

La denture can also refer to the teeth on a saw, or on a gear in a piece of machinery.

To translate the English word dentures into French, use *un dentier* or *une prothèse dentaire.*

> She wears dentures – *Elle porte un dentier.*

And, just as an aside, *la dentelle* has nothing to do with teeth, but is lace.

l'optique – the optics

L'optique does mean the optics.

> *Il utilise des instruments d'optique* – He uses optical instruments.

And, when *optique* is used as an adjective, *le nerf optique* is indeed the optic nerve.

However, *l'optique* can also refer to the perspective or the orientation. This can result in some sentences that make no sense at first to an English speaker. Consider these, for example:

Le changement d'optique est renversant – *The change in perspective is astounding.* (Talking about the view from earth as photographed from a satellite).

Ils travaillent dans une optique différente – They have different orientations / They have different perspectives about the work / They are working toward different goals.

Vu sous cette optique… – Seen from that point of view… / Seen from that perspective…

dans l'optique de la vente – in the sales orientation (used in marketing)

dans l'optique du produit – in the positioning of the product (also from marketing)

And finally, *un crayon optique* is used for writing on computer or phone screens.

une baraque – a barracks

Une baraque is not a barracks, but a temporary structure built out of planks of wood. By extension, it can be a temporary place to live: a hut, a shed, a <u>shack</u>.

Speaking negatively in slang, calling something *une baraque* means it's a dump, a hole, a joint, etc.

And, *baraque* can also be used ironically, with the opposite meaning.

> *C'est pas mal, cette baraque* – That's a pretty nice joint.

le basket, la basket – the basket

Le basket does **not** mean the basket. Neither does **la basket**.

Le basket means the game of <u>basketball</u>. (It's *un anglicisme*, of course).

La basket is a <u>sports shoe</u>. Thus, *les baskets (fem)* is the usual name for sneakers, tennis shoes, basketball shoes, etc.

You can remember which is the masculine and which the feminine by <u>le</u> *basket* being *un jeu* (masc), and <u>la</u> *basket* being *une chaussure* (fem).

A couple of slang expressions also use *les baskets*:

> *Lâche-moi les baskets !* – Leave me alone / Get off my back / Quit hassling me!

> *Il est bien dans ses baskets / Il est à l'aise dans ses baskets* – He's at peace with himself / He's very together.

In translating the English word basket into French there are many specialized words, but the two most common are *une corbeille* (for a fruit basket, for instance) and *un panier* (for a shopping basket).

oppresser – to oppress
oppressé – oppressed
oppressant – oppressive

The French verb *oppresser* only corresponds with half of the meaning of to oppress in English.

In English, to oppress has two primary meanings. When talking about tasks, resposibilities or problems it means that they are heavy and weigh you down. Here, to oppress refers to an emotional state.

*In French, the verb **oppresser** is used in the same way:* in talking about a mood, an atmosphere or a situation it means that it is "suffocating"; in talking about tasks, responsibilities or problems it implies that they are heavy and weigh you down. It also refers to an emotional state.

If you are translating the English verb oppress into French in terms of an emotional state or feelings, use *oppresser.*

> The anguish was oppressing me / suffocating me – *L'angoisse m'oppressait.*

> All these responsibilities are oppressing me / are weighing me down – *Toutes ces responsabilités m'oppressent.*

On the other hand, **in English**, to oppress frequently

has a different meaning. It means to take away a people's liberty and freedom.

If you want to translate the English verb oppress into French in this <u>political sense</u>, you have to translate it by *opprimer*.

> The conquerers are oppressing the country – *Les conquérants oppriment le pays.*

It's the same distinction for *oppressé* and *opprimé* when you want to translate the English adjective <u>oppressed</u>:

> He was feeling oppressed / suffocated by fear and anguish – *Il était oppressé par la peur et l'angoisse.*

> The people were oppressed by the conquerers – *Le peuple était opprimé par les conquérants.*

To translate another English adjective, <u>oppressive</u>, in talking about the emotional sense you'd use *oppressant*.

> The heat is oppressive / suffocating – *C'est une chaleur oppressante.*

> My resposibilties are oppressive / oppressing / weighing me down – *Mes responsabilités sont oppressantes.*

If you are talking about a government being oppressive, you'd expect to use *opprimant*. However *opprimant* is a rarely used word. Instead, the French use **oppressif** (masc) or **oppressive** (fem) thus making a distinction between *oppressant* for an oppressive mood and *oppressif* for an oppressive government, etc.

> It's an oppressive government – *C'est un gouvernement oppressif.*

If you want to translate the English noun <u>oppression</u> into French, you can use *l'oppression* for either sense of the word. In other words, *oppression* is not a *faux ami*.

> With the extreme heat, I felt an oppression / I felt painfully oppressed – *Avec cette grande chaleur j'ai ressenti une oppression douleureuse.*

> To struggle against oppression is a duty – *Lutter contre l'oppression est un devoir.*

Finally, an <u>oppressor</u> is un **oppresseur**. There is no corresponding derivative of *opprimer*. *Oppresseur* is *un vrai ami*, not *un faux ami*. You can thus have this interesting definition:

> *Un oppresseur est une personne qui opprime.*

Let's summarize:

- If you are talking about being oppressed by a

mood, by a situation or by responsibilities use **oppresser, oppressé** and **oppressant,** for to oppress, oppressed and oppressive.

- If you are talking about being oppressed by a government with consequent loss of freedoms, use **opprimer, opprimé, oppressif** and **oppresseur** for to oppress, oppressed, oppressive and oppressor.

- You can use **oppression** in talking about oppression in either sense.

affecter – to affect

Affecter has some meanings in common with to affect in English, but *affecter* has other meanings that you do not find in English at all.

To begin, *affecter* and to affect can **both** mean to act on, to <u>have an effect on</u>.

> The strike has affected three airports – *La grève a affecté trois aéroports.*

Secondly, *affecter* and to affect can **both** mean to <u>touch emotionally</u>.

> She was strongly affected by his concern about her health – *Elle était vivement affectée par son inquiétude pour sa santé.*

Thirdly, *affecter* and to affect can **both** mean to <u>feign</u>

<u>an emotion</u> or feeling, to make believe to have it, or to exagerate it.

> He affected an attitude of lack of concern – *Il a affecté une attitude désinvolte / une pose désinvolte.*

In French, however, *affecter* can often mean to <u>assign or allocate</u> (money, usually). To affect does **not** have this meaning in English.

> *Le budget a affecté ces fonds à l'Éducation nationale* – The budget has allocated those funds to national education.

And finally *affecter* can mean to post, to assign or to <u>appoint</u> an employee or a soldier to a post or position. To affect certainly does **not** mean this in English.

> *Il a été affecté à l'usine de Marseille* – He has been assigned to the factory at Marseille.

> *Il s'est fait affecter sur un navire à Brest* – He got himself assigned to a ship at Brest.

désaffecté – disaffected

This brings us to another nice *faux ami*, *désaffecté* and disaffected.

In English, disaffected refers to people (or a group of people such as a disaffected army unit) and means dissatisfied, disgruntled, malcontent or rebellious.

> It was a rebellion by several disaffected units of the President's Personal Guard.

In French, on the other hand, *désaffecté* usually refers to a public building and means that it is out of use and closed down, or that it has been <u>decommissioned</u> and put to another use.

> *Cette église désaffectée est maintenant utilisée comme bibliothèque* – That ex-church / That decommissioned church now serves as a library.

> *L'ancienne mairie a été désaffectée et est maintenant en ruines* – The old town hall was closed down and is now in ruins.

The meaning of *désaffecté* is undoubtedly related to the last meaning we gave you for *affecter* just above (to assign to a post), even though *affecter* in that sense usually refers to a person.

To translate the English word disaffected into French, the best choice is probably *mécontent*.

la commotion – the commotion

In English the primary sense for a commotion is a

confused, noisy bustle and running about. Especially a confused noise.

> Quit making all that commotion! (Mother to kids).

> She was disturbed by all the commotion coming from across the street.

In French, *une commotion* has three senses, but none of them mean a commotion. First, in medical terms, *une commotion* is a <u>concussion</u>.

> *Elle s'est heurté la tête et a eu une commotion / une commotion cérébrale* – She banged her head and had a (cerebral) concussion.

Secondly, *une commotion* can be an <u>emotional shock</u>.

> *Quand elle a reçu les nouvelles elle a souffert d'une commotion / elle a été commotionnée* – When she received the news it was a shock for her.

Finally, in a figurative literary sense, *une commotion* can also be extended to <u>a shock felt by society</u>, for example as a result of civil unrest.

If you want **to translate** the English word commotion into French, the best words are probably *agitation* and *bruit confus*.

> Quit making all that commotion! – *Arrêtez*

tout ce bruit et cette agitation ! / Arrêtez de faire tout ce bruit !

She was disturbed by all the commotion coming from across the street – *Elle était troublée par le bruit et l'agitation qui venaient de l'autre côté de la rue / Elle était tracassée par le charivari / le tumulte qui venait...*

It's interesting that *commotionner* is also used as a verb in French:

Elle a été commotionnée quand elle s'est heurté la tête – She received a concussion when she banged her head.

Elle était commotionnée par les nouvelles – She was shocked by the news.

Historical Note: Finally, I'll note that I found mental agitation and civil uprising both listed as archaic uses for commotion in a twenty-five year old English language dictionary. While this indicates that these meanings were already obsolete twenty-five years ago, it does show that a commotion and *une commotion* were closer in meaning years ago than they are now.

le devise – the device

In French, *une devise* doesn't mean a device. *Une devise* is a foreign currency, or it refers to the currency of one country compared to the currency of another.

> *L'Euro est une devise forte* – The euro is a strong currency.

> *C'est dangereux de spéculer sur les devises* – It's dangerous to speculate in foreign currencies.

> *Celle-là est une devise non convertible* – That's a non-convertible currency.

In both languages *une devise* and a device can refer to an emblem or motto, but it is not a meaning which is frequently used in either, and in English it's mostly used in descriptions of heraldry, and it's obsolete in normal speech:

> *"Liberté, Égalité, Fraternité" est la devise de la République française.*

> *Telle est sa devise* – That is his motto / his guide for living. (This is a rather literary usage.)

> The device on his shield was… (referring to motto or emblem or both)

To translate the English word device into French, use *un dispositif*. (See the discussion of *un dispositif* earlier). You could also use *un appareil,* and in casual slang you could even say *un truc.*

en puissance – in power, in puissance

In French, *puissance* and *puissant* mean power and powerful.

In English, puissance and puissant mean the same thing, although they are usually used only poetically and are almost obsolete in daily language.

However, if you encounter the French term **en puissance** it will leave you perplexed because it doesn't mean powerful, it means <u>potential</u>. For example, consider the following:

> *Il y a plusieurs assassins en puissance à Paris* – There are several potential assassins in Paris.

(It's really a pretty peculiar usage from an Anglophone's point of view).

solvable – solvable

In French, *solvable* means financially <u>solvent</u> and able to pay one's debts. *Solvable* doesn't mean solvable at all.

> *C'est un client solvable* – He's a client who can pay his bills.

> *La France est un pays solvable* – France is a country that is solvent and can pay its debts.

If you want to translate solvable into French, use *sol-*

uble, résoluble, qui peut être résolu, or *qui peut être solutionné.* The most frequently used is probably *qui peut être résolu.*

> It's a solvable problem – *C'est un problème soluble / qui peut être résolu.*

Similarly, *solvabilité* means <u>solvency</u> or, when discussing a loan, credit rating.

un suppléant – a supplicant

In English, a supplicant is someone who asks, or even pleads, for something, earnestly and even humbly.

The **French** word *suppléant* has nothing to do with that. *Un suppléant* is a replacement, a substitute, a deputy who fills in, a substitute teacher, etc. It derives from *suppléer,* which means to replace, to stand in for.

> *Elle n'est pas la gérante, mais elle en est la suppléante* – She's not the manager but she acts as his deputy / but she replaces him when he's out.

There is, however, a French word, *suppliant*, which does have the same meaning as suppliant. *Un suppliant* does indeed mean someone who is begging or pleading. It comes from the verb *supplier* which means to beg or plead.

Supplication has the same meaning in both languages.

Supplier was discussed earlier as a *faux ami* for the English verb supply.

l'opportunité – the opportunity

In English, the opportunity usually refers to the chance or the occasion to do something. (You can also think of it as a combination of circumstances which will allow you to do something.)

> I'll have an opportunity to go to the supermarket tomorrow.

> We may have the opportunity to sell that stock at a profit next month.

In French, the noun *opportunité* is related to the adjective *opportun* (opportune in English). Thus, when one speaks of the *opportunité* of something, or of doing something, it refers to its opportuneness, its timeliness, its advisability and appropriateness at the moment. It's written as *l'opportunité de…*

> *Nous avons discuté de l'opportunité de sa visite* – We discussed the opportuneness of his visit / the timeliness of his visit / <u>whether his visit comes at a good time</u>.

You can see that while the two meanings are related, they **are not** the same. "whether his visit comes at a good time" isn't the same as "whether he has an opportunity to visit."

The English meaning of opportunity has actually also crept into the French language in recent years, but French dictionaries list this usage as an *anglicisme* and an *emploi critiqué* (a criticized usage).

Thus, in a sentence like this, you can indeed **translate** opportunity by *opportunité:*

> If you have the opportunity to buy that for me... – *Si vous avez l'opportunité d'acheter cela pour moi...*

and you will be understood, but the best translation would probably be:

> Si vous avez l'occasion d'acheter cela pour moi...

importuner – to importune
importun – importunate

In English, to importune and importunate have the feeling of persistent and unpleasant pleading, begging or demanding.

In French, however, while the verb *importuner* can have the same sense, it can also mean to be annoying or unpleasant by a simple presence, and it can refer to a thing as well as to a person. It comes from the idea of being inopportune.

Je ne veux pas vous importuner – I don't want to bother you (by my presence).

You can even say:

La fumée l'importune – The smoke bothers him.

The adjective *importun* can mean inopportune, (annoying, indiscreet, intruding, coming at the wrong time, undesired, unwanted).

Je ne veux pas vous être importun – I don't want to be annoying to you.

C'était une visite importune – It was an inopportune visit.

The noun **un importun** can refer to an intruder. (Not an "intruder" in the sense of a burglar, but an intruder on a scene, in a room, between other people, etc). Possible French synonyms would be *un intrus* (someone who wandered in where he wasn't wanted) or *un gêneur* (someone who was annoying or in the way).

Quand je suis entré dans le salon, j'ai eu l'impression d'être un importun – When I entered the room, I felt like an intruder / I felt like I was intruding / I had the impression that I was an intruder.

Note that the same thought could be expressed using *importun* as an adjective and it works equally well:

Quand je suis entré dans le salon, je me suis senti importun.

un lot – a lot

In English, the term "a lot" can have numerous meanings. A very common meaning, of course, for a lot (of), or lots, is as a pronoun meaning <u>a great deal</u> or a large number (of).

In French, the noun *un lot* does **not** have this meaning. The correct **translation** of a lot of into French is *beaucoup de*.

> I saw a lot of birds yesterday – *J'ai vu beaucoup d'oiseaux hier.*

As I said, there are other meanings for a lot **in English**. When one uses the noun lot in the sense of drawing lots or deciding by lot, it means <u>deciding by random choice</u>.

> They drew lots – *Ils ont tiré au sort.*

His lot in life can mean a person's <u>condition in life</u>, especially as decided by fate. It's primarily a literary usage in English. In French this is usually translated by *le sort* as in:

> He's trying to improve his lot – *Il essaie d'améliorer son sort.*

However, the French word *lot* can have the same

meaning (of fate) when used in a literary or poetical context.

> *Mon lot est de toujours regretter* – My lot in life is to always regret / My fate is to regret always.

A lot can refer to an item or group of <u>items meant to be sold together</u>. This usually, but not always, refers to a sale in an auction. *Un lot* can have the same meaning in French.

> They decided to sell the paintings in lots – *Ils ont décidé de vendre les tableaux par lots.*

> Three lots didn't sell – *Il y avait trois lots qu'ils n'ont pas vendus.*

Another sense for a lot is <u>a patch of land</u> set aside for sale, for building a house on, or for a special purpose. The usual translation for that would be *terrain*, but there are special cases.

> a vacant lot – *un terrain vague.*

> My lot is three hectares – *Mon terrain fait trois hectares.*

> the parking lot – *le parking, le parc de stationnement*

In French, *un lot* can also mean a patch of land, but the meaning is different as it comes from a different direction. *Un lot* is <u>a part</u> of a whole which has been divided or shared between several people. Thus we can have:

> *L'héritage était partagé en lots égaux –* The inheritance was divided into equal shares.

> *Ils ont divisé le terrain en lots pour le vendre –* They divided the land into parcels to sell it (more easily).

You can see that *un lot* derived in this fashion is different in meaning than the English meaning of a lot just above, even though they both may refer to a plot of land.

A very common meaning in French for *le lot* is the jackpot or <u>prize</u>. The lot doesn't have this meaning in English.

> *Il a gagné le gros lot –* He won the jackpot.

> *Ce n'est que le lot de consolation –* It's just the consolation prize.

> *Qui a gagné le lot ? –* Who won the prize?

Finally, *un lot* can refer to a group or <u>assemblage of people or things</u>. While not common, a lot can have this meaning in English as well:

> *Il a lu beaucoup de lettres, et dans le lot, il a trouvé ce qu'il cherchait –* He read a

lot of letters, and in the lot he found what he was looking for.

All the different meanings may seem pretty complicated so let's **review and summarize:**

- Meanings in English but not in French:

    a lot of birds

    drawing lots

    a vacant lot

- Meanings in both English and French:

    his lot in life – *son lot dans la vie*

    three lots of paintings – *trois lots de tableaux*

    in the lot he found – *dans le lot il a trouvé*

- Meanings in French but not in English:

    divisé en lots égaux (equal parts)

    gagner le gros lot

le signalement – the signaling

Le signalement in French has nothing to do with signaling. It means the <u>description</u> and usually refers to the description of a person.

Donnez-moi son signalement s'il vous plaît – Give me her description, please.

La police a son signalement – The police have his description.

Donner le signalement de quelqu'un is a fairly commonly used expression, but it's used mostly in a legal or police context. If you were asking for the description of a pretty girl, you wouldn't ask for her *signalement* but you'd say something like:

Elle est comment, cette fille ? – What is that girl like? What does she look like?

or:

Décris-la-moi. – Describe her to me.

excité – excited

This is a *faux ami* on which I was recently corrected sharply by my daughter: "You don't use *excité* like that, Dad!". It's one of the problems in having a bilingual daughter. (I had said something like: *Je suis excité d'apprendre ça).*

In French, the adjective *excité* means <u>"hyper", agitated, unable to sit still, worked up</u>. It's the opposite of *calme.*

Elle est très excitée – She's really hyper / She's very agitated.

In English, therefore, you can use excited in quite a

number of different ways which should **not** be translated into French by *excité*. For example:

If you are saying you are excited about the prospect of going someplace (or about the prospect of something happening), that means that you are <u>looking forward</u> to going, you are anxious to go, you are very happy to go.

If what you mean to say is that you are looking forward to, or that you are anxious to do something, you should **not translate** it as *excité*. Try one of these choices instead:

> I'm excited that we can go together – *Je suis ravi / très heureux que nous puissions y aller ensemble.*

> I'm excited that I'll be seeing you again soon – *J'ai hâte de te revoir / Il me tarde de te revoir.*

If you say you are excited to hear something, that means you are <u>very happy</u> to hear it.

If what you want to say is that you are very happy, you should **not translate** it as *exité*.

> I'm excited to hear that they won – *Je suis heureux d'entendre qu'ils ont gagné / Ça me plaît beaucoup qu'ils aient gagné / J'étais enthousiasmé d'entendre qu'ils ont gagné.*

If you say, in English, that you get excited about

doing something (going skiing, for instance), that means that you have a lot of <u>enthusiasm</u> about it, it thrills you.

Excited in the sense of being thrilled, or of having a lot of enthusiasm, is also **not translated** by *excité*.

> I still get excited about going skiing –
> *Faire du ski m'enthousiasme toujours.*

Note that excited and *excité* can **both** be used for <u>sexual arousement</u>, and be aware that this is a common meaning for *excité* in French.

To summarize, in French *excité* can mean agitated and hyper, or it can mean sexually excited, but it doesn't have the other senses that excited can have in English. Avoid the trap of saying "Je serais excité d'y aller!". It's wrong!

l'affuence – the affluence
l'affluent – affluent

In English, affuence is wealth.

In French, the usual meaning of *affuence* has nothing to do with wealth, but it refers to a crowd of people all going to the same place. It's more usually found in written rather than spoken French.

> *L'affluence de gens qui entraient était telle que j'étouffais* – The crowd of people who where entering was so great that / was such that I felt suffocated. (Note

that this doesn't mean "The wealth of the people who were entering...". It means "The number of people who were entering...")

Je prends le métro aux heures d'affluence – I take the subway at rush hour.

Il y a une grande affluence à ce salon – There's a large crowd at that salon / There's a large crowd entering that salon.

The French noun **affluent** also has nothing to do with wealth. *Un affluent* is a tributary (of a river or stream). Since the *affluents* all empty into the same river, you can see how this relates to the meaning of *affluence*.

les affluents de la Seine – the tributaries of the Seine

To translate the English word affluence into French, use *abondance* or *richesse*.

To translate the English word affluent into French, use *riche*.

Side Note: It's interesting to note that one of my English dictionaries gives a tributary stream as an archaic meaning of affluent, and one of my French dictionaries gives *abondance* as an obsolescent meaning for *affluence*, showing that the English and French words were once closer in meaning, but have since drifted apart.

un exposé – an exposé

In English, an exposé is usually a jounalistic report, either in the newspapers or on television, which exposes or brings to light something scandalous which had been hidden.

> The paper published an exposé of graft in the city government.

In French, on the other hand, *un exposé* is a simple talk, usually an account of facts, with or without analysis. There is nothing necessarily pejorative about *un exposé* as there is in an English exposé. In school, or at work, *un exposé* is simply a presentation, a dissertation or a report.

> *Elle a fait un simple exposé des faits / exposé de la situation* – She gave a simple account of the facts / account of the situation.

> *Il nous a fait un exposé verbal de la mission* – He gave us a verbal briefing on the mission.

> *Il a fait un exposé sur la théorie de...* – He gave a presentation on the theory of...

You can see from these examples that *un exposé* in French is not at all the same thing as an exposé in English. If you wish **to translate** the English word exposé in French, try something like this:

> The newspaper's exposé of graft in the

city government... – *Les révélations /
L'enquête par le journal sur des pots-de-
vin dans l'administration de la ville...*

l'instance – the instance

In English, an instance means an example or occurrence, or a particular case.

There were many instances (occurenc-
es) of poaching during the winter.

In this instance (particular case), I think
we should go ahead.

In French, *instance* has several meanings but it
does not mean instance.

Instance, in French, can mean <u>insistance</u>, although
it's a usage that's a bit dated. (Nowadays one would
use the French word *insistance*).

*Il a demandé avec instance / avec insis-
tance* – He asked with insistance.

And, following from that, *instances* can mean <u>en-
treaties</u> or pleas.

*Il a cédé aux instances de sa femme / Il
a renoncé à le faire devant les instances
de sa femme* – He gave up doing it because of his wife's pleas.

In a completely unrelated meaning, *une instance* can
mean an <u>authority</u> with power to make decisions.

les instances dirigeantes – the governing body

Finally, in a legal setting, *"en instance"* means <u>in court</u>, or <u>in proceedings</u>.

une affaire en instance – a case in court

Ils sont en instance de divorce – They are in the process of divorce.

Je crains qu'il n'introduise une instance – I'm afraid that he's going to institute court proceedings / going to file suit.

Il a été acquité en seconde instance – He was acquitted on appeal. (Literally "in the second proceedings")

En instance is sometimes gereralized to cover anything that is "in course" of happening.

Toutes les décisions sont encore en instance – All the decisions are still pending.

Cette lettre est en instance – That letter is in the process of going out / is waiting to go out.

To translate the English word instance into French in the sense of <u>an example</u>, use *l'exemple* or *le cas*.

There are many instances where he contradicts himself – *Il y a beaucoup d'exemples où il se contredit / beaucoup de cas où il se contredit.*

To translate the English word instance into French in the sense of <u>a particular case</u>, use *dans ce cas*.

In this instance, I think we should go ahead – *Dans ce cas, je crois qu'il vaut mieux continuer.*

l'alimentation – the alimentation

English speakers will recognize alimentation as an older, somewhat outdated, word for nourishment, or for the providing of nourishment.

In French, as well, *alimentation* means <u>nourishment</u> or the <u>providing of nourishment</u>.

Il faut avoir une alimentation équilibrée – It's necessary to have a balanced diet.

Les généraux ont pensé à l'alimentation des troupes – The generals planned for feeding the soldiers / the army.

However, in French, *alimentation* can be extended to all sorts of provision in ways that we don't usually use it in English. For example:

C'est l'alimentation de la ville en eau – It's the provision of water to the city.

l'alimentation de l'usine en matières pre-

mières – the provision of raw materials to the factory

Donnez-moi le fil de alimentation / le câble d'alimentation de l'ordinateur, s'il vous plaît – Give me the power cord of the computer, if you please.

However, the most common usage for *alimentation* that you are likely to encounter in everyday speech, and which is very foreign to our ears, is *l'alimentation* meaning the <u>corner grocery store</u>. (It's probably short for *magasin d'alimentation* but no one ever says *magasin d'alimentation*). *L'alimentation* in this sense is a synonym for *l'épicerie*.

Je vais chercher des pommes à l'alimentation – I'll get some apples at the grocery store.

volatil – volatile
volatile – volatile

The adjective ***volatil*** can mean volatile in the sense of something which can <u>evaporate easily</u>:

L'éther est volatil – Ether is volatile.

and in a literary sense *volatil* can be extended to what can evaporate suddenly in a figurative sense:

le bonheur volatil – the fragile happiness

mémoire volatile – computer memory

which is lost when the the computer is turned off, which is not saved.

However, The French word *volatil* **is not** used either for a personality or for a situation in the way that it is in English. **To translate** volatile into French in these senses consider the following examples:

> Her moods are really volatile – *Elle est bien <u>versatile.</u>*

> It's a volatile situation – *C'est une situation <u>explosive</u>.*

There is also a noun, ***volatile***, which looks very similar to *volatil*, but which has a completely different meaning:

> *le volatile* – the bird, the flying creature, winged creature (it undoubtedly comes from the verb *voler*, to fly)

Les volatiles (in the plural), now usually refers to poultry, but it's an uncommon word. The usual word for poultry is *la volaille*.

le crayon – the crayon
le pinceau – the pencil

Le crayon is a really elementary *faux ami* that you are most probably well aware of. *Un crayon* in French, is not a crayon, but a <u>pencil</u>.

Un crayon de couleur is a colored pencil.

To translate, if you are referring to a child's coloring crayon the correct word in French is *une craie grasse* or *un crayon de cire*.

And *un pinceau* doesn't mean a pencil --- even if you see something described as *dessiné avec un pinceau* (drawn with *un pinceau*). *Un pinceau* is a (paint)<u>brush</u>.

le faste – the fast
faste – fast

If you are not expecting this *faux ami* it can be a bit confusing.

In French, the noun *le faste* doesn't mean a fast, but rather has almost an opposite connotation. Instead of a period of deprivation, *faste* means <u>splendor</u> or <u>sumptuousness</u>.

> *Le faste de cette cérémonie était étonnant* – The splendor of that ceremony was astonishing.

> *un exemple de faste oriental* – an example of oriental splendor

> *Ce sera un mariage sans faste* – It will be a simple wedding.

To translate the English <u>noun</u>, a fast, into French, the correct word is *un jeûne*.

It is a hunger fast – *C'est une grève de la faim / un jeûne de protestation.*

He has broken the fast – *Il a rompu le jeûne.*

In English, the <u>adjective</u> fast usually means <u>speedy</u>.

That's a fast car.

and by extension:

She leads a fast life. (She leads an exciting life which may be morally questionable at times.)

The adjective fast can, however, mean <u>pertaining to a fast</u>, as in the expression:

a fast day (a day when one is supposed to fast)

Finally, fast can mean <u>firmly attached</u>.

It's tied down fast. (It's tied tightly and won't move.)

He's a fast friend. (He's a friend who you can rely on.)

It's a fast dye. (It won't fade.)

These last usages aren't heard much in modern speech.

None of the meanings of the adjective fast in English can be translated as the adjective *faste* in French. The adjective *faste* is opposed to *néfaste* and means lucky or fortunate. It's usually used in an expression like:

> *mon jour faste* – my lucky day (Note that this does **not** mean a day of fasting!)

> *une période faste* – a lucky period of time (when you are in the money, for instance)

l'exploitation – the exploitation

In English, exploitation theoretically means to make full use of (a resource). In actual usage though, exploitation is often used in a pejorative sense and refers to taking unfair advantage of, or to profiting unfairly and selfishly from, the work of someone else, or of other people..

> He engaged in terrible exploitation of his workers.

In French, the noun ***exploitation*** can have three different meanings. First, *une exploitation* means <u>a business or concern</u>, very often a <u>farm</u>.

> *une exploitation agricole* – a farm

> *son exploitation* – his farm

Il a plusieurs exploitations dans la vallée – He has several farms in the valley.

C'est une grosse exploitation de trois cents hectares – It's a large farm of three hundred hectares.

une exploitation minière – a mine

une exploitation industrielle – an industrial business

Secondly, *l'exploitation* refers to the act of <u>farming</u> or, in referring to a business, a mine, an airline, the act of working or <u>running the business</u>.

l'exploitation d'une mine – the working of a mine

l'exploitation d'un terrain – the farming of a piece of land

Il a mis son terrain en exploitation – He started cultivating his land.

Ils ont mis en exploitation presque toute la terre qu'ils ont achetée – They have put under cultivation almost all of the terrain that they bought.

Finally, *exploitation* can be used to mean an <u>abuse</u>, as in English,

l'exploitation de l'homme par l'homme – the exploitation of man by man

C'était l'exploitation des ouvriers par l'entreprise – The company was exploiting the workers.

From the first two meanings of exploitation, you can guess that **un exploitant** is most commonly a farmer, or he can be the person running a business.

On the other hand, the verb **exploiter** is not a *faux ami*, and means pretty much the same as to exploit in English, that is, to make the most of, or to use (to exploit) a situation or a talent, on the one hand --- or to take unfair advantage of on the other. It can also mean to cultivate a farm or to run a business.

Exploitable, usually refers to terrain, where it means able to be worked or farmed, or to natural resources, where it means able to be exploited.

Finally, **un exploit** is also not a *faux ami* and means the same thing as it's English counterpart, a feat or achievement.

C'était un exploit fabuleux – It was a fabulous exploit.

fantaisie – fantasy
fantastique – fantastic
fantaisiste – fantastic
fantasque – fantastic

In English fantasy can mean the <u>act of imagining things</u>, especially things that are improbable or unrealistic.

He's lost in fantasy.

It's in the realm of fantasy.

A fantasy can also be the thing or <u>scene that is imagined</u>. It is assumed that it is probably something improbable or unrealistic.

> It's always been his fantasy to retire on a tropical island.

> He has lots of sexual fantasies.

> That's nothing but a fantasy.

To translate the English word fantasy into French, use *fantasme*, or even *rêve*.

> He's lost in fantasy – *Il est perdu dans ses fantasmes.*

> It's always been her fantasy to retire on a tropical island – *Son rêve a toujours été de se retirer sur une île dans les tropiques.*

> He has lots of sexual fantasies – *Il a beaucoup de fantasmes sexuels.*

> That's nothing but a fantasy – *Ce n'est rien qu'un rêve / Ce n'est pas réaliste.*

In French, on the other hand, **la fantaisie** has several meanings, but it does **not** mean *fantasme* or *rêve*, it doesn't mean the act of day-dreaming about, or imagining, improbable things, nor does it refer to the improbable dreams themselves.

In current usage, *une fantaisie* can refer to a whim, a sudden desire which usually doesn't correspond to a real need, really more of a <u>fancy</u>. A French synonyme would be *un caprice*.

> *Il lui a pris la fantaisie de manger des huîtres* – He got the idea that he wanted to eat oysters / He got it into his head that he wanted to eat oysters / He got a whim… / He's taken a fancy to eating…

> *C'est quoi, cette fantaisie ?* – What's come over you? / What's got into you?

Fantaisie also can refer to creative <u>originality</u> and imagination. By extension, this can refer to the little unexpected pleasant things which give spice to life.

> *Il a trop de fantaisie pour être un bon fonctionnaire* – He has too much originality and imagination to be a good government employee.

> *pain de fantaisie* – fancy bread

> *Ça donne un peu de fantaisie à la vie* – That adds a little excitement to life.

> *C'est une vie qui manque de fantaisie* – It's a dull life, monotonous, uninteresting and unexciting.

> *Elle porte un pantalon de fantaisie* – Her
> pants are very original / are really wild.

Finally, *fantaisie* can also be used for a product
which is <u>an imitation</u>.

> *C'est un Calvados de fantaisie* – It's an
> *eau de vie* imitating a *Calvados*.

> *bijoux de fantaisie* – costume jewelry

As you might expect, since the English noun fantasy
can be translated by *fantasme* or *rêve*, the verbs
fantasmer and *rêver* mean to fantasize or to day-
dream.

> *Il fantasme sur son avenir* – He's fanta-
> sizing about his future.

Now, for some related words: We'll start with the adjective **fantaisiste**. *Fantaisiste*, when talking about
a person, means not serious and is often used for
someone who is unreliable or who doesn't devote
himself to his task.

> *un étudiant fantaisiste* – one who is not
> a reliable student, skips class, doesn't
> study

> *un historien fantaisiste* – an unreliable
> historian, who perhaps invents things

When *fantaisiste* refers to a thing instead of a person, it means it's not serious, not reliable, or that

it's fake, and when it refers to an idea or theory, it means that it's made-up, false.

> *un remède fantaisiste* – a fake remedy

> *C'est une nouvelle fantaisiste* – It's a piece of news that's fake, false, or at least very questionable.

Note that *fantaisiste* **does not** mean fantastic.

While *fantaisie* doesn't mean fantasy, **fantastique** does mean fantastic most (but not all) of the time. *Fantastique* can have several senses. The first meaning is imaginary, fabulous, unreal, created by the imagination. This is better translated as <u>full of fantasy</u>.

> *un conte / un film fantastique* – a fantasy story / a fantasy movie

> *les tableaux fantastiques de Brueghel* – the fantasy filled paintings of Brueghel

The second sense of *fantastique* is <u>bizarre</u> or grotesque. We can use the <u>same</u> example here.

> *les tableaux fantastiques de Brueghel* – the bizarre paintings of Brueghel

Whether you would translate it as fantasy filled, or bizarre, (or both), would depend on context.

The final, and most common, meaning of *fantastique*

is <u>fantastic</u>, astonishing, sensational, unbelievable, just like it's English counterpart.

> *une réussite fantastique* – a fantastic success

> *un faste fantastique* – a fantastic splendor

By extension, this can mean super, terrific, remarkable, amazing, wonderful, as in:

> *Cette femme est absolument fantastique* – That woman is absolutely fantastic / terrific / remarkable.

Some French synonyms for this sense of the word would be *formidable*, *génial* and (informally) *super*.

Finally, the adjective **fantasque** usually refers to a person or his mood or character. It means <u>whimsical</u>, capricious, or odd. It can also refer to a thing: to a story or to a shape, for instance, and then it means odd or <u>bizarre</u>.

> *C'est un homme fantasque* – He's a really odd type.

> *Sur le sable le vent a créé des formes fantasques* – The wind has made strange shapes in the sand.

To Summarize: There are quite a number of similar words here, which can be confusing. I suggest that instead of trying to memorize all the meanings, it will make more sense to reread this section, especially the examples, to get a feel how each of the six words *fantaisie, fantasme, fantasmer, fantaisiste, fantastique,* and *fantasque* are used. Sentences and phrases will stick in your mind better than definitions.

le travail – the travail

In English, travail is, more often than not, a literary word. It means painful or laborous effort and toil. A travail is a struggle, a trial, a tribulation. It implies a certain amount of suffering:

> They went through a lot of sorrow and travail during the war / during their marriage / before arriving at their goal.

In French, on the other hand, *le travail* is simply work. One of my French dictionaries has an entire page of examples of the use of *travail*, but when you boil it down, all of the uses can be translated by work, or labor.

Speaking of labor, *travail* and travail can both refer to labor during childbirth.

Note also that the pronounciation of the two words is different. The last syllable of the English word is pronounced the same as "ale" or "ail", while the last syllable of the French *travail* is pronounced fairly similarly to the English word "eye".

If you wish **to translate** the English word travail into

French you can perhaps use some combination of *le dur labeur, l'épreuve*, et *la souffrance*.

> They went through a lot of sorrow and travail during the war – *Ils ont passé un temps d'épreuves dures, de souffrance et de tristesse pendant la guerre.*

> They had a lot of travail before arriving at their goal – *Ils ont eu beaucoup de labeur dur et d'épreuves avant d'atteindre leur but.*

le labeur, le labour – the labor

This brings us to *le labeur* and *le labour*.

In French, ***le labeur*** (with an "e"), is a literary word which has a meaning which is fairly close to that of the English word labor. *Le labeur* means toil and sustained hard work, like its English counterpart.

> *C'était un labeur accablant* – It was an overwhelming amount of hard work.

On the other hand, ***le labour*** (with an "o"), is a farming word which means plowing and tilling. It is a *faux ami*.

> *un cheval de labour* – a plow horse

In translating the English word labor into French, the word you use depends on the sense you want.

It was a lot of labor – *C'était beaucoup de <u>travail</u>*.

It was really hard labor – *C'était du <u>labeur</u>*.

She started into labor (childbirth) – *Le <u>travail</u> a commencé*.

the cost of labor – *le prix de la <u>main-d'oeuvre</u>*

capital and labor – *le capital et la <u>main-d'oeuvre</u>*

The Secretary of Labor – *le ministre du <u>Travail</u>*

raser – to raze

In French, the verb *raser* does indeed mean to <u>raze</u> (a building or a city, for instance) to the ground. However, unless you are in the demolition business, you are much more likely to hear *raser* used in one of several other contexts, which it's English counterpart, to raze, doesn't have.

First of all, *raser* is the word meaning to <u>shave</u>,

> *Elle a rasé son mari quand il était malade* – She shaved her husband when he was sick.

and *se raser* means to <u>shave oneself</u>.

Il faut que je me rase chaque jour – I have to shave every day.

Elle se rase les jambes / les aisselles dans la douche – She shaves her legs / her armpits in the shower.

(While in English to raze doesn't mean to shave, you can see the relationship of the words in the noun razor, which you use to shave).

Thirdly, *raser* means to <u>barely touch</u> or <u>almost touch</u>, to graze, to just lightly brush against, the surface of something.

Un épervier a rasé l'herbe et est remonté dans le ciel – A sparrow-hawk skimmed the grass and climbed back up in the sky.

Il a eu peur, et il a rasé les murs en descendant la rue / Il a eu peur et il a descendu la rue en rasant les murs – He was scared and he hugged the walls as he descended the street / and he went down the street sticking close to the walls.

Ce camion m'a rasé ! – That truck almost hit me!

Finally, in the *langue familière*, *raser* can mean to <u>bore</u>.

Il n'imagine pas combien il rase ses élèves – He has no idea how much he bores his students.

Ça me rase beaucoup d'aller les voir – It really bores me to go to see them.

Since the English verb to raze has only the first of these meanings (to destroy to the ground), you'll want to be aware of the additional meanings of the French verb *raser*.

accuser – to accuse

The **French** verb *accuser* is another word that can have the same meaning as its English counterpart, to accuse, but which also has several other meanings that have nothing to do with accuse, and which will leave you really perplexed if you don't expect them.

First of all, as I just said, *accuser* can mean to ac-cuse.

Ils l'accusent de meurtre / de cambriolage / d'avoir empoisonné sa femme – They are accusing him of murder / of burglary / of having poisoned his wife.

Il accuse le sort – He blames it all on fate.

Surprisingly, *accuser* can also mean to show, to indicate or to <u>reveal</u>. This is a sense of the word that sounds very strange to an Anglophone ear.

> *Son visage accuse la fatigue* – His face shows his fatigue / reveals that he's tired.

> *Il commence à accuser son âge* – He's starting to look his age / to show his age.

> *Rien dans son comportement n'accuse sa détresse* – Nothing in her behavior indicates her distress / betrays her distress / reveals her distress.

> *Il accuse le coup* – He's showing the effects (of whatever the blow was) / He was shaken by it.

In a similar vein, *accuser* can mean to define, to <u>accentuate</u>, to make manifest. This is only slightly different than the previous usage.

> *Sa robe moulante accuse les formes de son corps / Les formes de son corps sont accusées par sa robe moulante* – Her clinging dress accentuates (or shows) the shape of her body / The form of her body is accentuated / is clearly defined by her clinging dress.

> *Sa malveillance s'est accusée avec le temps* – His nastiness / His malicious-

ness has become more accentuated / more clearly defined with time.

Finally, *un accusé de reception* is a <u>receipt</u>. This is especially confusing the first time you see it as it has absolutely nothing to do with accused.

l'acceptation, l'acception – the acceptation

In French, the noun *acceptation* is a formal word meaning the <u>acceptance</u>.

> une acceptation sous condition – a conditional acceptance

In English, acceptation is also a formal literary word but it has a different meaning. The acceptation refers to the <u>generally accepted meaning</u> of a word.

There is a French word which means the same thing as acceptation, but it's not *acceptation*, it's ***acception***.

> The acceptation (the generally accepted meaning) of that word is… – *L'acception de ce mot est…*

These are not common words, but they are used. I discovered them when a French friend referred to *l'acception* of a word and I had to ask what that meant.

incessamment – incessantly

In English, the word incessantly means continuously, constantly, without cease, and usually refers to something unpleasant.

In French, on the other hand, the word *incessamment* means <u>momentarily,</u> <u>immediately,</u> <u>any moment now</u>, right away, without delay. It's completely different than the English meaning.

> *Elle doit arriver incessamment* – She should arrive right away / momentarily.

When someone has been "coming any minute" for some time now you can even say humorously:

> *Elle doit arriver incessamment sous peu* – (The redundency of *incessamment sous peu* means something like: She <u>really</u> should be getting here any minute now!)

Some **French synonyms** for *incessamment* are *sans délai, sans retard, tout de suite, sous peu, très prochainement*.

To translate the English word incessantly into French the correct words to use are *sans cesse* or *continuellement*.

> *It has been raining incessantly!* – Il a plu sans cesse !

graduation – graduation
graduer – *to graduate*

It's always tempting to say *graduation* when you are talking about the ceremony marking the end of a course of studies. However, if you use *graduation* in French to refer to this ceremony, a French person will look at you blankly. **In French**, *la graduation* refers **only** to the divisions on a measuring device.

> *La graduation de cette règle est en centimètres* – That ruler is divided into centimeters / The graduation of that ruler is in centimeters.

Remember, *"ma graduation"* simply **doesn't work** in French. To translate graduation try one of these.

> He went to the graduation – *Il est allé à la cérémonie de remise des diplômes.*

> It will be my graduation – *Je vais recevoir mon diplôme.*

The French verb *graduer* has nothing to do with to graduate. *Graduer* usually means to increase something gradually, like intensity or pressure for example..

To translate the English verb to graduate into French, try one of the following:

> I am going to graduate from college next June – *Je vais recevoir mon diplôme (de licence) en juin.*

She graduated in 2007 – *Elle a eu sa licence en 2007.*

I graduated from the University of Texas – *J'ai fait mes études à l'Université de Texas.*

She graduated from high school three years ago – *Elle a terminé ses études au lycée il y a trois années.*

exténuer – to extenuate
exténuant – extenuating

In English, the verb **to extenuate** is fairly rare. It refers back to some transgression and means to make excuses for, make allowances for, to justify, to diminish, as in:

I don't want to extenuate his guilt / his transgressions.

On the other hand, the adjective **extenuating** is commonly used, especially in the phrase "extenuating circumstances". These are circumstances that make a transgression seem more understandable and more forgivable.

He did do it, but there were extenuating circumstances that can help explain his actions.

In French, the verb *exténuer* is used much more commonly and has an altogether different meaning.

Exténuer means to exhaust (physically), tire out, wear out. *S'exténuer* means to tire oneself out.

> *Cette longue marche m'a exténué* – That long walk exhausted me.

> *Elle s'exténue avec tant de travail* – She's wearing herself out with so much work.

The French adjective *exténuant* means exhausting or fatiguing.

> *Cette marche est exténuante* – This walk is exhausting.

> *C'est un travail exténuant* – It's tiring / exhausting work.

To translate the phrase "extenuating circumstances" into French, try *circonstances atténuantes*.

To translate the verb extenuate (referring to a crime or a transgression), use *amoindrir* or *atténuer*.

Historical Note: It's interesting to note that in older literature you may find the French verb *exténuer*, which now means to exhaust, meaning to make thin *(rendre mince, amaigrir)*. This illustrates perhaps that extenuate and *exténuer* were once a bit closer in meaning.

obédience – obedience

To translate the English word obedience into French, the correct and normal translation is ***obéis-***

sance (except for an obedience class for dogs which is *un cours de dressage*).

You should **not** normally use **obédience**, which is a peculiar word not having any common English counterpart and meaning (approximately) the bond between a spiritual or political power and those people who submit to its rule. For example:

> *Elle est d'obédience chrétienne / catholique* – She's a strict practicing Christian / Catholic.

> *C'était un communiste d'obédience trotskiste* – He was a Trotskyite communist.

> *Ce sont des pays d'obédience communiste* – They are countries under communist rule / control.

In a literary context *obédience* can mean obedience in the sense of submission.

génial – genial

In English, genial means friendly and warm, cordial. It's a somewhat literary word and tends to be used especially for a greeting or for someone's manner.

> He's always genial in his relations with others.

She gave Peter a little wave which was genial but nothing more.

In French, on the other hand, since *le génie* means the genius, *génial* usually means inspired by genius, brilliant, ingenious.

> *C'est un romancier génial* – He's a brilliant novelist.

> *C'est une oeuvre géniale* – It's a brilliant work, a work inspired by genius.

> *Tu es génial !* – You're a genius! / What a great idea!

As an exclamation by itself in casual speech, ***Génial !*** is similar to *Super !,* or *Chic !* or *Chouette !* and means Terrific! or Great idea!

> *Veux-tu sortir manger une pizza ? --- Génial !* – Do you want to go out for a pizza? --- Terrific! Great idea!

To translate the English word genial into French, the closest fit is probably *affable*, but *accueillant, poli, aimable, gracieux, bienveillant* and *sympathique* each capture a part of its meaning.

> He's always genial with his friends – *Il est toujours affable / aimable / gracieux / sympathique avec ses amis.*

le grief – the grief

In English, grief means deep <u>sorrow</u>, often the sorrow felt after someones death.

> She felt a great deal of grief after the death of her mother.

In slang, grief can mean irritation or trouble, as in the expression:

> Don't give me any grief!

> My kids have been giving me a lot of grief lately.

In French, on the other hand, *grief* or *griefs* (it is, as often as not, used in the plural) means <u>grievances</u>, reasons for reproach, or reasons for complaint. The grievances are usually directed against a person, rather than an institution, etc.

> *J'ai beaucoup de griefs contre Pierre* – I have a lot of grievances against Pierre.

> *Elle fait grief à Pierre à cause de ce qu'il a dit / à cause de ses propos* – She has a grievance against Pierre because of what he said / because of his remarks.

> *Il m'a fait grief d'être parti* – He held it against me that I left.

It's not that you are likely to hear the French word *grief* often. What you need to remember is that you

can't translate the English word grief with *grief*. It just doesn't work at all.

To translate the English word grief into French, in the sense of <u>grieving</u> or sorrow, *chagrin* is probably best although *tristesse, peine* or *douleur* could work in some contexts. (The *faux ami* chagrin and *chagrin* was discussed earlier in the book).

> She felt a great deal of grief after the death of her mother – *Elle a eu beaucoup de chagrin après la mort de sa mère / Elle a été très chagrinée après la mort de sa mère.*

If you want to translate grief into French in the sense of <u>annoyance</u> and trouble, try something like this:

> Don't give me any grief! – *Ne m'embête pas !*

> My kids gave me a lot of grief yesterday – *Mes enfants m'ont beaucoup embêté hier.*

ballon – balloon
balle – ball

In French, the word *un ballon* does indeed refer to a child's balloon, or a hot air balloon (which is also called *une montgolfière),* or a weather balloon, or figuratively, a trial balloon *(un ballon d'essai).*

However, the balls used in many sports which are

inflated with air and covered with leather or thick rubber, are also called *ballons* and are not called *balles*. Specifically, the balls used in soccer *(football)*, basketball *(basket-ball, basket)*, rugby *(rugby)* and American football *(football américain)*, are all called *ballons*.

On the other hand, the balls that you use in tennis, golf, ping-pong, handball and baseball are all called **une balle** and not *un ballon*. Note that none of them is inflatable, although tennis balls and ping-pong balls etc. do have air in them.

Une balle in French has other meanings, as well, that a ball may or may not have in English. *Une balle,* in addition to referring to a ball, can refer to a bullet, in slang to a testicle (as in English), and *une balle de coton* or *laine* is a bale of cotton or wool. Finally *la balle de blé* is the husk or chaff of the wheat.

In English a ball can mean a ball to play with, a musket ball, or, in slang, a testicle. These three senses are common to French. By extension, balls (testicles) can mean courage (in slang) as in "He's got balls". Interestingly, in (vulgar) French slang *"Il a des couilles"* which also means "He's got balls", has the same implication: "He's got courage".

A ball can also mean a formal dance, which is translated in French by *un bal* and not by *une balle*. Also, in slang, one can say "We had a ball" which could be translated by *"Nous nous sommes éclatés"*.

This is a lot to absorb so let's summarize:

- **In French**

  un ballon

  > a child's balloon
  > a weather balloon
  > <u>but also</u>
  > > an inflatable ball for sports

  une balle

  > a non-inflatable ball for sports
  > a bullet
  > a testicle
  > <u>and also</u>:
  > > a bale (of cotton, etc)
  > > a husk of wheat

  un bal

  > a ball (a formal dance)

- **In English**

  a balloon

  > a child's balloon
  > a weather balloon
  > <u>but not</u>:
  > > a ball for sports

  a ball

  > a ball for sports
  > a musket ball
  > a testicle
  > <u>and also</u>:
  > > courage (He's got balls")
  > > a great time ("I had a ball")
  > > a formal dance

une histoire – a history

in French, *l'histoire* can refer to the <u>subject history</u> as in English, and *une histoire de France* is a <u>book</u> about the history of France. However, *une histoire* in French is **most often** a <u>story or a narrative</u>, and sometimes it refers to <u>a made-up story</u>, a lie, or a fib.

> *C'est une histoire d'intrigue* – It's a story of intrigue.

> *Ça, c'est une histoire merveilleuse* – That's a wonderful story.

> *Son histoire ne tient pas debout* – His story doesn't hold water.

> *Est-ce que tu me racontes une histoire ?* – Are you feeding me a line? / Are you kidding me?

> *Quelle histoire !* – What a story!

> *Ce ne sont que des histoires. Il n y a pas un mot de vrai dedans !* – It's nothing but lies. There isn't a word of truth in it!

In English, a history **never** means a made up story or even a regular story. (Falsified history may be made-up, of course, but that is not what "a history" means.)

la rétribution – the retribution

In English, retribution almost always refers to what is considered to be <u>just punishment</u>, that is, punishment which is deserved because of some evil act or crime.

> We'll crush them in retribution for what they've done.

In French, on the other hand, *rétribution* simply means <u>pay or reward for services rendered</u>.

> *Je n'accepterai aucune rétribution* – I won't accept any pay.

> *Ce sont des fonctions sans rétribution* – They are honorary duties.

It's apparent that if you translate the English word retribution by *rétribution*, it won't make any sense. **To correctly translate** the English word retribution into French, use *châtiment*.

> We'll crush them in retribution for what they've done – *Nous allons les écraser comme châtiment pour ce qu'ils ont fait.*

spirituel – spiritual

In French, the adjective *spirituel* can mean <u>spiritual</u>, but *spirituel* has another meaning which will really take you aback if you don't expect it. In talking of a person, or especially of a remark, *spirituel* means <u>witty, sharp, bright</u>. etc.

> *Cette farce n'est pas du tout spirituelle* – This prank isn't very funny / very witty.

> *C'est une caricature spirituelle* – It's a witty caricature.

> *Que c'est spirituel !* – Very funny! (ironic)

a farce – une farce

In English, a farce is a crude <u>slapstick comedy</u> using silliness, buffoonery, coarseness and horseplay with ludicrous situations. *Une farce* in French can have the same meaning.

By extension a farce in English can also mean a mockery, an <u>absurd event</u>. This would usually be translated in French as follows:

> The trial turned into a farce – *Le procès est devenu grotesque / devenue comme une farce.*

In French, however, you are very likely to hear ***une farce*** used in other contexts entirely:

First of all, in a culinary setting, *une farce* can mean a <u>stuffing</u> for a meat or vegetable dish.

Secondly, *une farce* is a <u>practical joke or prank</u>. You can see its relationship to the theatrical meaning of *farce*, but a practical joke is not at all the same thing as a slapstick comedy.

We can start with the same example that we used in the *faux ami* spiritual just above:

> *Cette farce n'est pas du tout spirituelle* – This prank isn't very funny / This practical joke isn't very witty.

> *un magasin de farces* – a practical joke shop

> *Il aime faire des farces à tout le monde* – He likes to play practical jokes on everybody.

*Un **farceur*** is, as you might expect, a joker or a practical joker.

> *C'est un vieux farceur !* – He's an old joker! / He's pulling your leg!

Historical Note: One of my English dictionaries states that the theatrical meaning of a farce derives from the culinary "stuffing", as comic interludes were "stuffed" into the texts of religious plays of the 16th century, to keep the interest of the audience.

virtuel – virtual

In English, virtual has two meanings. The first meaning is <u>almost but not quite</u>, as in:

> We noted the virtual absence of trees.

(We noted the near absence of trees / that there were almost no trees.)

It's a virtual impossibility. (It's almost an impossibility.)

It was a virtual admission of guilt. (It was practically an admission of guilt).

She's a virtual prisoner in her own house – (She's practically a prisoner in her own house).

The second meaning of virtual is <u>simulated</u> or computer-generated, as in "virtual reality" or in "a virtual bookstore on the web". (You can see how this meaning probably came from "almost but not quite.")

In French, the meaning of *virtuel* has slipped a bit from the English meaning of virtual. Instead of meaning almost, *virtuel* means <u>potential</u> or possible. This is **not** the same meaning. For example:

C'est un candidat virtuel à la présidence – He's a potential candidate for the presidency. (You can see that the English word virtual **could not** be substituted here at all, nor in the examples which follow.)

Ils réfléchissent au marché virtuel de ce produit / à la vente virtuelle de la maison – They are considering the potential marketing of that product / the possible sale of the house.

To translate the English word virtual into French in the sense of almost but not quite, use *quasiment* or *presque*.

> It was a virtual admission of guilt – *C'était presque un aveu de culpabilité.*

> She's a virtual prisoner in her own house – *Elle est quasiment prisonnière dans sa propre maison.*

On the other hand, in French *virtuel* **does** have the same computer meaning of something which appears functionally for the computer user although it might not have an actual physical existance.

> *la mémoire virtuelle, un disque virtuel, une image virtuelle* – virtual memory, a virtual disc, a virtual image

virtuellement – virtually

The French word *virtuellement* has both the English meaning of virtually, practically, almost, for all intents and purposes, and also the French meaning of potentially or possibly (coming from *virtuel*), as discussed above).

> *Elle est virtuellement prisonnière dans sa propre maison* – She's virtually / practically / almost a prisoner in her own house.

> *Il est virtuellement candidat pour la*

présidence – He's potentially a candidate for the presidency.

The English word virtually means practically or almost but does **not** mean possibly or potentially.

pervers – perverse

In English, perverse usually refers to a person or their behavior and implies an obstinate and stubborn insistance on behaving in ways that are unacceptable, unreasonable or illogical (even inspite of consequences).

He took a perverse pleasure in continually giving the wrong answers. (obstinate and stubborn)

She's being deliberately perverse. (obstinate and stubborn)

It would be perverse to continue to insist that they were there. (illogical and obstinate)

the perverse decision of the court (illogical)

The second and secondary meaning of perverse is sexually perverted. The word perverted is actually used much more commonly in this sense, and is probably the preferred word in English, although perverse can be used.

perverse pleasures, perverse lifestyle
(perverted pleasures, perverted lifestyle)

In French, *pervers* means only sexually perverted
and **does not** mean stubborn or obstinate.

les goûts pervers – perverted tastes

On the other hand, *un effet pervers* can refer to an
unlooked for consequence of an action which is contrary to the expected result.

la circulation – the circulation

In French, *la circulation* can mean circulation as in
the circulation of air, the circulation of the blood, the
circulation of money, putting a book into circulation,
etc, but the context in which you are most likely to
hear it is for (road) <u>traffic</u>.

Il y a beaucoup de circulation aujourd'hui
– There is a lot of traffic today.

*Peut-être cette route aura moins de cir-
culation* – Maybe that route will have less
traffic.

Circulation interdite ! – No thoroughfare!
You are not allowed to drive through
here!

In English, circulation **is not** used as a synonym for
traffic. Note also that there is a French word *trafic*,
but that *circulation* is used much more commonly.

ressentir – to resent

The French word **ressentir** doesn't mean to resent. It means to <u>experience or feel</u>. (It refers to feeling in an emotional sense, not feeling in a physical sense).

> *Elle ressentait pour la première fois l'amour* – She was feeling love for the first time. (literary)

> *Il ne montre pas ce qu'il ressent* – He doesn't show what he feels.

> *Il ne ressent aucune tendresse pour Marie* – He doesn't feel any tenderness for Marie.

> *Il ressentait le besoin d'être seul* – He felt the need to be alone.

> *Il a durement ressenti ses années en prison* – His years in prison were very painful for him / really had an impact on him. (**Note** that this doesn't mean that he resented his years in prison, but that he felt them.)

The reflexive **se ressentir de quelque chose** means to continue to feel the effects of something.

> *Il se ressent de sa maladie* – He still feels the effect of his illness.

> *Je me ressens de la perte de ma mère*

– I still feel the effects of the loss of my mother.

Jean se ressent de sa chute – Jean still feels the effects of his fall.

In very slangy speech, **s'en ressentir pour** (followed by a noun or the infinitive of a verb) means to be up for, to be ready for, to be in shape for.

Alors, tu t'en ressens pour une longue marche ce matin ? (*s'en ressentir pour* followed by a noun) -Well, are you up for a long march this morning?

Alors, tu t'en ressens pour marcher un peu ce matin ? (*s'en ressentir pour* followed by a verb infinitive) – Well, do you feel ready to walk a bit this morning?

estampe – stamp

Une estampe is not a postage stamp. It's a <u>fine arts print</u>.

C'est un livre illustré de plusieurs estampes – It's a book illustrated with several prints.

des estampes de Dali – prints by Dali

le cabinet des estampes (du musée) – the print room (of the museum)

Une estampe can also be a tool or a <u>machine to</u>

make <u>prints</u> or to stamp a design, similarly to it's counterpart word, a stamp, in English.

To translate the English word postage stamp into French, the correct word is *un timbre*.

un pamphlet – a pamphlet

In English, a pamphlet is a small booklet or leaflet containing information or arguments, usually about a single subject. It's a general word for any small brochure, from an instruction pamphlet or fact sheet to a political pamphlet.

In French, on the other hand, *un pamphlet* is **always** a tract written as a (violent) satirical attack against the government, church, other institutions or a well known person.

Thus most pamphlets in English **would not** be translated as *un pamphlet*, and would usually be **translated** as *une brochure*.

pathétique – pathetic

Both *pathétique* and pathetic can mean emotionally moving, and their meanings in this sense are close enough to be recognizable by a speaker of the other language, even if the usage isn't exactly identical. (In French, by the way, *pathétique* is a rather literary word.)

She came in out of the cold looking hungry, cold and a little pathetic.

Sa souffrance était pathétique – His suffering was very moving.

C'est un roman pathétique – It's a moving novel.

However, in English slang, pathetic often means appalling, useless, worthless or lamentable.

He's pathetic!

How pathetic!

Isn't she pathetic!

The French word *pathétique* is **never** a translation for pathetic in this sense. Thus:

C'est un roman pathétique

never means it's a pathetic (worthless) novel, but **always** means it's a moving novel.

To translate the English word pathetic into French in the sense of appalling or worthless, use *lamentable*.

How pathetic! – *C'est (fortement, vraiment) lamentable !*

It's a pathetic book! – *C'est un livre lamentable ! / C'est un navet !*

la mécanique – the mechanic

If you are looking for a mechanic, the correct word to use is *un mécanicien* because *la mécanique* is the science of mechanics.

l'exhibition – the exhibition

In English, the most common usage of exhibition is a public <u>display of works of art</u> (at a museum or gallery, for example), <u>or of goods</u> or merchandise (at a trade fair, for example).

The **correct translation** for this kind of exhibition is *une exposition.*

> We went to an exhibition of Monet's paintings – *Nous sommes allés à une exposition des peintures de Monet.*

> the exhibition center – *le centre d'expositions*

In English, an exhibition can also mean a <u>display of skills</u>.

This is probably **best translated** by *une démonstration.*

> It was a nice exhibition of what they could accomplish in a short time – *C'était une bonne démonstration de ce qu'ils peuvent accomplir en peu de temps.*

Finally, an exhibition can be used pejoratively to refer to an <u>ostentatious display</u>, in bad taste, of either emotion or of some other quality.

> It was a disgraceful exhibition – *C'était un spectacle de mauvais goût.*

In French, while *une exhibition* can be used for a wild animal show, or for the presenting of documents in a legal setting, you are quite unlikely to see it used in either of these senses very often.

Exhibition in French has one other sense. It is used pejoratively, quite similarly to the pejorative sense in English, for a <u>display which is ostentatious and immodest</u>. It is, however, a much more literary word than its counterpart in English.

> *Chacun se sentit choqué par cette exhibition de sentiments* – Everyone felt shocked by this exhibition of emotion.

> *Sa robe est très courte. Elle fait exhibition de ses jambes* – Her dress is very short. She's making a virtual exhibition of her legs. (pejorative)

Thus,

> It was a disgraceful exhibition.

which we translated "*C'était un spectacle de mauvais goût*", could also be translated: "*C'était une exhibition de mauvais goût*".

Historical Note: You should note that in the past

une exhibition was used for an exhibition of art, etc, as in English, but this usage is now obsolete and *une exposition* is now the correct word, but you may still see the word *exhibition* in older works.

exhiber – to exhibit

Consistent with the meanings of *exhibition*, **exhiber** in French means to <u>produce your official papers</u> (carte d'identité, driver's license, passport), or to <u>exhibit wild animals</u>, etc., but most often *exhiber* is used pejoratively to mean to <u>show off ostentatiously</u> and immodestly, to flaunt.

> *Elle porte des chemisiers si décolletés qu'elle exhibe ses seins* – She wears blouses that are so low cut that she shows off her breasts / displays her breasts / flaunts her breasts.

> *Il m'a exhibé toutes ses médailles* – He showed off all his medals to me.

The reflexive, *s'exhiber*, means to show oneself off in public and it is also used pejoratively.

> *Il n'aime pas s'exhiber en public* – He doesn't like to make a display of himself in public. (He thinks it's in bad taste.)

To translate:

To exhibit paintings or sculpture is not translated by

exhiber, but *exposer*. (You will remember that an art show is not *une exhibition,* but *une exposition*.)

> She's going to exhibit her paintings next week – *Elle va exposer ses tableaux la semaine prochaine.*

To exhibit goods in a shop window is also translated by *exposer*.

To exhibit bad manners, or courage, or cowardice is better translated by *faire preuve de*, as in:

> He exhibited a lot of courage when his son was in danger – *Il a fait preuve de beaucoup de courage quand son fils était en danger.*

Finally, to exhibit remorse or grief is translated by *manifester*. (The difference is that manners, courage and cowardice are shown by behavior. To exhibit one of them is translated by *faire preuve de*. On the other hand remorse and grief, etc are emotions. To exhibit one of them is translated by *manifester*.)

> She didn't exhibit any grief after the death of her father – *Elle n'a manifesté aucun chagrin après la mort de son père.*

guérilla – guerrilla

The French translation for the English word guerrilla (irregular soldier, partisan), is *un guérillero*.

In French, *la guérilla* means the guerrilla warfare.

> *C'était une guérilla sanglante et longue –*
> It was a long and bloody guerrilla war.

la société – the society

In French, the noun *société* can mean society in the same senses as in English. One can say

> *un danger pour la société* – a danger to society (in talking about the <u>community</u> as a whole)

> *la haute société* – (referring to what we would call <u>high society</u>)

> *une société primitive* – a primitive society (referring to a <u>people</u> or to a culture)

> *une société secrète /* or *une société de pêcheurs à la ligne* – a secret society / or a fishing club (referring to a <u>group of people</u>, a club, an <u>association</u>)

One can also hear *société* used as in:

> *Il préfere la société de jeunes femmes* – He prefers the <u>company</u> / the <u>companionship</u> of young women. (We could conceivably say "the society of young women", but "the company of young women" is better in English.)

However the usage which will be the most confusing to an English-speaking person is the common use of *une société* to refer to <u>a business, a firm or a company</u>.

> *une société d'assurances* – an insurance company

> *une société anonyme* – an incorporated business (*société anonyme* is often abbreviated *S.A.* and has the same meaning as "Inc." in English.)

> *une société multinationale* – a multinational company

> *une société d'édition* – a publishing company

> *une société d'État* – a state-owned company

The English word society is not used in this sense at all.

transpirer – to transpire

In English, to transpire means to <u>happen</u> or to occur.

> I wonder what transpired while we were gone. (I wonder what happened...)

As a second meaning, transpire can mean to <u>prove to be the case</u>, to turn out. For example:

As it transpired, she was wrong in expecting that he would come. (As it turned out…)

In French, on the other hand, *transpirer* has a completely different meaning. The verb *transpirer* means to <u>sweat or perspire</u>. To transpire never means to sweat in English.

> *Il avait transpiré pendant la nuit* – He had perspired during the night.

> *Il a transpiré à grosses gouttes pendant son travail* – He sweated heavily while he was working.

> *Il a transpiré sur ce boulot* – He sweated over this job. (casual language)

> *Il transpire des aisselles* – He's sweating under his armpits.

In French, transpirer can be used figuratively when talking about a secret or about some news. In this sense, *transpirer* can mean to <u>gradually come to light</u>, to slip out, to leak out (through the pores, so to speak).

This is a more literary (as well as figurative) usage, and it may also help us to make a better guess at where the English meaning "to turn out to be the case" came from.

> *Le secret a transpiré presqu'à la veille de*

l'élection – The secret leaked out almost on the eve of the election.

In both languages, in a botanical context, *transpirer* and to transpire have the same meaning: to give off water through the stomata of the leaves.

forger – to forge

The French verb *forger* doesn't mean to forge or to counterfeit but to <u>work at a forge</u>.

To translate the English verb to forge into French in the sense of to counterfeit, use *contrefaire* or *fabriquer un faux de*. For example:

> He forged my signature – *Il a contrefait ma signature.*

> He forged the will – *Il a fabriqué un faux testament.*

étranger – stranger

The **English** word stranger can mean either someone <u>from somewhere else</u>:

> He was a stranger in our town.

or someone <u>that you don't know</u>:

> He was a stranger to me.

> Don't talk to strangers!

To translate a stranger into French in the sense of someone from somewhere else, use *un étranger*.

To translate a stranger into French in the sense of someone you don't know, use *un inconnu*.

The **French** word *un étranger* can also have two meanings. *Un étranger* can mean a person <u>from somewhere else</u>, which we would translate as "a stranger", or it can mean a person <u>from another country</u>, which we would translate as "a foreigner".

The two different meanings are represented by the same word, *étranger*, in French, and people tell from context, while in English we have the two different words, stranger and foreigner. Note that a stranger and a foreigner are not same thing. Someone could be a foreigner but not a stranger at all, perhaps even a friend. And, of course, someone could be a stranger without being a foreigner.

Finally, in French, *l'étranger* can mean <u>a foreign country</u>, or <u>abroad</u>, as in:

> *Il vient de l'étranger* – He comes from abroad / from a foreign country.

Depending on context, *l'étranger* can also mean the stranger or the foreigner, of course, if you are talking about a specific person:

> *L'étranger est venu d'Angleterre* – The stranger / The foreigner came from England.

le collège – the college

If you have children of school age, this *faux ami* can trip you up. **Un collège** in France runs from the sixth to ninth grades, inclusive. In other words, what we would call middle school, or junior high school.

And the grades count backwards, so that you enter *le collège* in *sixième*, pass through *cinquième*, and *quatrième*, on your way to *troisième*, which would be the equivalent of ninth grade in the U.S.

In *troisième*, the kids take a competitive national exam, referred to informally as *le Brevet* (although it has a longer official name). This exam decides what *lycée* or high school they can be admitted to.

Now let's consider the English word **college**. Translating the idea of an American-style liberal arts college into French can be difficult, as there is no counterpart in France. The French kids are placed into a fixed educational track (Science, etc) by the time they enter *lycée* (tenth grade), and the French are mystified by an American student entering university without an idea what he or she will be doing for a lifelong career, and the idea that the student may take courses in a variety of different fields in the university, with no other goal but to broaden his education, is more mystifying still.

Probably the best way to say that a student is in college is to say that he or she *fait des études supérieures*, is *à l'université*, or is *à la fac* or *en fac* (which is casual language).

dilapidé – dilapidated
dilapider – to dilapidate
dilapidation – dilapidation
un dilapidateur / une dilapidatrice

In English, the adjective **dilapidated** means <u>deteriorated</u> and fallen into a state of disrepair. It usually implies that this disrepair is as a result of neglect and of aging. The verb, **to dilapidate**, is now archaic, but meant (as you would expect), to cause something to fall into a state of (partial) ruin and disrepair by neglect.

> The sofa was dilapidated and seemed to be falling apart.

In French, although it appears so similar, ***dilapider*** has a different meaning. I should say <u>two</u> different meanings:

Dilapider in French almost always refers to money or property. When it refers to someone's personal fortune it means <u>to waste or to squander</u>. French synonyms would be *gaspiller* and *dissiper*. In this context, *dilapidé* doesn't mean dilapidated, it means wasted or squandered.

> *J'ai peur qu'il dilapide sa fortune* – I'm afraid that he will squander his fortune.

> *Malheureusement, il a dilapidé son argent* – Unfortunately, he has squandered his money.

When *dilapider* refers to public funds instead of personal funds it means to <u>embezzle or misappropriate</u>.

> *Il a dilapidé des fonds publics* – He has isappropriated public funds.

Similarly, the French word **dilapidation** doesn't mean dilapidation but means the squandering or embezzlement of funds.

> *C'est forcément la dilapidation de sa fortune* – It's certainly the squandering of his fortune.

> *C'était la dilapidation de fonds public* – It was the embezzlement of public funds.

Finally **dilapidateur** and **dilapidatrice** as adjectives means spendthrift, and as nouns means a spendthrift or embezzler, depending on context. (They are not commonly used words).

> *C'est un homme dilapidateur* (adj) – He's a spendthrift.

> *C'est un dilapidateur* (noun) – He's a spendthrift / embezzler.

Historical Note: As an interesting aside, one of my English dictionaries lists dilapidate as coming from the Latin *dilapidare*, meaning to squander, to demolish. It appears that the French *dilapider* has kept the meaning squander, while the English meaning of dilapidate leans more in the direction of demolish.

To translate the English word dilapidated into French, the best choice is probably *délabré*.

> in a state of dilapidation – *dans un état de délabrement*

> the dilapidated sofa – *le canapé délabré*

le canapé – the canapé

The example we used just above brings us to another *faux ami, canapé*. **In French**, *un canapé* can have two different meanings. It can refer to a small piece of bread or pastry with a topping such as salmon, caviar, asparagus tips, a slice of hard boiled egg, et cetera, which is served at a formal party, or even at a cocktail party. This meaning is identical to the English meaning.

However, **in French**, a common, and probably the most common, meaning for *un canapé* is as another word for a <u>sofa</u>. The difference between *sofa* and *canapé* being that it is usually assumed that one can sleep on *un canapé* if necessary.

Canapé does not have this sense in English, or if it does it is a very, very rare usage, while it's the most common usage in French.

> *Asseyez-vous là, sur le canapé* – Sit down there, on the sofa.

> *Il va passer la nuit sur le canapé* – He's going to spend the night on the sofa.

molester – to molest

In English, to molest used to mean to verbally pester, annoy or harass somebody, usually in an aggressive and persistent manner.

In current usage however, to molest usually means to <u>force sexual attentions</u> on a woman against her will, or force sexual attentions on a child. This second meaning (sexual molestation), has become the dominant one in current English.

In French, on the other hand, *molester* means to <u>manhandle</u> or to maul physically, especially in public. French synonyms are *maltraiter physiquement, brutaliser, malmener* and *rudoyer.*

> *Quelques voyous l'ont molesté dans la rue* – Some young toughs roughed him up in the street.

> *Il s'est fait molester par la police* – He got himself manhandled by the police.

As you can see, if you were to encounter the French word *molester* you could probably figure out the meaning from the English meaning and from context, but it is not the way molest is usually used in English.

To translate the English meaning of to molest in the sense of pester aggressively you can use *importuner* or *embêter.*

To translate the English meaning of to molest in the sense of sexual molestation try something like:

> He sexually molested her – *Il lui a fait subir des sévices sexuels.*

Historical Note: As an interesting aside, in older French sources *molester* can mean to annoy or harass someone, but this usage is dated and was not even mentioned in most of my dictionaries. Thus in both languages, *molester* and molest used to mean to annoy, pester or harass someone, but this usage is now dated in both languages. The current senses of the words have drifted in different directions --- to manhandling in French, and to sexual molestation in English.

une compote – a compote

The differences between these *faux amis* are a little less obvious. **In French**, *une compote* is made up of <u>fruit which is mashed</u> or finely diced, then cooked in water, usually with sugar. Something like applesauce for example.

In English, on the other hand, a compote of fruit is usually <u>whole stewed fruit,</u> often with syrup. While this difference may not seem like a big deal, when you see *une compote* on a menu, or when you, yourself, are trying to describe what you are serving, or what you had for dinner, it can make a difference to you, and it can save you from misunderstanding what you will be served, or from incorrectly describing a dish.

> *Ma femme a préparé une compote de coings pour le dessert* – My wife has prepared applesauce (but made out of quince) for dessert.

In English a compote can also refer to a long stemmed dish for serving candy, nuts or fruit. It **does not** have this meaning in French.

un souvenir – a souvenir

While *un souvenir* **in French** can mean a memento, a keepsake or a tourist memento, just like in English, the most common meaning for *un souvenir* in French is a memory.

> *J'ai de mauvais souvenirs de ce voyage* – I have bad memories of that trip.

> *Elle n'en a pas souvenir* – She has no recollection of it.

> *Si mes souvenirs sont corrects, je suis arrivé ici il y a environ quatorze ans* – If my memories are correct / If my memory is correct, I arrived here about fourteen years ago.

A souvenir **does not** mean a memory or a recollection in English.

la confidence – the confidence

In English, confidence usually means <u>assurance</u>. It can be assurance in oneself, in something else, or in someone else.

He has a lot of confidence.

I have a lot of confidence in the staff of the hospital.

She has confidence that the job will be finished on time.

However, a confidence can also be a <u>secret or private matter</u> that you share with someone. And if you tell someone something "in confidence" you expect them to keep it secret.

I want to tell you something in confidence (in secret).

The two girls loved to share confidences (private matters to be held in secret).

I think that we should take him into our confidence (let him in on the secret).

In French, on the other hand, *la confidence* **only** refers to the second of these meanings: a <u>secret or private matter</u>:

I want to tell you something in confidence – *Je veux te dire quelque chose en confidence.*

She shared confidences with her friend – *Elle a fait confidence de ses secrets à son amie / Elle a fait des confidences à son amie.*

But, if you want **to translate** the English word confidence in the sense of assurance, you **can not** use *confidence*, you have to use an entirely different French word, *confiance.*

He has a lot of confidence – *Il a fort confiance (en lui-même).*

I have confidence in the staff of the hospital – *J'ai confiance en l'équipe de l'hôpital / Je fais confiance à l'équipe de l'hôpital.*

You can buy it with full confidence (assurance). – *Vous pouvez l'acheter en toute confiance.*

consumer – to consume

I'm putting *consumer* and to consume here because these two words are very much like *confidence* and confidence which we just discussed.

You recall that the French word *confidence* expresses just one of the two senses that confidence can have in English, and that there is a very similar word, *confiance*, to express the other, perhaps more common, sense. Well, in just the same way, *consumer* expresses just one of the two senses that "to consume" can have in English, and there is a very similar word, *consommer*, to express the other, perhaps more common, sense.

In French, **consommer** means to <u>eat or drink</u>, to consume by <u>ingesting</u>, by <u>using up</u>. It therefore holds for a car consuming gas as well.

> *Cette voiture ne consomme pas beaucoup d'essence* – This car doesn't consume much gas.

> *Ils ont consommé tout ce qui était sur la table* – They ate everything that was on the table.

> *Elle a déjà consommé trois bouteilles de bière* – She's already consumed three bottles of beer.

> *Ils ont consommé presque toutes leurs provisions pendant les deux premières semaines* – They consumed almost all their provisions in the first two weeks.

On the other hand, **consumer**, the French word with the same spelling as the English word, means to consume only in the sense of being <u>eaten up as by a fire</u>.

> *Le feu a consumé la maison pendant que nous regardions* – The fire burned down the house while we were watching.

> *Il a été consumé par la fièvre* – He was eaten up by the fever.

Elle est consumée par l'ambition / par les soucis / par la jalousie – She is consumed by ambition / by worries / by jealousy.

Elle se consume de chagrin – She's wasting away with grief.

The two senses are quite distinct, as you see. The pronounciations are close enough that if you use the wrong word in speech, a French person will probably make allowances, but when you write one of them, you'll want to use the correct word.

la dévotion – the devotion

And finally, we have a third set of words with the same format as the two sets just above: an English word, devotion, whose French counterpart, *dévotion*, is a translation for only a less common meaning of the English word, and where there again exists a not-very-different French word, *dévouement*, that matches with the most common meaning of the English word.

In French, the word ***dévotion*** primarily means <u>religious fervour</u>, <u>devoutness</u> and <u>piety</u>. For example:

Elle fait ses dévotions – She's saying her prayers, going to confession, etc.

Elle est en état de dévotion mystique – She is in a mystical state of religious fervour.

Le chapelet est un objet de dévotion – The rosary beads are an object of religious devotion.

C'est une fausse dévotion – It's hypocrisy.

La dévotion can also be used figuratively to mean <u>adoration</u> or <u>veneration</u>, but this is very much a secondary and literary sense:

Il a une grande dévotion pour Racine – He has a verneration for Racine / He worships Racine.

Il écoutait avec dévotion – He listened fervently.

On the other hand, there is another French word, **dévouement** which means devotion in the sense of <u>self-sacrifice</u> and <u>dedication</u> to a duty or a cause.

Il a un dévouement total à son parti / à son boulot – He is totally devoted (or dedicated) to his party / to his job.

C'est un dévouement aveugle – It's a blind devotion.

Ma femme m'a soigné avec dévouement quand je me suis cassé la jambe – My wife cared for me with dedication / devotion when I broke my leg.

The verb that goes with *dévouement* is **dévouer.**

Il est très dévoué à sa femme – He is very devoted to his wife.

Il est totalement dévoué à son emploi – He is totally devoted to his job.

Elle se dévoue aux gens qui vivent dans la misère – She devotes herself / dedicates herself to helping people who are living in poverty.

le placard – the placard

In English, a placard has just a single meaning. It refers to a poster or sign for public display, often with a political message, either fixed to a wall or carried in a demonstration.

The demonstrators all carried placards saying...

In French, on the other hand, while *un placard* can mean a <u>poster</u>, as in English, you are **much more likely** to encounter it as a <u>closet or cupboard</u>.

Je vais mettre ces boîtes vides dans le placard – I'm going to put these empty boxes in the closet.

Le placard can also have figurative uses in slang:

Il a des squelettes dans le placard – He has some skeletons in his closet.

Ils vont mettre le projet au placard – They

are going to put the project on hold / to put the project on ice. (Literally translated: they're going to stick it in the closet).

Tu peux faire vingt ans de placard – You could do twenty years in prison.

la figure – the figure

In French, when referring to a person's body, *la figure* refers to the person's <u>face</u> and **does not** refer to the person's shape. (A French synonym is *le visage*).

Je vais lui casser la figure – I'm going to smash his face.

Il fait une drôle de figure – He has a funny look on his face.

To translate the English word figure into French in the sense of body shape, use *la silhouette*.

She has a thin figure – *Elle a une silhouette fine.*

Other meanings for figure are similar in French and English:

une figure de mots / une figure de rhétorique – a figure of speech

une grande figure de l'histoire – a great figure of history *une figure géometrique* – a geometrical figure

une figure d'argile – a clay figure

Cela commence à prendre figure – That is starting to take shape.

la démonstration – the demonstration

In French, *la démonstration* is used for the most part just like demonstration in English. For example:

une démonstration de force – a demonstration of force (military)

de grandes démonstrations de joie – a great show of joy

Le professeur de chimie a fait une démonstration – The chemistry professor did a demonstration.

C'était une démonstration du fonctionnement de l'appareil – It was a demonstration of the functionning of the apparatus.

On ne peut pas vendre cette voiture, elle est en démonstration – We can't sell this car. It's for demonstration.

However, **in English,** one often calls a political or labor protest a demonstration. **In French**, *une démonstration* **never** means a protest.

To translate the English word demonstration into French in the sense of a protest, the correct word is *une manifestation.*

> It's an anti-war demonstration – *C'est une manifestation contre la guerre.*

> They took part in the demonstration – *Ils ont participé à la manifestation.*

inusable – unusable

These *faux amis* come close to being opposites. The French adjective ***Inusable*** comes from the verb *user* which means "to wear out". Thus, as you would guess, *inusable* means <u>unable to be worn out</u>. Thus:

> *Sa robe s'était révelée inusable* – Her dress proved to be impervious to wear / Her dress never wore out.

> *J'ai ce pull depuis dix ans / J'utilise ce marteau depuis dix ans maintenant. Il est practiquement inusable* – I've had this sweater for ten years / I've used this drill for ten years now. It doesn't seem to ever wear out / It seems impervious to wear.

If you contrast

> *Ce pull est inusable.*

with

This sweater is unusable.

you will quickly see how close *inusable* and unusable are to being opposites.

To translate the English word unusable into French, you can use *inutilisable*, or you can say that the thing *ne peut pas être utilisé*.

la carnation – the carnation

Here's an odd little *faux ami:*

In English, a carnation is a <u>flower</u>. And carnation can also refer to a rosy pink color, but this meaning is rarely used.

In French, *la carnation* is the (facial) <u>complexion</u>.

> *Elle a la carnation de blonde* – She has fair skin, a fair complexion.

In fine arts, *carnation* can also refer to flesh-color tint.

To translate the English word carnation into French, the name of the flower in French is *un oeillet* and the name of the color is *incarnat*.

Side Note: That *carnation* in French means flesh-color undoubtedly comes from the Latin stem *carne* meaning meat (think "carnivore"). Interestingly, while *carnation* means flesh tint in fine arts, there's a French adjective *carné* which means flesh-colored in regular speech.

la complexion – the complexion

This brings us to another *faux ami*, complexion and *complexion*.

In English, the complexion is the natural color and appearance of the skin of a person's face.

In French, la complexion is a <u>person's constitution</u>.

> *Elle a une complexion robuste, faible, délicate* – She has a robust, feeble, delicate constitution.

> *Il est maigre de complexion* – He's naturally skinny.

To translate the English word complexion into French, the correct word is *la carnation*, as we just learned.

To summarize these last two *faux amis*:

- The **constitution** in English is *la complexion* in French.

- The **complexion** in English is *la carnation* in French.

- The **carnation** in English is *l'oeillet* in French.

coquetterie – coquetry, coquettishness
coquet, coquette, coqueter – a coquette
un flirt – a flirt

In English, a coquette is a woman who flirts for the pleasure of making conquests, coquettishness is flirtatiousness, and coquetry is flirtatious behaviour or a flirtatious manner.

In French, these words have pretty much lost that connotation, and flirtatious and flirtatiousness are listed as meanings which are *vieillis* (out of date and old-fashioned, if not obsolescent).

The French meanings of **coquet** and **coquette** evolved from flirtatious, to desiring to please members of the opposite sex by means of ones appearance, to the current meaning of <u>appearance consciousness</u>. For example:

> *Il est trop coquet* – He's a dandy / He's too fussy about his appearance.

> *C'est une petite fille coquette* – She's a little girl who is very conscious of her appearance / who likes to dress up and look nice.

Coquet and *coquette* can also be used for objects to say that they are <u>attractive</u> in appearance. For example:

> *une maison coquette, un jardin coquet,*

> *une robe coquette* – a charming house, a charming garden, a stylish dress

In slang *coquet* and *coquette* can be used figuratively to mean <u>attractive</u>:

> *C'est une coquette somme* – It's an attractive sum.

> *C'est un héritage assez coquet* – That's a pretty nice inheritance.

To say that someone is ***une coquette***, meaning that she is a flirt, or that she is coquettish in the English sense of the word, is an <u>outdated</u> usage in French.

Similarly, the verb ***coqueter*** meaning to flirt is also <u>outdated</u>.

And ***coquetterie*** no longer means flirtatiousness but means <u>appearance-consciousness</u> in current day French.

> *Elle s'habille avec coquetterie* – She dresses stylishly, with good taste, (but perhaps in a bit of an affected manner).

> *Il fait des coquetteries* – He behaves in an affected manner / He puts on airs.

To translate the English word flirtatious into French, use *charmeur / charmeuse* or *enjôleur / enjôleuse*.

There were French adjectives ***flirteur / flirteuse***, which meant flirtatious and the noun ***un flirt*** which meant a person who is flirtatious, but these are listed as <u>no longer in use</u> and currently <u>obsolete</u>.

The French verb **flirter,** is still in use however. It does mean to <u>flirt</u>, and it is used similarly to the English word flirt, even in a figurative sense.

> *Mais lorsque la température a commencé à flirter avec le zéro, la maison a dû être bien froide* – But when the temperature began to flirt with zero, the house must have been really cold.

You can also still use the noun **un flirt**. However, *un flirt* doesn't refer to a flirtatious person, but to a <u>brief romantic relationship</u>, like a flirtation but maybe a bit more, as in:

> *Elle a eu un flirt avec Jean. C'était son premier flirt* – She had a brief romantic relationship with Jean. It was her first romance.

To say she is being flirtatious with him, try the following:

> She's very flirtatious – *Elle est très charmeuse.*

> Anne is flirting with Jean / being flirtatious with Jean – *Anne fait du charme à Jean / Anne et Jean flirtent ensemble.*

surveiller – to survey

In English, to survey can mean to <u>examine the contours of a piece of land</u>, usually with the idea of making or improving a map, or verifying property lines.

>They had someone survey the lines of their new property.

To survey can also mean to <u>get the opinions</u> of a number of people, to do a survey.

>They surveyed the opinions of all the residents of the town over twenty years of age.

Finally, to survey can mean to <u>look at someone or something closely</u> to evaluate or appraise them or it.

>He surveyed the damage.

>His cold blue eyes surveyed her dispassionately.

In French, on the other hand, *surveiller* has a different meaning. It usually means <u>keep an eye on</u> or to <u>watch over</u>. It's meaning is more closely related to the English word surveillance (obviously originally a French word) than it is to survey.

>*Il faut surveiller ces enfants tout le temps* – You have to keep an eye on those kids all the time.

La police surveille la foule – The police are keeping an eye on the crowd.

Il surveillait ses bagages pour éviter un vol éventuel – He kept an eye on his baggage / watched over his baggage to avoid any possibility of a theft.

Le contremaître surveillait le chantier – The foreman kept an eye on the workplace / was watching over the workplace.

Note that while the English word to survey can also have a sense of looking at something to appraise it, it is not at all the same meaning. The French word *surveiller* has **none** of the three meanings that survey can have in English.

To translate the English verb to survey into French, try one of the following suggestions:

He had someone survey his new property – *Il a fait expertiser sa nouvelle propriété.*

They surveyed the opinions of all the residents – *Ils ont enquêté sur les opinions des résidents.*

He surveyed the damage – *Il a évalué les dégâts.*

Her cold blue eyes surveyed him dispassionately – *Ses yeux bleus et froids l'ont regardé sans émotion.*

Note again that none of these sentences was translated with *surveiller*.

la mutation – the mutation

The French word *mutation* has the same meaning as <u>mutation</u> if you are talking biology.

However, the most common usage that you will hear for *une mutation* is a <u>transfer</u>. For example, the transfer of an employee or a soldier from position to position, or from city to city.

> *Elle a eu une mutation dans une autre ville* – She was transferred to another city.

> *Jean a obtenu une mutation pour raison de santé* – Jean obtained a transfer for health reasons.

This usage sounds completely foreign, of course, in English. The associated verb is *muter.*

> *Elle a été mutée dans une autre ville.*

Another general meaning of the French word *mutation* is a <u>change</u> or an alteration. Thus in a legal sense *une mutation* can refer to a transfer or <u>change of ownership</u> of property.

Finally, in referring to a deep, and presumeably lasting, change, one can say:

> *La Chine est en pleine mutation économique* – China is in the midst of / is undergoing profound economic change.

You could probably figure out the meaning of *mutation* in this example even if you didn't know it, but you would probably never use it that way in English.

l'alternative – the alternative

I learned that you can't use *l'alternative* for the alternative in most cases when I commented to friends that *"Vieillir n'est pas si mal si on pense à l'alternative"* and I received that blank and somewhat puzzled stare that means I used a word in a way that doesn't quite make sense in French.

In English, an alternative is a <u>possibility or choice</u>, and can refer to actions or objects.

> Her only alternative was…

> You have three alternatives.

> He should consider another alternative.

In French, *l'alternative* is not usually used in the same way. *L'alternative* is a more literary word than its English counterpart, is less used in oral conversation, and is used differently.

To start with, *les alternatives* refer to opposing phenomena or states which succeed each other regularly. In other words, <u>phenomena which alternate</u>. For example:

> *Des alternatives... d'exaltation et d'abattement"* (Flaubert).

Secondly, *une alternative* can refer to a <u>situation or obligation in which you have only two possible choices</u>:

> *Je suis dans une affreuse alternative, ou bien accepter l'affectation et perdre mon épouse, ou bien la refuser et perdre mon emploi* – I'm in a terrible predicament. Either I accept the assignment and lose my wife, or refuse it and lose my job.

Note that here *l'alternative* refers to the situation of being forced into one of the choices, and **not** to one of the choices itself.

You may occasionally see *l'alternative* used, as in English, to refer to an alternate choice, but this usage is considered *un anglicisme* and *un emploi critiqué* (a usage which is frowned upon and, as I discovered, not even understood at times).

If you want **to translate** the English noun alternative into French, try something like this:

> He has no other alternative – *Il n'a pas d'autre choix / d'autre solution.*

> You have three alternatives – *Vous avez*

trois choix possibles / trois solutions pos-sibles.

To get older isn't so bad if you consider the alternatives – *Vieillir n'est pas si mal si on pense à l'autre choix.*

ancien – ancient

In English, ancient means belonging to the distant past and no longer in existence, as in

> the ancient civilizations of the Sumerians

or it means very old, as in

> an ancient forest.

In French, *ancien* can also mean can mean <u>very old</u> or <u>belonging to the distant past</u>, as in:

> *des livres anciens*

> *Cette partie de l'immeuble est plus ancienne que le reste.*

> *les civilisations anciennes*

If you are referring to something which is old but still existing *(un monument ancien),* French synonyms would be *vieux* or *antique.*

If you are referring to something which is very old but

no longer exists *(une civilisation ancienne)*, a French synonym would be *passé*.

In French, however, *ancien* has other meanings that ancient **does not** have in English. When *ancien* is used before the noun it usually means <u>ex-</u> or <u>former</u>.

> *C'est un de mes anciens élèves* – He's one of my ex-pupils / former pupils.

> *C'est mon ancienne épouse* – She's my ex-wife. (Note that this doesn't mean "She is my old wife". [It says nothing about her age], just as *un de mes anciens élèves* doesn't mean that the student is old).

> *C'est un ancien policier* – He's an ex-policeman / He's a former policeman.

> *Ah ! oui, c'était le dentiste. Un ancien dentiste, plus exactement* – Ah, yes, it was the dentist. An ex-dentist, actually. *(Simenon)*

Finally, *ancien* can mean <u>having seniority</u>.

> *Il est plus ancien que moi dans le métier* – He's been in the profession longer than me.

la perception – the perception

In French, *la perception* may indeed mean the <u>per-</u>

<u>ception</u> (by the senses). However, common alternate meanings for *la perception* are the <u>tax office</u>, or the <u>collection of taxes</u>.

Perception **never** means tax office or tax collection in English.

un percepteur – a preceptor

In English, a preceptor is a literary word for a teacher or an instructor. There is a corresponding French word *un précepteur / une préceptrice* with the same meaning.

However, don't confuse preceptor with *percepteur*. *Un percepteur* is a <u>tax collector</u> and has nothing to do with teaching.

futile – futile
la futilité – the futility

These are excellent *faux amis*. When you first come across a word like *futile* or *futilité* in French, you are likely to simply assume without further reflection that they mean the same thing as the English words. Unfortunately, they don't!

In English, futile refers to an action and means that it is or was <u>doomed to failure</u>. For example:

That would be futile. (It won't work)

They made a futile attempt to hold back the flood waters with sandbags.

They tried to hold back the flood waters with sandbags but the attempt was futile.

In French, however, *futile* refers to a remark, reason, a pretext or an action and says that it is <u>frivolous, trivial and unimportant.</u>

> *...presque toujours pour une raison futile* – ...almost always for a frivolous reason. *(Simenon)*

> *Il n'aimait pas voir mêler les questions futiles aux solemnités du bridge* – He didn't like to see frivolous questions mixed with the solemnity of bridge. *(Simenon)*

> *Elle l'a fait sous le prétexte le plus futile / sous le plus futile des prétextes* – She did it on the most frivolous pretext.

You can also refer to a person as *futile*, which means that he or she is <u>frivolous</u> and not serious.

Historical Note: In English, futile also used to have a secondary meaning of frivolous, but this meaning is now rarely used (and would not even be recognozed by most English speakers).

The nouns **futility** and *futilité* have the same difference in meanings. **In English** futility is the property of being <u>doomed to failure</u>.

He didn't recognize the futility of his actions (…that his actions were doomed to failure).

She was filled with a sense of futility. (She felt that whatever she did was bound to fail.

In French, *futilité* means <u>frivolity, silliness, insignificance, childishness</u>. As you can see, it's a completely different meaning.

la futlité de son raisonnement / de son objection – the frivolity or silliness of his reasoning / of his objection.

(Note again *that la futilité de son objection* doesn't mean that his objection was doomed to failure, but that it was frivolous).

Une futilité can also, by extension, refer to a frivilous action or remark.

Il dit des futilités – He's spouting nonsense / What he's saying is silly.

To translate the English word futile into French, you can use *inutile* but it's probably not as strong as futile. *Qui ne va pas marcher* is probably better. For example:

That would be futile – *Ça serait inutile / Ça ne peut pas marcher / Ça ne va pas marcher, c'est sûr !*

To translate the English word futility into French you have to use the same methods:

> He didn't recognize the futility of his actions – *Il ne s'est pas rendu compte que ses actions vont être inutiles / que ce qu'il faisait ne marchera pas / que ce qu'il faisait ne marchera jamais.*

ulcérer – to ulcerate
ulcéré – ulcerated

In French, in a medical context, *ulcérer* can mean to <u>ulcerate</u>.

However, in the figurative sense **ulcérer** means to <u>cause a strong resentment</u> in someone, <u>to embitter</u> someone. This figurative sense has indeed become the most common meaning of *ulcérer* (my Petit Larousse doesn't even bother to list the medical meaning).

Ulcéré, therefore, naturally means <u>resentful or bitter</u>. Here are some examples:

> *Tes critiques l'ont vraiment ulcéré* – Your criticism has really embittered him.

> *Il en est ulcéré* – He's really bitter about it.

> *Ses propos m'ont ulcéré* – His remarks really irritated me / I really resent his remarks.

Il mangeait en silence, ulcéré et sombre – He was eating in silence, resentful and gloomy.

Ulcerated and to ulcerate **are not** used this way in English.

fumer – to fume

In English, to fume can mean to emit gas, vapors or smoke. This is an uncommon usage however, and it is used only in specific circumstances, as for noxious chemicals, for example, which can be said to "fume".

The most common meaning of to fume is to <u>seethe with anger</u>, to feel, show or express a great anger.

I could see that he was fuming after the remark that she made.

He was fuming against the injustice of the situation.

In French, *fumer* can also mean to fume with anger, but this is slang, *le langage familier*. **To translate** the English word to fume into good French for a more formal situation, use *rager, fulminer, être exasperé,* etc.

He was fuming against the injustice of the situation – *Il rageait contre l'injustice de la situation.*

In proper French, the primary meaning of *fumer* is <u>to smoke</u>, in any of the same three senses that to smoke has in English:

First, *fumer* means to smoke as regards to tobacco or other substances.

> *Il fume une cigarette / un pipe / un joint / du tabac / de l'herbe / un paquet par jour* – He smokes a cigarette / a pipe / a joint / tobacco / grass / a pack a day.

Second, *fumer* means to give off smoke or vapor.

> *La bouche du canon fumait / La cheminée fumait / Le feu fumait / La soupe chaude fumait* – The barrel of the cannon was smoking / The chimney was smoking / The fire was smoking / The hot soup was steaming.

> (While the English verb to fume can mean to give off noxious vapors, it wasn't and wouldn't be used as a translation in any of these examples. In English, we would use to smoke or to steam in all of them.)

Finally, *fumer* can refer to smoking meat, salmon, etc.

> *Sa spécialité est de fumer de la viande* – Her specialty is smoking meat.

To summarize, in English you can't use to fume to translate *fumer* (meaning to smoke) in any of these senses. And to fume only means to give off vapors in the limited sense of giving off noxious fumes, as noted above.

un as – **an ass**

If you think that you hear someone calling you an "ass" in French, it's probably a compliment. He's calling you *un as*, which is <u>an ace</u>. *Un as* can refer to an ace at a particular activity as in

> *un as du volant* – an ace driver
>
> *un as de petanque* – an ace petanque player

or it can be a general compliment as in:

> *C'est un as* – He (or she) is a neat person / He (or she) is really great / *Il (ou elle) est très fort(e).*

To translate the English word ass into French, it depends which type of ass you are talking about. If it's the animal it's *un âne*, if it's a person that you are calling an ass, it's *un idiot* or *un âne* , and if it's a backside it's *une fesse,* or more vulgarly, *un cul*, as in:

> She has a nice little ass – *Elle a un joli petit cul.* (The final *"l"* is not pronounced in *cul).*

But remember that this is a vulgar usage and you should be very, very careful about using it.

Side Note: The "ace" in a deck of cards is also *un as*.

une fabrique – a fabric

In French, *une fabrique* is a factory.

> *Ils ont une grande fabrique près de Paris* – They have a large factory near Paris.

To translate the English word fabric into French, the correct word is *le tissu*. (The *faux ami* "tissue – *tissu*" was discussed earlier).

> It's a pretty fabric – *C'est un joli tissu.*

la prévention – the prevention

In French, the word *prévention* does mean <u>prevention</u> if you are talking about an illness or an accident, etc.

> *la prévention de la malaria / du paludisme* – the prevention of malaria
>
> *la prévention des accidents* – the prevention of accidents
>
> *les mesures de prévention routière* – measures of road safety

However, *prévention* has other meanings that will

leave you scratching your head when you come across them, especially in reading. First of all *la prévention* means the prejudice, the bias, or the preconceived ideas.

> *Il faut examiner les choses sans préventions* – It's necessary to look at things without preconceived bias. (It does sound strange, doesn't it!)

> *Il essayait de dissiper les préventions que le commissaire aurait pu nourir contre lui* – He was trying to dissipate the prejudices / the preconceived notions that the commissaire might have had against him.

Sentences like that make no sense when you first come across them unless you are aware of the *faux ami*.

Finallly, *en prévention* has a use in legal language and is roughly equivalent to in custody or in detention.

> *Il est maintenant en prévention* – He is now in custody.

la correction – the correction

As with *prévention,* which we have just discussed, *la correction* does mean correction in the English sense, but then has other meanings it doesn't have in English.

First we'll give some examples of *la correction* meaning the correction:

> *Les corrections dans le texte sont toutes indiquées en rouge* – The corrections in the text are all indicated in red.

> *Il faut faire quelques corrections* – It's necessary to make some corrections.

However, *correction* can also mean <u>correctness</u>, which correction never means in English:

> *La traduction était d'une correction parfaite* – The translation conformed exactly to the original / was faithful to the original.

Next, *correction* can mean <u>correct behavior</u>, <u>propriety</u>. French near-synonyms are *bienséance* and *politesse*.

> *Il se comportait avec une correction parfaite* – He behaved with perfect manners / He behaved very properly.

> *C'est la plus élémentaire des corrections* – It's basic good manners.

> *C'était l'impeccable correction de M. Pyke qui l'embêtait* – It was the perfect correctness of M. Pike that was annoying him.

And finally, *une correction* can mean a <u>spanking</u> or a <u>thrashing</u>. This is from the langage familier.

> *Si tu n'es pas sage, je vais te donner une bonne correction* – If you don't behave I'm going to give you a thrashing.

un homme du monde – a man of the world

The French expression *un homme du monde* isn't a strict *faux ami* as it doesn't sound like it's English counterpart. However it is a *faux ami* in that using your knowledge of English you are likely to mistake its meaning.

If you see or hear the expression *un homme du monde* you are naturally likely to translate it to yourself as a man of the world. However that's not what it means. *Un homme du monde* is a man who belongs to high society.

> *Elle est familière avec moi et elle épluche tous les comptes. --- En somme, selon vous, ce n'est pas une vraie femme du monde ?*
>
> She is overly familiar with me (her housekeeper), and she goes over all the bills with a fine-tooth comb. --- In sum, in your opinion, she is not a true woman of high society? / she's not a real society woman? (Simenon)

To translate the English expression man of the world

into French, probably the closest you can come is *un homme d'expérience* or *un homme de grande expérience.*

la résignation – the resignation

In English the word resignation has two different meanings. It can mean <u>acceptance without challenge</u> of something undesirable but inevitable, in other words: submission. This can refer to news, the authority of someone else, etc.

> He accepted the decision with resignation / He accepted the news with resignation.

Resignation can also mean a <u>decision to give up a post or a job</u>.

> He submitted his resignation.

In French, résignation has **only** the first meaning (<u>acceptance without challenge, submission</u>).

> *Il a accepté la décision avec résignation.*

To translate the English word resignation in the sense of giving up a job or post, use *la démission.*

> He submitted his resignation – *Il a donné sa démission.*

crier – to cry

In English, to cry can mean to exclaim or to cry out:

> "I don't believe it!" he cried.

> He cried out with pain.

> "James!" he cried out from across the room.

In French, the verb crier has the same primary sense: to <u>cry out</u> , to <u>shout</u>, to <u>scold in a loud voice</u>.

> *Il a crié de douleur* – He cried out with pain.

> *Il criait comme un fou* – He was screaming like a crazy person / He was shouting as loud as he could.

> *Ta mère va crier* – Your mother is going to scold you / shout at you.

> *Il a crié un ordre* – He cried out an order.

> *Il criait vengeance* – He cried out for vengeance

> *Les poissonières criaient les prix des poissons* – The fish merchants call out the prices of the fish.

However, by far the most common **English** meaning of to cry is to cry tears, which must be translated by *pleurer*. You **can not** translate to cry in the sense of tears with *crier*.

> He saw her in the bedroom crying – *Il l'a vue dans la chambre en train de pleurer.*

> I'm afraid I'm going to cry – *Je crains de me mettre à pleurer.*

> He must be very sad. He cries all the time – *Il doit être très triste. Il pleure tout le temps / continuellement / sans arrêt.*

In French as well *crier* has a few minor meanings that it doesn't have in English. If you are talking of a door, *crier* means to squeak or creak. If you are talking about a bird, *crier* means to call. Finally, if you are talking about colors *crier* means to clash, as in:

> *Ce rouge crie avec le rose de ta jupe* – This red clashes with the pink of your skirt.

un regard – a regard

In French, *un regard* is a <u>look</u> or a <u>glance</u>.

> *Tapez les chiffres à l'abri des regards indiscrets* – Type in the numbers while sheltering them from indiscrete glances (referring to credit card codes).

Elle m'a lancé un regard furieux – She gave me a furious look.

Je l'ai cherché du regard – I looked around for him.

Il m'a envoyé un regard goguenard – He gave me a mocking glance.

In English, on the other hand, while the verb to regard often means to look at, the noun a regard rarely means a look.

Regard can mean <u>admiration</u> or <u>respect</u>.

To translate regard into French in this sense use *l'estime, le respect,* or *l'admiration.*

I have great regard for him / I hold him in high regard – *J'ai beaucoup d'estime / de respect pour lui.*

Regard can also mean <u>consideration</u>.

To translate regard into French in the sense of consideration, use *considération* or *égard.*

She saved him without regard for her own life – *Elle l'a sauvé sans égard pour sa propre vie.*

I didn't say it, out of regard for his feelings – *Je ne l'ai pas dit, par égard pour sa sensibilité.*

Regard can also mean <u>attention</u>.

To translate regard into French in this sense use *l'attention*.

> He doesn't pay any regard to what he's doing – *Il ne fait aucune attention à ce qu'il fait.*

> She doesn't pay any regard to what I say – *Elle ne fait aucune attention à ce que je dis.*

With regard to can mean in connection with.

To translate regard into French in this sense try one of these suggestions:

> with regard to what she said – *quant à ses propos / en ce qui concerne ses propos*

> in that regard – *à cet égard*

Finally, Regards (in the plural), or Best regards, is used at the end of a letter to say best wishes or something equivalent.

There are many very, very flowery French phrases for ending a letter. They are much more elaborate than their English counterparts and some use forms of speech that people haven't used in a hundred years. Some more simple ones that you might be more comfortable using include *amitiés, mes amitiés, mes sincères amitiés, toutes mes amitiés, amicalement* in writing to a friend, and *cordialement* in a more business-type letter.

la charge – the charge
charger – to charge

These words have an enormous number of meanings in both French and English. Many of the meanings are the same for both languages:

> We need to charge the new battery – *Il faut charger la nouvelle batterie / pile.* (This is if you are charging a new battery for the first time. Otherwise it's *Il faut recharger la batterie* as you are recharging it).

> The soldiers charged / The bull charged – *Les soldats ont chargé / Le taureau a chargé.*

> It was a cavalry charge – *C'était une charge de cavalerie.*

> He took charge of it – *Il l'a pris en charge.*

> I'll take charge of that – *Je me chargerai de cela.*

> He was charged with the responsibility to get it done – *Il a été chargé de le faire.*

> What he said had an emotional charge – *Ce qu'il a dit avait une charge affective.*

I'm not going to make any attempt to list all of the meanings in either language. What I'm going to do first is tell you about a use of the French verb *char-ger* where you normally **wouldn't** use the English verb charge.

Then I'll describe two important uses of the English verb charge which **can't** be translated into French as *charger*.

Here they are:

In French, *charger* can mean to fill up or to load:

> *Le mur était chargé de tableaux* – The wall was covered with / loaded with pictures.

> *Sa voix a chargé ce mot d'une intonation étrange* – His voice loaded this word with a strange intonation / His voice gave this word a strange intonation.

> *C'était une table chargée de gâteaux* – It was a table loaded with cakes.

To charge is not usually used in this way in English, although it possibly could be in some cases..

In English, on the other hand, we use charge in the areas of money and the judiciary. These are two areas where you'll get those blank stares if you mistakenly try to translate the English word charge by *charger* or *charge*.

First let's talk about money:

a charge card – *une carte de crédit*

What are your charges for delivery? / What do you charge for delivery? – *Quels sont les frais de livraison ?* (You use *les frais* for the charge for <u>services</u>).

What do you charge for that? – *Quel est le prix de cela ?* (You use *le prix* when you are <u>buying something</u>, whether bread in a *boulangerie* or the *plat du jour* in a *restaurant.* You could also ask *Combien ça coûte ?* in very informal language).

There is no charge for admission – *L'entrée est gratuite.*

The bookstore charged me ten euros for this book – *La librairie m'a fait payer dix euros pour ce livre.*

How much do you charge by the hour – *Combien prenez-vous de l'heure ?*

Can I charge it to my account? / Can I charge it to my bill? – *Puis je mettre ça sur mon compte ? / Puis je mettre ça sur la note ?*

What is important to remember is that you **can not** use the French words *charger* or *la charge* in any of these examples. If you say *Qu'est-ce que la charge pour ça ?*, you won't be understood!

Now let's look at some of the ways that charge is

used in the <u>legal</u> arena in English. Remember that these also **should not** be be translated into French with *charge* or *charger*.

First using the verb charge to mean <u>accuse</u>:

> What crime is he charged with? -- (If he's just accused...) *De quel crime est-il accusé ?* -- (If he's formally charged...) *De quel crime est-il inculpé ?*

> I charge him with having killed his wife – *Je l'accuse d'avoir tué sa femme.*

Now using the noun charge to mean <u>accusation</u>:

> What is the charge against him? / What are the charges against him? – *Que sont les accusations portées contre lui ? De quoi est-il accusé ?*

Side Note: Note that *charger quelqu'un de quelque chose* can mean to put the responsibility for something on the person or to give him the responsibility for it.

For example: *Il a essayé de répondre honnêtement sans charger ses camarades* can mean he tried to respond honestly without putting the responsibility on his companions, or it could even be translated as "without accusing" them, but this is a stretch and not at all the same thing as the English meaning of charge which clearly means to accuse someone formally of a crime.

résumer – to resume

This *faux ami* is straightforward and simple. The French verb *résumer* **doesn't** mean to resume. *Résumer* means to <u>summarize</u>, to sum up, to recapitulate.

> *Pour résumer ce qui est arrivé...* – To summarize what happened...

> *Je vais essayer de résumer la situation en quelques mots* – I'm going to try to summarize / to recapitulate the situation in a few words.

> *Pour me résumer, je dirai que je ne suis pas du tout heureux de cette situation* – To sum up what I have already said, I will say that I'm not at all happy with this situation.

If you want **to translate** the English word to resume into French, it's probably best to use *reprendre*, but you can also use *se remettre à*:

> I'm going to resume work tomorrow – *Je vais reprendre le travail demain / Je vais me remettre au travail demain.*

> I think he is going to resume his journey – *Je crois qu'il va reprendre son voyage.*

Side Note: The English word résumé meaning a summing up of a person's previous employment, etc. was evidently imported directly from the French.

particulier – particular

In English, the word particular has three main senses.

First, particular singles out a <u>specific</u> member of a group:

> He has a particular way of dressing.

> He seems to be looking for a particular person.

> There are particular colors that she doesn't like.

Second, particular can mean <u>special</u> or unusual, as in:

> He needs to exercise particular care / He needs to be particularly careful.

Thirdly, particular can mean <u>fastidious</u>, meticulous, careful, very concerned with everything being proper and correct.

> He's a very particular person.

> She's very particular about neatness.

Finally, the two-word phrase "in particular" means <u>especially</u>, more than others.

> I like this color in particular.

In French, *particulier* can refer to something which singles out a <u>specific</u> person or thing, as in English.

> *Il a une façon particulière de s'habiller –* He has a particular way of dressing.

> *Il y a une couleur verte très particulière qu'elle n'aime pas du tout –* There is a particular color of green that she doesn't like at all.

> *Le coquelicot était d'un rouge particulier à l'espèce –* The poppy was in a red particular to the species.

The French word *particulier* can also mean <u>special</u> or unusual, also as its English counterpart.

> *Il faut prendre un soin particulier –* It's necessary to take particular care.

> *Il a écouté avec une patience toute particulière –* He listened with particular patience.

However, in French, *particulier* **never** means fastidious. To translate the English word particular in the sense of fastidious or meticulous, try one of the following:

> He's a very particular person – *C'est un homme très méticuleux.*

> She's very particular about neatness –

Elle exige que tout soit bien rangé dans sa maison.

And one of the most common meanings that you will encounter for *particulier* in French is **not found** at all in English and will puzzle you when you hear it. *Particulier* often means <u>private or personal.</u>

Ce n'est pas un immeuble de bureaux, c'est une maison particulière – It's not an office building, it's a private house.

Il a des raisons particulières pour... – He has his own private / personal reasons for...

Ce n'est pas une voiture de l'entreprise, c'est ma voiture particulière – It's not a company car, it's my own personal car.

Il lui reste un hôtel particulier qui est la plus belle demeure de la ville – He still has a private mansion which is the most beautiful home in the city.

And *particulier* can be used as a noun in this sense too, to mean <u>a private person</u> or an individual person:

Cet immeuble n'appartient pas à une entreprise, il appartient à un particulier – That building doesn't belong to a company, it belongs to a private person.

Particular **is not** used this way in English.

Now let's consider **en particulier**. *En particulier* can be used like "in particular" to mean <u>specially</u>:

> *De toute sa famille, j'aime son frère en particulier* – Of all his family, I like his brother in particular.

> *J'aime les romans policiers de Simenon en particulier* – I like Simenon's detective stories in particular.

But, *en particulier* can also mean <u>privately</u>, which it **does not** mean in English.

> *Je voudrais vous parler en particulier* – I would like to talk to you in private.

Here's what you need to remember: *particulier* in French **never** means meticulous or fastidious (as particular often does in English), but *particulier* in French **often** means private or personal (which particular never does in English).

se formaliser – to formalize

Just as in English, French words that are used in speech vary from common everyday words to others which are somewhat more formal or sophisticated, but still very much a part of the oral language. The French verb, *se formaliser (de),* is a word like that. It's used in speech but is a slightly more sophisticated word than some of its synonyms.

In English, to formalize means to <u>make formal</u> or to give formal status to.

In French, however, the verb *formaliser* has nothing at all to do with formality. *Se formaliser* de means to <u>take offense at</u>. Some more common French synonyms include: *s'offenser, s'offusquer, se vexer, se piquer.*

Thus, in English:

> We will formalize our offer to buy the building. (We will make the offer we have been talking about into a formal offer).

While, in French:

> *Vous pouvez parlez franchement, je ne vais pas me formaliser* – You can talk frankly. I won't take offense.

> *Il se formalise pour un rien* – He gets offended over nothing / He's getting offended over nothing at all.

> *Ne vous formalisez pas* – Don't get offended / Don't be offended.

To translate the English verb to formalize into French, in talking about a business contract, for instance, try something like this:

> We will formalize our offer to buy the building – *Nous allons donner une forme officielle à notre offre d'achat pour*

l'immeuble / Nous allons faire une offre d'achat officielle.

la fourniture – the furniture

You can't use *la fourniture* to translate the furniture. *La fourniture* has nothing to do with furniture. It means <u>the act of supplying or provisioning</u>.

> *C'est lui qui est chargé de la fourniture des vivres à l''hôtel* – It's he who is responsible for supplying the hotel with food supplies / provisions.

And *les fournitures* are the supplies and provisions themselves.

To translate the English word furniture into French, the correct word is *les meubles* or *le mobilier*.

vulgaire – vulgar

This is a tricky faux ami because the English and French meanings overlap somewhat.

In English, in current speech, vulgar means <u>coarse and rude</u>. Vulgar often means <u>obscene</u> and refers to a remark that <u>makes explicit and offensive reference to sex or bodily functions</u>. A vulgar person is someone who would make that kind of remark, someone who is coarse and crude. A vulgar display (of wealth, for example), is one lacking good taste.

There was a second meaning which is now dated

in English and rarely used. This is vulgar meaning pertaining to the masses, to the common man (in a pejorative sense).

In French, the adjective *vulgaire* used to mean <u>widespread</u>, common to all. Thus, *une expression vulgaire* which would mean an expression known to everyone, and *la langue vulgaire*, refers to the popular language, spoken by the masses, by everyone. This usage has now evolved slightly to mean <u>common, ordinary, without distinction, mediocre.</u>

> *le nom vulgaire d'une plante* – the common name as opposd to the scientific name

> *la langue vulgaire* – the popular language spoken by the people, used historically for French and Provencal as opposed to Latin.

> *C'est un homme vulgaire* – He's a mediocre person without an original idea. (**Note** that this doesn't necessarily mean that he is vulgar in the English sense of the word).

> *Il a beau être riche, ses manières et son comportement sont affreusement vulgaires* – He may be rich but his manners and his behavior are truly common, commonplace and ordinary (or worse). He's a mediocre person.

By extension, *vulgaire* can <u>mean totally lacking in distinction, finesse, and délicatesse</u>, and thus appropriate for the lowest levels of society.

And finally, depending on context, *un mot vulgaire (un gros mot),* or *une expression vulgaire* means <u>vulgar speech</u>, as in English.

To summarize:

- **Vulgar** in English leans toward coarse and obscene. A second meaning, referring to the masses, has mostly faded out of use.

- *Vulgaire* in French primarily means common, either common in the sense of widespread, or common in the sense of ordinary and mediocre. When specifically used for a remark or word, it can mean vulgar.

To translate the English word vulgar into French, use *grossier* or *obscène*, or both, to be sure to be understood in the sense that you mean it.

vulgariser – to vulgarise
vulgarisation – vulgarisation

The French verb *vulgariser* means to <u>popularise</u>, to <u>make understandable for the common man</u>. This is somewhat predictable from what we just learned about vulgaire.

> *C'est un journaliste qui vulgarise la science* – He's a journalist who popularis-

es scientific knowledge for the common man.

We are used to the English meaning of vulgar so this sounds strange and pejorative to us, but in French it's not necessarily pejorative unless the speaker doesn't like popularisations.

The French noun *une vulgarisation* means a popularisation.

> *Sa spécialité est la vulgarisation de la biologie* – His specialty is the popularisation of biology.

> *Ce livre est une vulgarisation des théories d'Einstein* – This book is a popularisation of Einstein's theories.

le chauvinisme – chauvinism

It's giving away my age, but I can remember studying vocabulary words for the SAT exam many years ago, and one of the words I learned was chauvinism. At that time, chauvinism meant excessive patriotism or nationalism. "Male chauvinism" hadn't been coined yet.

Well, in French, *le chauvinisme* still means excessive patriotism and nationalism, just the way I learned it in school. It doesn't mean male chauvinism, and if you use it that way you probably will be misunderstood. *Un chauvin* is the word for a person who has *chauvinisme:* what we would call a chauvinist or ultra-nationalist.

To translate the English term male chauvinism into French use *machisme.*

To translate a male chauvinist into French, use *un homme macho, un macho,* or *un machiste.*

un engagement – an engagement

The **French** word *engagement* has a couple of senses which are more or less similar to their English counterparts, or at least close enough to be recognizable.

For example in a military context, *un engagement* can mean a <u>military engagement</u> (battle) or it can mean an enlistment.

With regard to employment, *un engagement* can refer to engaging or <u>hiring</u> a new employee, or booking a musician or an act.

So far, these two usages would probably be close enough to Engllish that you'd be able to recognize them, or at least figure them out, if you ran across them. However, if you are putting something up for security, *l'engagement* means <u>pawning</u>, <u>pledging</u> or mortgaging the article. (Since the French word for pledging or pawning is *mettre <u>en gage</u>,* I'd be willing to risk a speculation that the word <u>*engagement*</u> comes from this).

Finally, *un engagement* has another meaning in French which doesn't jump to the eye of an English speaker, at all! Here are some examples:

> *Ma femme a été emmenée dans les camps pendant la Révolution Culturelle et elle n'est jamais rentrée. Et le plus étrange, c'est que je suis plus attaché à elle maintenant que lorsque nous vivions ensemble. C'est une question de…d'engagement. Oui. C'est ça. Un engagement. Très chinois, l'engagement. J'ai pris un engagement vers ma femme, et je dois m'y tenir –*

> My wife was taken to the camps during the Cultural Revolution and she never has come back. And the strangest thing is that I am more attached to her now than when we were living together. It's a question of…of <u>commitment</u>. Yes. That's it. A <u>commitment</u>. It's very Chinese, <u>commitment</u>. I made a <u>commitment</u> to my wife and I have to stick by it. (Modified from *La femme perdue*, Nicole Mones).

This sense of commitment is also used in a political or even ideological sense as in:

> *Son engagement au parti communiste date des années trente –* Her <u>commitment</u> to the communist party dates back to the thirties.

Finally, when talking about investing money it refers to a commitment or tying up of the money for a period of time.

> *C'est un engagement de trois années au minimum* – It's a <u>commitment</u> (of money) for at least three years.

To translate the English word an engagement, in terms of an agreement to marry, into French, the correct word is **not** *l'engagement*, **but** *les fiançailles*.

> She has broken her engagement – *Elle a rompu ses fiançailles.*

> She has a pretty engagement ring – *Elle a une jolie bague de fiançailles.*

I'll grant you that an agreement to be married is a commitment, so if *engagement* means commitment it ought to work, but *engagement* is not used that way in French. The correct word is *les fiançailles*.

To translate an engagement in the sense of prior plans, try one of the following:

> I have a previous engagement – *Je suis déjà prise / J'ai déjà un rendez-vous à cette heure-là.*

évincer – to evince

Inspite of their identical spelling, evince and *évincer* have nothing to do with each other and thus are bona fide *faux amis*. However I'm going to cover them fairly quickly as neither evince or *évincer* is a commonly encountered word.

In English, to evince is a formal or literary word that means to show, in the sense of revealing the presence of.

> Her letters evince the love she feels for him.

In French, on the other hand, *évincer* has two meanings both coming from the stem of dispossessing someone of something.

The first meaning is to <u>evict</u> someone legally.

The second meaning is to <u>oust or supplant</u> somebody from a position <u>by intrigue</u>, usually in a political context.

> *Il est arrivé / est parvenu à évincer son rival de la présidence* – He succeeded in ousting his rival from the presidency / chairmanship.

une manie – a mania
un maniaque – a maniac

In both French and English, *une manie* and a mania can refer to a <u>period of insanity</u>, especially a manic episode in a patient with manic-depressive illness or, as it is now called, bipolar illness.

In both languages a mania and *une manie* can also refer to an <u>obsession</u>, or overly intense preoccupation, in someone who is otherwise quite well.

> He has a mania for old cars / for cleanliness – *Il a la manie des voitures anciennes / de la propreté.*

In French, used in the plural, **les manies** can also mean <u>odd little habits</u>. This usage blends somewhat with the idea of obsession on the milder end, but mania wouldn't be used in this way in English:

> *C'est un homme célibataire avec beaucoup de petites manies* – He's a man who has never married and who has a lot of odd little fussy habits.

The French adjective (and noun) **maniaque** can also mean crazy, but usually refers to either of the latter two meanings that we listed above for *manie*. That is to say, someone either with an obsessional idea and <u>obsessional behavior</u>, or someone unduly controlled by his little obsessional habits, a fussbudget, someone who is <u>finicky, fussy, and pernickety.</u>

The English word **maniac** does **not** have these meanings. It doesn't mean obsessional or fussbudgety, neither as a noun, nor as an adjective.

Here is an example of *maniaque* referring to someone with an obsessional idea:

> *C'est une maniaque de la propreté* – She's obsessed with cleanliness.

And here's an example of *maniaque* referring to someone who is fussy and finicky:

> *Maintenant qu'il a vieilli, il est vraiment devenu maniaque* – Now that he has gotten older he has really become a persnickety fussbudget.

une conférence – a conference

What you need to remember about *conférence*, is that, while it can mean a <u>conference</u> or meeting as in English, it **also** can mean a <u>lecture</u> or presentation.

> *une conférence de presse* – a press conference
>
> *une conférence au sommet* – a summit conference
>
> *M. Blanc est en conférence* – Mr. Blanc is in conference / in a meeting.
>
> *Il va faire / Il va donner une conférence sur les faux amis dans la salle de conférences* – He's going to give a lecture on faux amis in the lecture hall.
>
> *le maître de conférences* – the lecturer

une carpette – a carpet

In English, a **carpet** usually refers to a wall-to-wall floor covering which is nailed or glued down to the floor, and meant to cover the entire floor surface. Figuratively, it can be used for something totally covering a surface. For example, a carpet of snow.

A **rug**, on the other hand, refers to a free-standing floor covering which does not cover the whole floor. (An exception to this is the expression oriental carpet or Persian carpet, which usually refers to a large to medium sized oriental rug). A **throw rug** is a small decorative rug which can be moved easily from place to place.

In French, the word for what we would call a wall-to-wall carpet is **une moquette**. The word for what we would call a large to medium sized rug is **un tapis**. And the word for a small floor covering, perhaps what we would call a throw rug, is **un petit tapis** or **une carpette**.

The two key things to remember are first, that instead of being a fixed wall to wall covering like a carpet in English, *une carpette* is roughly a small throw rug (and it's a word which is not used nearly as often as *tapis*). And second, that the French word for a carpet is *une moquette*.

In French slang, *une carpette* can also be used to refer to a person who lets himself be figuratively walked all over by other people. You'll recognize that this is an exact parallel to calling someone a doormat in English.

la gratification – the gratification

In ordinary spoken and written French, *une gratification* refers to a <u>payment</u> made, usually to a person rather than to a business, which is <u>above and beyond what is due</u>. Thus it could refer to a bonus *(une prime, une bonification),* a tip *(un pourboire),* a Christmas bonus or end-of-the-year bonus *(les étrennes),* or an illicit under-the-table exhange of funds *(un pot-de-vin).*

> *Il a donné des gratifications aux salariés* – He gave bonuses to the salaried employees.

> *Je crois qu'il a pris cette décision parce qu'il a reçu une bonne gratification* – I think he decided in that way because he received some money under the table / he received a bribe.

> *J'ai reçu ma gratification de fin d'année* – I received my year-end bonus.

To translate the English word gratification into French, it is best to use *la satisfaction.* (The French word *gratification* only means gratification in the field of psychology).

> I'm doing it for my own gratification – *Je le fais pour ma propre satisfaction.*

le relief – the relief

The words relief and *relief* mean the same things in both languages when you are talking about painting or sculpture or a countryside. In other words, the character of the piece of art, or of the place, which gives a sense of <u>depth</u>, of foreground and background.

And putting something in relief or *en relief* means <u>making it stand out</u>, emphasizing it, making it clearly visible or obvious due to it being accentuated in some way. This also is true in both languages.

> *L'idée était bien mise en relief* – The idea was very well put in relief / was made to stand out.

> *Je l'ai mis en relief* – I highlighted it (on the computer, etc).

> *Ce paysage me paraît sans relief* – This countryside seems to me to be without relief / to be flat, without interest.

> *Le soleil couchant a mis les sommets des montagnes en relief* – The setting sun put the mountain peaks in relief / made the mountain peaks stand out.

> *L'homme pénétra à la nuit tombée dans la courte allée. Il connaissait par coeur les reliefs des pavés déchaussés* – The man entered the short alley at night-

fall. He knew by heart the outlines / the shapes of the loose paving stones.

In English, however, relief has several other entirely different senses that it doesn't have at all in French.

When we talk about a sense of relief we are referring to a <u>release from anxiety or worry or pain.</u>

You **can not translate** this sense of the English word relief into French with *le relief.* the correct word is *soulagement.*

> What a relief! – *Quel soulagement !*

> It was a relief to find a hotel with an available room – *J'étais soulagé de trouver un hôtel avec une chambre libre.*

> I have some pills that are recommended for the relief of headache – *J'ai quelques pilules qui sont conseillées pour soulager les maux de tête.*

In English, relief can also refer to <u>assistance</u>, usually in food, clothing or money, to people in need. *Le relief* **never** means assistance in French.

> The disaster relief didn't arrive fast enough – *Les secours aux victimes du désastre ne sont pas arrivés quand il fallait / ne sont pas arrivés assez vite.*

> They sent out a relief expedition – *Ils ont envoyé une expéditon de secours.*

Finally a relief nurse, a relief driver, etc., refers to someone <u>replacing</u> someone who has been on duty. *Le relief* isn't used this way either in French.

> His relief didn't show up – *Son remplaçant n'est pas arrivé.*

The key thing to remember is that the French word *relief* has **only** the sense of something which <u>stands out</u>. It has none of the other senses that relief has in English, all of which have to do with release from discomfort or with assistance in some form or another.

célébrer – to celebrate
la célébration – the celebration

In English, to celebrate usually means to <u>mark a special happy day</u> by doing something enjoyable, usually in a social setting, but not necessarily. For example:

> They went out to a night club to celebrate their first anniversary together.

> She celebrated her birthday with a big party.

> She celebrated her success with a glass of champagne. (alone, this time)

A much less common meaning of to celebrate is to <u>perform a religious ceremony</u>, especially a mass.

> The priest celebrated mass at ten o'clock.

And much less common still, to celebrate can mean to praise publically.

> He was a much celebrated author.

In French, *célébrer* usually **does not** mean "to mark a special happy day by doing something enjoyable" which is the primary meaning in English. *Célébrer* usually means to accomplish a ceremony in a solemn way, to mark with a formal ceremony, to solemnise (which, as we saw, is just a minor meaning in English).

> *Le maire a célébré leur mariage* – The mayor performed their marriage.

> *Le prêtre n'a pas encore célébré la messe* – The priest hasn't yet celebrated the mass.

> *Ils vont célébrer la grande victoire en faisant un défilé* – The are going to celebrate the great victory with a parade.

Célébrer can also mean to praise publically, the other minor meaning of to celebrate in English.

> *La cérémonie était pour célébrer la mémoire de…* – The ceremony was to celebrate the memory of…

To translate the English word to celebrate in it's

usual sense (of marking a special day with a pleasant activity), into French, the correct word is *fêter*.

> They went out to a night club to celebrate their first anniversary together – *Ils sont sortis en boîte pour fêter leur premier anniversaire ensemble.*

> She celebrated her birthday with a party – *Elle a fêté son anniversaire en donnant une soirée.*

> She celebrated her success with a glass of champagne – *Elle a fêté sa réussite avec un verre de champagne.*

It's the same with **a celebration** and *une célébration*. Unless you are talking about the celebration of a mass, a funeral, a wedding, or something of the sort, the correct word is *une fête*.

> It's our anniverary and we are going to have a big celebration at our house – *C'est notre anniversaire et nous allons donner une grande fête chez nous.*

> We are going to party, celebrate, live it up tonight – *Nous allons faire la fête ce soir.*

séduire – to seduce
séduisant – seductive
la séduction – the séduction

These aren't complete *faux amis*, as *séduire* can mean to seduce (either a man or a woman), *séduisant* can mean seductive, and *séduction* can mean seduction.

However, what often confuses anglophones is that, **in French**, *séduisant* often simply means charming, tempting, or strongly attractive, without any implication of being sexually seductive, *séduire* often means to charm, to captivate, to fascinate, to please, to tempt, also without any necessary sexual connotation, and *séduction* often just means attraction without a necessary sexual element.

On the contrary, **in English**, although seductive, seduction and to seduce can mean to charm when used figuratively (I was seduced by his proposal), the **usual** usage implies sexual seduction.

It's a question of emphasis, which in French is further along the spectrum in the direction of charm, and in English more towards sexuality.

> *Ce sont des propositions séduisantes* – They are attractive proposals.

> *C'est une personne séduisante* – She's a charming / attractive person.

J'ai été séduite tout de suite – It appealed to me right away.

Il exerçait une séduction mystérieuse sur les autres étudiants – He exercised a mysterious attraction over the other students / He charmed or attracted the other students in a mysterious way.

C'est une offre séduisante – It's an attractive / tempting offer.

la partition – the partitiion

In French, *une partition* does mean a <u>political division</u>, as in English. For example:

la partition de l'ancienne Yougoslavie en cinq pays – the partition of the former Yugoslavia into five countries

However, in French, *la partition* also means the <u>musical score</u>, and often refers to the actual sheets of paper that the notes are written on. The partition **does not** have this meaning in English, and this sense of the word will not at all be self-evident when you first hear it:

Ma fille a oublié la partition – My daughter forgot to bring the sheet music.

Heureusement elle peut jouer le morceau sans partition – Fortunately she can play the piece without having the music.

la partition de piano / la partition d'orchestre – the musical score for piano / for full orchestra

In English, the partition can mean a thin <u>divider</u> breaking up a space. *La partition* **does not** mean this in French, and to translate the English word partition into French in the sense of a divider you should use *la cloison.*

The large room was broken up by a series of partitions – *La grande pièce a été divisée avec plusieurs cloisons / a été cloisonnée (en plusieurs petites pièces).*

Finally, in English, **to partition** is a <u>verb</u>, as in:

It was decided in an international conference to partition the country.

There **isn't any** corresponding <u>verb</u> *partitionner* in French, except perhaps in computer language where *partitionner* can refer to dividing up the hard drive, but it's considered an anglicism.

Therefore, **to translate** the English verb to partition into French, you can use *diviser* if you mean to divide, *partager* if you mean to divide up something like an inheritance, *démembrer* if you are talking about partitioning a country, and *cloisonner* or *compartimenter* if you are talking about partitioning a space or a room.

la monnaie – the money

The French word *la monnaie* has lots of meanings, most of which correspond to the English words money or currency. I won't go into those here but will focus on the *faux amis*, the meanings which don't correspond.

In French, the most common meanings that you will hear for *la monnaie* are <u>small change</u> (as in small coins) and <u>change</u> (as in the change you get when you break a large bill or as in the change you get back after paying for a purchase). Money **does not** have these meanings in English.

> *Désolé. Il faut que je vous donne un gros billet. Je n'ai pas de monnaie* – I'm sorry but I have to give you a large bill. I don't have change.

> *Avez-vous de la monnaie pour le parc-mètre ? Je n'ai rien qu'un billet de vingt euros* – Do you have the change for the parking meter ? I don't have anything but a twenty euro bill.

> *Est-ce que vous avez la monnaie de cent euros ?* – Do you have change for one hundred euros?

> *Gardez la monnaie !* – Keep the change!

Please also see the discussion of the *faux amis* change and *change* earlier in the book.

un cliché – a cliché

In French, as in English, *un cliché* can refer to an <u>expression or remark which has been used too often</u>.

However, *un cliché* can also mean a <u>film negative</u>, and it is often also used for a <u>photo,</u> snapshot, or print itself.

spécial – special

The French word *spécial* can mean <u>special</u> with the same sense as in English.

> *un train spécial* – a special train

> *une salle spéciale pour les malades contagieux* – a special room for contagious patients

> *un privilège spécial* – a special privilege

> *une édition spéciale* – a special edition

However, in French, *spécial* can have a second meaning that special **does not** normally have in English. *Spécial* can mean <u>strange, odd, peculiar,</u> even <u>bizarre</u>. For example:

> *Il est un peu spécial* – He's a bit odd / peculiar.

> *C'est un plat spécial. Il faut aimer* – It's a peculiar dish. You gotta like it. / Not everyone likes it.

C'est une fille très spéciale – She's a peculiar girl.

You can almost always tell whether *spécial* is meant in the positive sense or in the peculiar sense by context and by the tone of voice of the speaker.

la peste – the pest

In English, a pest is a person who is annoying or irritating, or an insect or animal which is annoying or even destructive.

That kid is a real pest.

The farmers are complaining of a lot of insect pests this year.

In French, on the other hand, *la peste* is a <u>medical illness</u>, specifically <u>plague</u>, although it can be used figuratively to mean any severe problem.

la peste bubonique – bubonic plague

Il faut l'éviter comme la peste – You have to avoid him like the plague.

It is possible to use *une petite peste* for a young girl or adolescent but it is a much harsher word than calling someone a pest in English and means something more like "She's a little devil".

To translate the English word pest into French, try one of these suggestions:

That kid is a real pest – *Ce garçon / Cet enfant embête tout le monde. Ce garçon est vraiment agaçant.*

The farmers are complaining of a lot of insect pests this year – *Les fermiers se plaignent qu'il y a beaucoup d'insectes nuisibles cette année.*

accommoder – to accommodate
l'accommodation – the accommodation

In English, to accommodate to means to fit to the needs or requirements of, to <u>adapt to</u>, to satisfy.

We have to accommodate to his wishes. (fit the requirements of, adapt to, satisfy)

I have to accommodate to the situation as it is. (adapt to)

Consumers have to accommodate to the realities of the marketplace (adapt to)

If you are talking about a building or a space accommodate means <u>have enough room for</u>.

The restaurant can accommodate fifty.

The big table can accommodate eight people comfortably. Ten will be a little tight.

The cabin accommodates up to eight people.

In French, *accommoder* can mean to <u>adapt to the needs of</u>, as in English:

> *Il accommode ses paroles à la situation* – He adapts his words to the situation.

> *Il s'accommode facilement aux exigences des circonstances* – He accommodates / adapts easily to the demands of circumstances.

> *Il a accommodé la deuxième chambre pour l'utiliser comme bureau* – He adapted the second bedroom to the needs of an office / to be used as an office. (This is a bit different than English usage, but the idea of adapting is there).

However, *accommoder* can also mean to <u>be content with</u>, to be satisfied with. You could stretch the English meaning to include this too:

> *Je peux m'accommoder à tout* – I can adapt to / accommodate to anything / I can be content with whatever.

And *accommoder* can also mean to <u>come to agreement with</u> someone (perhaps by compromise).

> *Il s'est accommodé avec Jean* – He came to an agreement / He came to an accomodation with Jean.

However, in French you **would not** use *accommoder* for a space or building.

The restaurant can accommodate fifty – *Le restaurant est assez grand pour cinquante personnes.*

And in French, in cooking, accommoder can mean to prepare, which is an entirely different meaning which it **doesn't** have in English.

> *Elle sait bien accommoder les restes* – She knows well how to prepare leftovers.

> *Je vais accommoder la salade* – I'm going to get the salad ready / put the dressing on the salad.

> *Sa spécialité est d'accommoder du poisson avec une sauce délicieuse* – Her specialty is to prepare fish with a delicious sauce.

Accommodate **does not** mean to prepare by cooking in English.

Similarly with ***accommodation*** and **accommodation**. The French word accommodation means only the act of adapting, and the accommodation of the eye.

In French, *accommodations* **never** means lodgings:

> We are looking for accommodations for the night – *Nous cherchons un logement pour ce soir.*

And, **in French**, while the verb *accommonder* can mean to reach an agreement, the noun, *une accommodation*, **never** means an agreement or compromise.

> We came to an accommodation with them – *Nous sommes arrivés à un compromis / à un arrangement avec eux.*

la formation – the formation

In French, *une formation* can mean a <u>rock formation</u>, like in English.

> C'est une formation sédimentaire.

La formation can mean the <u>act of forming</u>, as it does in English.

> *C'était la formation de la nation / de notre équipe* – It was the formation of the nation / of our team.

In military terms *une formation* can mean a <u>military formation</u>, again as in English.

> *L'escadre était en formation de combat* – The squadron was in combat formation.

However *formation* can have some meanings in French which **are not** seen in English. First *une formation* can mean a <u>group</u>.

> *une formation politique* – a political group

une formation syndicale – a union group

une formation de jazz – a jazz group

Finally, *une formation* often is used to refer to a <u>period of training and education</u>.

Elle a eu une formation excellente / Sa formation a été excellente – She's had an excellent training / education.

J'ai reçu une solide formation littéraire – I've had a solid literary education / foundation.

Elle va avoir trois semaine de formation – She will have three weeks of training.

Il a eu quatorze années de formation musicale – He's had fourteen years of training in music.

Il est électricien de formation – He's an electrician by training.

Il lui faut une formation – He or she needs a training session.

If you had to, you possibly could intuit the meaning of some of these sentences but this usage sounds really strange to anglophones.

le vigile – the vigil
la vigile – the vigil

In English, a vigil is a period when one stays awake during the night, either on the alert, watching for something, or to pray (at the bedside of a sick person, for example).

The sentry kept a lonely vigil.

She kept a vigil at her mother's bedside.

In French, there are two corresponding words: *la vigile* and *le vigile*. Neither of them has the same meaning as vigil in English. They are both *faux amis*:

<u>La</u> *vigile* is used purely in a religious context and refers to the day before a major Catholic holiday, the eve of the holiday, when one is supposed to prepare for it. (The English word vigil can have this sense rarely as well, but again only in a ecclesiastical context).

<u>Le</u> *vigile* is a night watchman or security guard.

> *Il est un des vigiles du centre commercial* – He's one of the night watchmen at the shopping center.

It's interesting to look at the interplay of some of these words. If the study of words doesn't particularly interest you, just skip ahead to the next *faux amis*.

Let's look at the following words:

We have the English word **vigil** which means a period of staying awake during the night <u>on the alert</u> or <u>on watch</u>. Then we have the French words *le vigile*, the <u>night watchman</u> and *la vigile,* <u>the day before</u> a religious *fête*.

Let's follow the French meaning for *vigile,* "the day before", which is the furthest from the English "period of staying awake on the alert", and see where it leads us.

Well, another word for <u>the day before </u>in French is *la veille. (la veille de la bataille* for example). However, *la veille* has a second, entirely different meaning. Of all the possible second meanings it could have, the one it does have is: a <u>period of wakefulness</u>, especially one where one stays <u>awake on watch, alert.</u> *(Je vais prendre la veille ce soir).*

Thus starting off in the opposite direction we are brought back full circle to the meaning of the English word vigil (a period where one stays awake, on watch, alert).

Veiller is also a verb, and it means <u>to stay awake, on alert</u>. *(Je vais veiller auprès de ma mère, qui est malade, ce soir). Veiller* can also mean <u>to watch over</u> (or *surveiller*, which we have covered earlier in this book). *(Il faut veiller à ce qu'il n'y ait pas de problème. Il faux veiller à tes intérêts).* In this sense it refers solely to watchfulness and not to staying awake.

Un veilleur is a <u>lookout</u> or sentry in a military context, and a **veilleur de nuit** is a <u>night-watchman</u>, bringing us back to *un vigile*.

Going off in another direction, **vigil** and *vigile* can also lead us to **vigilance** and *vigilance* which in both English and French mean the state of <u>keeping a careful watch</u>, usually for danger. And to **vigilant** and *vigilant* which mean <u>alert and keeping watch</u>.

Thus, although **vigil** and *vigile* are actually *faux amis*, we see how these words are connected by a web of other words, and how they surely came originally from the same source but drifted apart in meaning over the years.

sanguin – sanguine

In English, the adjective sanguine means <u>optimistic</u>. It's a fairly literary word, but you can hear it in conversation, as in the first example below.

> I'm not at all sanguine about our chances.

> He has a very sanguine disposition.

In French, on the other hand, coming from *sang* (blood), the adjective *sanguin* can mean <u>having to do with blood</u> as in:

> *les groupes sanguins* – blood groups

> *la circulation sanguine* – the circulation of the blood

> *une transfusion sanguine* – a blood transfusion

Naturally, when *sanguin* refers to a color in French it's <u>red</u>, and when it refers to a complexion it's <u>ruddy</u>.

> *Il a le visage sanguin* – He has a ruddy complexion (as opposed to pale).

In French, *sanguin* can also refer to temperament, as in English, but it has an entirely different meaning. It means <u>impulsive</u> (with perhaps a hint of violence).

> *Il a un tempérament sanguin* – He's impulsive by nature.

Sanguin can also be a <u>noun</u> in French:

> *un sanguin* – a man with an impulsive personality

> *une sanguine* – a blood orange (It's a fruit, an orange whose flesh is red.)

To translate the English adjective sanguine into French, use *optimiste*.

> I'm not at all sanguine about our chances – *Je ne suis pas du tout optimiste quant à nos possibilités / en ce qui concerne nos possibilités.*

Side Note: There is another pair of adjectives with the same stem: *sanguinaire* and sanguinary. *San-*

guinaire and sanguinary are **not** faux amis. They both usually refer to combat and mean bloody or involving a lot of bloodshed. In French, *sanguinaire* can also refer to a man and mean bloodthirsty.

l'anniversaire – the anniversary

The French word *anniversaire* can cause confusion because it means <u>birthday</u> as well as <u>anniversary</u>.

> *C'est notre anniversaire (de mariage)* – It's our anniversary.

> *C'est l'anniversaire de la bataille de...* – It's the anniversary of the battle of...

> *Mon anniversaire est le quinze août* – My birthday is August fifteenth.

> *Joyeux anniversaire !* – Happy birthday!

candide – candid

In English, the adjective candid means <u>frank or truthful</u>, and refers either to a person and his personality or to a remark.

> He's a very candid person – He's a very frank person. He speaks frankly and truthfully.

> He spoke candidly – He spoke frankly (without censuring his remarks as to

whether they would be pleasing to his audience).

In French, on the other hand, the adjective *candide* means <u>innocent</u>, <u>ingenuous</u>, <u>naïve</u>, pure, simple. While ingenuous people may speak frankly, candid and *candide* don't mean at all the same thing. Consider:

> *C'est une personne candide* – He or she is a simple, innocent person.

This isn't at all the same as:

> He or she is a candid person.

Similarly, *il a un air candide* doesn't at all mean that he has a truthful air about him. It means that he seems simple and innocent.

If you want **to translate** the English word candid into French use *franc / franche* or *sincère*.

> He's a very candid person – *C'est un homme très franc / très sincère*

Side Note: An interesting example is the humorous satirical novel by Voltaire, in which his archetypal innocent wandering through the world was named Candide, in the book by the same name.

Another Side Note: Two of my English dictionaries point out that candid comes from the Latin *candidus* meaning white, and that the early meaning was pure and innocent, thus showing the common origin of the French and English words.

A Final Side Note: A secondary meaning for candid in English refers to a photograph. A "candid photograph" means that it's an informal photo, presumably showing the person as he is naturally, especially if taken without his (or her) knowledge.

Candide does not have this meaning in French. You **would not** speak of *une photo candide*. There isn't any good one word equivalent in French and you'd have to speak of *une photo prise à l'insu de la personne photographiée,* or something equivalent.

la candeur – the candor

In English, candor (or candour in Great Britian), means frankness and honesty.

In French *la candeur* means innocence, ingenuousness, naiveté, even *crédulité*.

Thus, the faux amis *la candeur* and the candor are parallel to *candide* and candid as you might expect. Here are some examples.

In English:

> He spoke with candor (He spoke frankly) – *Il a parlé franchement / Il a parlé avec franchise.*

> She has a lot of candor (She usually

speaks with frankness and sincerity) – *Elle a l'habitude de parler avec frachise / avec sincérité.*

I appreciate your candor (I appreciate your frankness and sincerity) – *Je vous suis reconnaissant de votre franchise et sincérité.*

In French:

Elle a parlé avec candeur – She spoke naively / She spoke with purity and innocence.

Il a un air de candeur – He has an air of simplicity.

un artiste – an artist

Un artiste usually means an <u>artist</u>.

However, where you may get tripped up, is in the common slangy usage of *un artiste* to mean an <u>eccentric</u>, odd, even bizarre, person. When used like this *artiste* is always a pejorative. You'll be able to tell by the context and by the sarcastic tone of voice of the speaker.

C'est un artiste, lui ! – He's a real eccentric / oddball.

femelle – female
la femelle – the female

As an adjective, the French word *femelle* can apply to an animal, a plant or an electrical plug *(une prise femelle),* but **never** to a woman. For a woman or her feminine charm you must use the word *féminine.*

As an aside, *féminine* is an interesting adjective. It's really *féminin / féminine* with both masculine and feminine forms. You may ask how can the word feminine ever be masculine? Well, how about *le sexe féminin* and *un mot du genre féminin,* for example. (For more on these interesting issues, see my book *The Rules for the Gender of French Nouns).*

As a noun, *une femelle* is used for an animal but **is not** used for a woman. You must be careful of this because if you call a woman *une femelle* it is *très familier* and *très péjoratif.* The correct word, of course, is *une femme.*

chanter – to chant

In French, *chanter* means to sing.

Elle chante juste, dans une chorale, à plein voix, doucement – She sings on tune, in choir, loudly, softly.

Le rossignol chantait – the nightingale was singing.

In English, the single verb to chant can refer to two different kinds of activities. The first activity is chanting slogans (in a demonstration, for instance), and the other activity is chanting religious hymns (by Bhuddist monks for instance). They are not at all the same thing, although they are both called chanting in English.

In French, on the other hand, there are two verbs for these two different activities. Neither verb is *chanter*.

The word for chanting slogans is *scander*.

> *Les manifestants scandaient des slogans contre le gouvernement* – The demonstrators were chanting slogans against the government.

The word for chanting religious hymns is *psalmodier*.

> *Le choeur psalmodiait dans l'église* – The choir was chanting in the church.

> *Les voix des moines étaient fortes et belles quand ils psalmodiaient* – The voices of the monks were strong and beautiful when they were chanting.

> *Les religieux psalmodiaient les prières des morts* – The monks chanted the prayers for the dead.

One other special usage in French that might confuse you, especially if you read mysteries in French: *faire chanter quelqu'un* means to <u>blackmail</u> someone.

> *Il m'a fait chanter* – He blackmailed me.

Blackmail itself is *le chantage*.

> *Elle est victime d'un chantage* – She's a victim of blackmail

supprimer – to suppress

Supprimer and suppress are two words that probably once meant the same thing but whose meanings have slipped apart over the years. Their current meanings are related but they **are not** the same.

As you know, **in English** to suppress means to <u>forcibly prevent the expression of</u>. For example:

> He tried to suppress a feeling of panic.

> They suppressed all stories about the election.

> That medicine can suppress excess secretions of the thyroid gland.

> The uprising was suppressed ruthlessly. (Did you know that there actually exists, or existed anyway, an old English word "ruth", now just about obsolete, which meant pity or compassion. Hence "ruth-

less", without pity. Where else would ruth-less come from, if there wasn't a ruth?).

The **French** word *supprimer* doesn't quite match these meanings. Its usual sense is to <u>delete, remove, cancel or abolish</u>, so you can see that the two words are related but you wouldn't translate one by the other. Here are some examples of *supprimer*:

> *Ces jours de congé ont été supprimé cette année* – Those vacation days / holiday days have been <u>canceled</u> this year.

> *Le service d'autobus est supprimé sur cette route* – The bus service is <u>cancelled</u> on this street.

> *Elle a supprimé plusieurs clauses du manuscrit* – She <u>deleted</u> several clauses from the manuscript.

> *Les gangsters ont supprimé un temoin gênant* – The gangsters <u>eliminated</u> / <u>did away with</u> a troublesome witness.

> *Nous avons supprimé une des cloisons dans notre bureau* – We <u>removed</u> one of the partitions in our offices.

Here's a case where you could translate *supprimer* with suppress:

> *Ils ont supprimé l'article* – They <u>suppressed</u> / <u>eliminated</u> / <u>did away with</u> the article.

To translate the English word suppress into French, try one of these suggestions:

> He tried to suppress a feeling of panic – *Il a essayé d'étouffer / de réprimer / de dominer une sensation de panique.*

> He suppressed a sob – *Il a étouffé / ravalé un sanglot.*

> He suppressed one important fact – *Il n'a pas révélé / il a dissimulé un fait important.*

> They suppressed all stories about the election – *Ils ont interdit / ont réprimé / ont étouffé / ont supprimé tout article sur les élections.*

> The uprising was suppressed ruthlessly – *L'insurrection a été réprimée impitoyablement.*

l'abattement – the abatement

In English, the abatement is the reduction, the <u>lessening</u>, the subsiding. Here are some examples:

> The storm raged on with no sign of abatement.

> Noise abatement is very important to the people living near the airport.

> a tax abatement – a reduction of taxes

In French, *l'abattement* most usually means the <u>despondency</u>, the discouragement, the hopelessness, (the emotional state of a person "beaten down").

> *Elle est dans un état d'abattement profond* – She's in a state of profound hopelessness and depression.

> *Il ne sentait aucune douleur, mais un étrange abattement, une sorte de stupeur inquiète* – He didn't feel any pain, but a strange despondency, a sort of restless or worried stupeur. (Simenon)

L'abattement can also mean a state of physical <u>enfeeblement</u>, due to exhaustion or depression, but this is a less common meaning.

If you want **to translate** the English word abatement into French it's probably best to use *la diminution* or *la réduction*.

> noise abatement – *diminution de bruit / réduction de bruit*

> the abatement of the storm – *la diminution / l'apaisement de l'orage*

Historical Note: It's interesting to note that my English dictionaries say that abatement comes from the Old French *abattre* (to cut down, beat down, kill, wear out, etc), and my French dictionaries say that *abattement* also comes from the same word. The two words however have gone off in directions which, while only partly different, are different enough that you usually can't use the one word for the other.

une charade – a charade

The **English** word charade can refer to a <u>word game</u> in which clues are given by acting out in pantomine. More commonly, and more generally, however, a charade refers to an <u>elaborate pretense</u>, an act to present things in an attractive light.

> It was nothing but a charade (It was nothing but a pretense).

> All those flowery words were just a charade (... were just a pretense, a fake).

In French, *charade* is <u>a different word game</u> in which the clues are given orally, instead of by pantomine as in the English game.

However, the French word *charade* **never** means an elaborate pretense, and *charade* is **never** a translation for charade in the sense of a pretense or fake.

To translate the English word charade in the sense of a pretense, use *une mascarade, un faux-semblant,* or *Ce n'est rien qu'un truc.*

un agenda – an agenda

In English, as you know, an agenda is a list of subjects to be covered at a meeting or (informally) a list of jobs to be done.

They put the subject on the agenda for the meeting.

I've put cleaning the attic far down on my agenda.

In French, on the other hand, *un agenda* is a <u>diary</u>, an <u>appointment book</u>, or a <u>personal organizer</u>. In a hotel, *l'agenda* is the hotel register or reservation book.

To translate the English word agenda into French, use *l'ordre du jour* or *le programme*.

They put the subject on the agenda – *Ils ont mis le sujet au programme.*

formidable – formidable

In English, formidable means inspiring fear and re-spect by ones size, power and bearing. It can thus secondarily mean powerful, dangerous and effec-tive.

He was a formidable opponent. (He in-spired fear. He would be powerful and dangerous as an opponent).

The new submarine will be a formidable weapon. (Powerful, effective and dan-gerous).

In French, the above meaning is considered obso-lete. The current meaning of *formidable* is <u>tremen-</u>

dous, fantastic, great, incredible (all used as words of praise).

Thus:

> C'est formidable ! – That's fantastic! / That's incredible!
>
> C'est une fille formidable ! – She's a terrific / fantastic girl!
>
> Jean est un gars formidable ! – Jean is a terrific guy!
>
> **Note** that this last sentence in French in no way implies a warning that Jean is frightening, that he inspires dread, or that he could be dangerous, as calling someone a "formidable" person might in English.

To translate the English word formidable into French, use redoutable, and you can throw in puissant as well.

> He was a formidable opponent – C'était un adversaire puissant et redoutable.

censurer – to censure
la censure – the censure

In English, the verb **to censure** means to express strong disapproval, to criticize, to reprimand, to rebuke formally. It's used usually, but not always, in a formal manner or formal setting.

> He was censured by his fellow students who were unhappy with what he had done.

> The judge was censured for improper conduct.

> He deserved to be censured.

> Congress censured one of its members for improperly taking money.

The noun, **the censure** is the <u>statement of criticism</u>, disapproval or reprimand referred to by the verb "to censure".

> He felt a certain degree of censure from the other students.

> The judge received a censure for improper conduct.

> He deserved the censure he received.

> Congress passed a resolution of censure against one of its members.

There is another similar English word **to censor**, which has a different meaning. To censor means to examine a book or a movie, et cetera, in an official capacity and to <u>remove unacceptable parts</u> of it, or to ban all of it. **The censor** is the person who does the censoring,

> The movie was censored.

> His mail was censored by the military censor.

> He censored what he was going to say.

In French, there is a switch! The verb *censurer* used to mean to criticize the words or actions of someone, and *la censure* used to mean the action of criticizing. These are now considered usages *vieillis* or obsolescent, although they can still be used when speaking of an official political body. For example:

> *L'assemblée a voté une motion de censure* – The assembly voted a motion of censure.

> *L'avocat a été censuré pour ce qu'il avait fait* – The attorney was censured for his actions.

These are uncommon uses as you might suspect. Far more commonly nowadays *censurer* means to censor and *la censure* is the censorship. *Le censeur* means the person doing the censoring (among other meanings). Thus:

> *Son courrier a été censuré par le censeur militaire* – His mail was censored by the military censor.

La censure a ordonné plusieurs coupures – The censor has ordered that certain parts be cut out.

Cette scène a été censurée – That scene was censored.

Le texte a été censuré par l'Église – The text was censored / banned by the Church.

In most cases **to translate** the English verb to censure into French you should use *blâmer, critiquer,* or *réprimander.*

And **to translate** the English noun censure into French you should use *la réprimande, le reproche* or *la critique.*

haineux – heinous

The **English** word heinous is a rather literary word meaning wicked, atrocious, or odious, and its usage is usually restricted to the word pairs heinous crimes and heinous acts.

The serial killer was finally arrested after a series of heinous crimes.

The **French** word *haineux / haineuse* come from the noun *la haine,* meaning the hatred, and *haineux* and *haineuse* mean full of hatred.

C'était un regard haineux – It was a look full of hate.

Il parle d'un ton haineux – He spoke in a tone of voice full of hatred.

C'est une femme haineuse – She's a woman full of hatred.

Note that *haineux* doesn't mean hateful, but full of hatred. Hateful is a different word which would be translated as *odieux* or *détestable and* thus is fairly close to heinous in meaning.

He commited a series of hateful acts / of heinous acts – *Il a commis une série d'actions détestables / odieuses.*

un amateur / une amatrice – an amateur

In English, an amateur is a <u>non-professional</u>, someone who participates in a sport or other interest for his or her own pleasure, as a hobby, either seriously or in just dabbling.

He's not a professional tennis player. He's an amateur.

The crew of the racing boat were all amateurs.

An amateur can be used as a pejorative:

What a botched-up job. It looks like it was done by a bunch of amateurs.

In English, probably the most common use of amateur is as an adjective:

> He's an amateur piano player / an amateur archeologist / an amateur painter.

> It's an amateur football league.

In French, the number one meaning for *un amateur* of something is someone <u>who is passionate</u> about it, who loves it. To paraphrase one of my French dictionaries, *quelqu'un qui aime, cultive et recherche quelque chose*. This can really throw you off. For example:

> *Il est amateur de bonne cuisine / de bon vin.*

doesn't mean that he's an amateur when it comes to good cuisine or good wine, but means that he is a lover of (and presumably quite knowledgeable about) good cuisine or good wine. It's a big difference in meaning.

> *C'est la collection d'objets d'art d'un amateur.*

doesn't mean that it's an amateurish collection, but that it's a collection put together by a knowledgeable collector and lover of fine art.

An amateur **does not** have this meaning in English.

Un amateur can also have the same meaning as an amateur in English, that is to say someone who cultivates an interest for his own pleasure and not as a professional.

> *Elle ne joue pas mal pour une amatrice* –
> She doesn't play badly for an amateur.

When referring to sports, *un amateur* can also mean (as in English) someone who is not paid, not a professional.

You can almost always tell whether *un amateur* means a lover of a subject, or a non-professional in that subject, by context.

And, although *un amateur* in French is officially only a noun and not an adjective, through common usage *amateur* has come to be used as an adjective in sentences like this:

> *C'est un peintre amateur / un musicien amateur* – He's an amateur painter / an amateur musician

What is most important to take away from this *faux ami* is that while *un amateur* can mean an amateur, probably the most common meaning for *un amateur* in French is someone who is a lover of the subject, and who is probably a knowledgeable expert besides.

Historical Note: As the word amateur comes from *amator*, the latin verb "to love", it's interesting to reflect that the meaning "lover of" a subject, which is now found only in French and not in English, was probably the original meaning for the word amateur in both languages.

lover – to love

This is an easy one. the French word *lover* has nothing to do with the English verb to love. It means to coil up if you are talking about a rope or a snake and it means to curl up if talking about a person or a cat, for instance. It also can be used as the reflexive *se lover* (to coil oneself up / to curl oneself up).

> *Le serpent se lovait lentement* – The snake coiled himself up slowly.

> *Le chat était lové dans le fauteuil* – The cat was curled up in the armchair.

> *Le chat se lovait dans le fauteuil* – The cat curled himself up in the armchair.

> *Marie était lovée dans le sofa* – Marie was curled up on the sofa.

hagard – haggard

In English, haggard usually means <u>looking exhausted</u>, worn out, drained, and unwell, and refers exclusively to a person or his facial expression.

> He struggled along behind the others, haggard and pale.

We saw the haggard faces of the hurricane survivors.

I discovered how different the usage of *hagard* could be **in French** when I came across the following sentence in my reading, spoken by a man who had received a letter in which the words were a confused rambling:

Il avait lu beaucoup de paroles hagardes mais cette lettre battait les records.

"paroles hagardes"?? I had to look it up to be sure of what it meant. I found that the primary meaning in French for *hagard* is <u>wild and distraught</u>: *"qui a un air effaré, égaré et bouleversé".*

As you can see from the example sentence above, this is using *hagard* in a way we would never use haggard in English. And, as you can also see, although *hagard* in French is most commonly used for a face or expression, it isn't restricted to a face, as haggard is in English. Here are some more examples:

Les amants séparés faisait des gestes hagards – The separated lovers made wild and distraught gestures.

Il a piqué une colère hagarde – He developed an anger which was wild and distraught.

The best **translation** of the English word haggard into French would probably be *épuisé et malade en apparence.*

Side Note: In falconry, haggard can also mean wild and untamed in English, but this is an uncommon usage which you've probably never even encountered.

l'antenne – the antenna

This is another *faux ami* that jumped out at me from my reading, this time of *un policier*. It was describing the policeman's new assignment:

> *Nouveaux locaux, nouvelle affectation, Brigade criminelle, groupe homicide, antenne du treizième* – New locale, new assignment, criminal brigade, homicide group, *antenne* of the thirteenth *(arrondissement)*.

But what did *antenne* mean? A little research quickly indicated that *l'antenne* can indeed mean the <u>antenna</u> (of a radio, a television, or an insect, for example). In broadcasting, *à l'antenne* means on the air and *hors antenne* means off the air.

However, *l'antenne* also can mean an <u>outpost</u> (military) or a <u>sub-branch</u> (of a chain of stores). Thus the example above says that the policeman's new assignment is in a branch of the thirteenth *arrondissement*. Here are some more examples:

> *C'est une antenne médicale / chirugicale* – It's an advance medical / surgical unit (military)

C'est une antenne de France Télécom –
It's a branch office of France Télécom.

afférent – afferent

I'll treat this faux ami somewhat cursorily as neither afferent in English nor *afférent* in French is at all common.

In English, afferent is a word from physiology and it means <u>conducting towards</u>, as in afferent blood vessels or afferent nerves.

> the afferent blood vessels of the spleen – the blood vessels conducting blood towards the spleen

In French, *afférent à* means <u>pertaining to</u> or relating to. It's a fairly literary word and not one you will hear in casual conversation, but you may encounter it in your reading.

> *les documents y afférents / des kilos de papiers y afférents* – the documents pertaining to it / kilos of paper pertaining to it.

> *la part afférente à chaque héritier* – the part pertaining to each heir

If you are talking physiology *afférent* does mean afferent.

le drame – the drama

In French, *un drame* can mean a <u>drama</u> in the same sense as the English word. For example:

> *un drame psychologique / un drame judiciaire* – a psychological drama / a courtroom drama

What is very different about the French use of *drame* is that *un drame* in common usage most often means a <u>catastrophe or tragedy</u>.

> *Il fait un drame d'un petit incident* – He's making a mountain out of a molehill.

> *Leur fils est encore à l'école. --- Malgré le drame ?* – Their son is still at school. --- Inspite of the tragedy ?.

> *D'habitude, quand un drame comme celui-ci se produit dans une famille, on trouve...* – Normally, when a tragedy like this takes place in a familly, one finds... (Simenon)

> *Il en fait tout un drame* – He's making a big deal out of it.

> *Ce n'est pas un drame !* – Don't get all worked up about it. It's not the end of the world.

> *N'en fais pas un drame !* – Don't make a big deal out of it. (This has pretty much

the same meaning as the sentence just above).

C'est ça, le drame ! – It's that that's the catastrophy.

This last expression is very common in current conversation and can be used for very minor "catastrophies". For example, in playing cards you might hear:

Mais la répartition des atouts a été mauvaise et Jean en a eu quatre. C'était ça, le drame ! – The division of trumps was very uneven and Jean had four of them. That was the tragedy!

dramatique – dramatic

This faux amis is similar to *drame* and drama just above. The French adjective ***dramatique*** can mean having to do with the theater (or theatre).

les arts dramatiques – the theatrical arts

And, in a theatrical setting, *dramatique* does mean dramatic in the sense of emotionally moving for the audience.

C'était un dénouement dramatique – It was a dramatic / moving climax.

However, by far the most common way that you will hear *dramatique* used is in the figurative sense where it means <u>tragic, awful, terrible, grave or dangerous</u>. It's often used in exclamations. For example:

> *La situation est dramatique !* – It's a dangerous situation!

> *Mais c'est dramatique !* – But that's terrible!

> *Mais ce n'est pas dramatique !* – It's not a tragedy. It's not the end of the world.

If you are not aware of the correct meaning of this usage of *dramatique*, it's easy to misinterpret and think that *"la situation est dramatique,"* for instance, means that the situation is dramatic, when it really means that it's terrible, awful, or dangerous.

dramatiquement – dramatically

While we are on *drame* and *dramatique*, we can briefly touch on *dramatiquement* and dramatically.

In English, dramatically usually means <u>greatly</u>, radically, etc.

> The rate of disease dramatically increased after the floods. (greatly increased)

In French, on the other hand, as you might guess from our discussion of *drame*, *dramatiquement* usually means <u>tragically</u>. The meaning can include a sense of drama as well.

Elle a été tuée dramatiquement dans un accident – She was killed tragically in an accident.

To translate the English word dramatically into French, try one of the following:

The rate of disease dramatically increased after the floods – *Le taux de maladie a augmenté de façon spectaculaire après les inondations / Le taux de maladie a beaucoup augmenté après les inondations / Le taux de maladie a sérieusement augmenté après les inondations.*

graphique – graphic

The **French** word *graphique* does mean graphic when you are talking about graphs.

In English, however, graphic has a second, unrelated, meaning which you would probably actually encounter much more commonly. Graphic often means shocking, detailed, vivid. For example:

He gave a graphic description of the events.

It was a graphic display of violence.

I couldn't deal with that movie. The murder scene was much too graphic for me.

In French, *graphique* **never** means vivid or shocking.

To translate the English word graphic into French in the sense of vivid, use *vivant* or *poignant.*

> He gave a graphic description of the events – *Il a fait un récit vivant / poignant des événements.*

To translate the English word graphic into French in the sense of detailed and shocking, use *détaillé* et *cru* :

> It was too graphic for me – *C'était trop détaillé et trop cru pour moi.*

l'humeur (fem) / l'humour (masc) – the humor

In English, the word humor has two different meanings. The first is the quality of being amusing or comic:

> He has a good sense of humor.

> There is a lot of humor in that film.

The second meaning of the English word humor is a mood or temperament:

> She's in a good humor today / a foul humor today.

In French, there are two different words, *l'humour*

and *l'humeur*, which correspond to these two different meanings.

L'humour refers to the first sense discussed above, the quality of being <u>amusing or comic</u>:

> *Il a de l'humour / Il a le sens de l'humour* – He has a good sense of humor.

> *C'était un récit plein d'humour* – It was a recount / narration which was full of humor.

> *C'est de l'humour noir / C'est de l'humour anglais* – It's black humor (macabre) / It's English humor.

On the other hand, ***l'humeur*** refers to a <u>mood or temperament</u>.

> *Elle est de bonne humeur / de mauvaise humeur / de méchante humeur aujourd'hui* – She's in a good mood / in a bad mood / in a wicked mood today.

> *C'est une personne de bonne humeur / de mauvaise humeur* – He or she is someone who is usually in a good mood, who has a good temperament / who is usually in a bad mood, who has a bad temperament.

> *Il a l'humeur vive* – He has a bad temper.

Elle est perpétuellement de bonne humeur – She is perpetually in a good humor.

Le déjeuner l'avait mis d'excellente humeur – The lunch had put him in an excellent mood.

sa mauvaise humeur légendaire – his legendary bad temper / bad mood

Il y a incompatibilité d'humeur entre nous – We are temperamentally incompatible.

You **cannot** use *l'humour* and *l'humeur* interchangeably.

différer – to differ

The French verb *différer* does mean to <u>differ</u> (to disagree), just as you would expect from English.

However, the same verb, or you could say another verb with identical spelling, has a second completely different meaning: *Différer* also means to <u>defer</u> (to put off doing).

It's as if the French language uses the same verb, *différer* for two truly unrelated meanings. It can confuse you if you are not expecting this second meaning.

First here are some examples of *différer* as to <u>differ</u>:

Ils diffèrent sur tous les points – They differ on every point.

Mon opinion diffère complètement de la sienne – My opinion differs completely from his / hers

C'est parce que leurs origines diffèrent – It's because their backgrounds differ.

Nous différons sur le choix de vin – We differ on the choice of wine.

Elles diffèrent par la couleur de leurs cheveux / Elles diffèrent par leur couleur de cheveux – They differ in hair color.

And here are some examples of *différer* as to defer:

Ils ont différé leur voyage – They deferred / put off their trip.

Elle n'a pas assez d'argent et elle veut différer le paiement – She doesn't have enough money and she wants to defer / put off the payment.

Je vais différer mon jugement sur la question – I am going to defer my judgement on the question.

Notre vengeance, pour être différée, n'en sera pas moins éclatante – Our vengeance won't be any less resounding, for being deferred. (Molière)

*Mais depuis six mois, ii différait son re-
tour sous des prétextes obscurs* – But for
six months he had deferred his return under obscur pretexts. (Fred Vargas)

déférer – to defer

That brings us immediately to another faux ami, *déférer* and to defer.

In English to defer has two different and fairly unrelated meanings. The first, as we have just noted, is
to <u>delay</u> or put off. And, as we have seen, this meaning of to defer is translated with *différer*:

> They deferred / put off their trip – *Ils ont
> différé leur voyage.*

> I am going to defer my judgement on the
> question – *Je vais différer mon jugement
> sur la question.*

However, to defer has a second meaning, which is
to <u>submit</u> to the opinion or wishes of someone. To
defer in this sense is translated by *déférer*:

> He deferred to her wishes – *Il a déféré à /
> s'est soumis à ses désirs / ses souhaits.*

> She deferred to his superior knowledge
> on the subject – *Elle a déféré / s'en est
> remise à son savoir supérieur / sa con-
> naissance supérieure dans ce domaine.*

And, the French word *déférer* has a second meaning as well, which is to bring an affair before a tribunal or court of justice. Thus:

> *Il défère une affaire au tribunal* – He brings an affair before the court.

> *Il défère un criminel à la justice* – He brings a criminal to justice / indicts a criminal.

> (*Déférer* actually has a third meaning, to accord, confer or bestow an honor. This meaning is listed as archaïc but you may run across it in reading older texts).

Thus, to translate from English to French:

- To differ is translated with *différer*.

- To defer (delay) is also translated with *différer*.

- To defer (submit) is translated with *déférer*.

To translate from French to English:

- *Différer* (to not be in agreement) is translated with to differ.

- *Différer* (to put off) is translated with to defer.

- *Déférer* (to submit) is also translated with to defer.

- *Déférer* (to bring to justice) is translated according to the specific cirumstances.

- *Déférer* (to bestow or confer an honor) is listed as archaïc, but would be translated with bestow..

alléguer – to allege

In English, to allege is usually to make an <u>accusation</u> without clear proof:

> He alleged that they had robbed him.

> It was alleged that he was the murderer.

> He is alleged to have lied.

> The children alleged that the babysitter had left them alone.

Alleged isn't always an accusation however, and can be an <u>excuse or alibi</u>:

> He alleged that he had been at home all night.

> He alleged that the reason he didn't show up was because he had been sick.

More rarely, to allege can also simply be an assertion or <u>claim</u>:

> They are alleged to be the most beautiful examples of that kind of pottery in all of France.

In French, on the other hand, *alléguer* is **never** used as an accusation, and is rarely simply an assertion or claim. It is **almost always** an <u>excuse</u>, an alibi, or a justification:

> *Il allègue que personne ne l'avait informé* – He alleges that no one told him.

> *Il a allégué comme raison qu'il avait été malade* – He claimed, as a excuse, that he had been sick.

> *Il n'est pas arrivé à l'heure, alléguant un problème de voiture* – He didn't show up on time, claiming that he had had car problems.

> *Elle a allégué qu'elle n'avait pas eu assez de temps / que le temps lui avait manqué* – She claimed that she didn't have enough time.

What is most important to remember is that you can't use *alléguer* as an accusation. Use *prétendre* or *dire* instead.

> He alleges that they robbed him – *Il prétend qu'ils l'ont volé.*

> It is alleged that he is the murderer – *Il est dit / On dit qu'il est le meurtrier.*

> He is alleged to have lied – *On dit que c'est lui qui a menti.*

or – or

The French <u>noun</u> *or* refers to the metal gold, but you won't confuse the English conjunction "or" with gold. The difference in context will be too obvious. What we are concerned with here is the French <u>conjunction</u> *or*, which has nothing to do with gold (and has nothing to do with the English word "or" either).

In English, or is used to link alternatives (tea or coffee), to link synonyms or an idea with its explanation (an espionage or spy film), or to link an action with its consequences (Don't do it or you'll be in trouble).

Or is not used like this in French. **In French,** *Or* marks a transition from one idea to another, or introduces a particular circumstance in the recital of a story.

Or can be translated as <u>then</u>, <u>but</u>, <u>now</u>, or <u>well</u>, depending on the situation, but none of these translations is really exact. *Or* is almost untranslatable.

Or is used more often in written French, but it can certainly be heard in speech as well. Here are some examples of its use:

> *Or, le moment qu'il redoutait arriva / est arrivé* – Then the moment he was dreading arrived. (This comes close).

> *Il ne boit jamais de vin. Or, hier soir il a bu quatre verres* – He never drinks wine. Well, yesterday evening, he drank

four glasses / But, yesterday evening he drank four glasses.

Or, un soir, son mari rentra et la trouva avec Pierre – Well, one evening her husband returned and found her with Pierre / Then, one evening her husband returned...

Or, à un moment imprévu... – But, at an unexpected moment... / But, unexpectedly...

As you can see, this is quite different than the English word or. **To translate** the English conjunction or into French, use *ou*.

tea or coffee – *thé ou café*

inepte – inept

In English, inept means <u>lacking skill, clumsy or awkward</u> and almost always refers to physical actions.

She was totally inept at cooking.

In French, *inepte* refers to a remark, a response, a book, or even the author of the remark or book, and it means <u>absurd, stupid or silly</u>, lacking good sense. French synonyms are *absurde, idiot, sot, stupide*.

Cette affaire semblait soudain une entreprise aléatoire, presque inepte – The affaire suddenly seemed uncertain, random, almost silly and absurd.

La requête de Jean lui paraissait inepte mais il ferait ce qu'il demandait – Jean's request seemed silly, but he would do what he asked.

Inepte also used to mean "not apt", or unsuited, but this meaning is now obsolete.

Although your English-French dictionary may translate inept by *inepte* out of lack of precision, you can see that it is not the same thing at all.

To translate the English word inept into French, the best words are *maladroit, balourd,* or say something like: *il n'est pas habile.*

confronter – to confront

The French verb *confronter* can mean to <u>confront</u>, as in:

Nous sommes confronté à un problème grave – We are confronted with as grave problem.

Ils ont confronté le prévenu avec le témoin – They confronted the accused with the witness.

But what would you make of this if you encountered it in reading?

Nous avons trouvé des empreintes ici, auprès de la victime. Ramassez tout ce que vous pouvez chez M. Dupont. On confrontera.

It starts out clearly: "We have found fingerprints here, near the victim. Gather all that you can at M. Dupont's house." But then what's the meaning of *"On confrontera"?* Does it mean we will confront? Clearly not!

Confronter in French also means to <u>compare</u>. That solves the mystery for us.

Confronter is often used in talking about comparing two texts, comparing what was said with what was written down, comparing two plans, two ideas, etc.

To confront **never** means to compare in English.

la finalité – the finality

In English, finality means <u>irreversibility</u>.

He said it with finality.

In French, *la finalité* has a completely different meaning. It means the <u>purpose, aim or goal</u>.

Qu'est-ce que la finalité de votre visite ?
– What is the purpose of your visit?

concret / concrète – concrete

In English, the <u>adjective</u> concrete means real, solid, tangible, not abstract, existing in material form.

> At last, it's a concrete proposal.

> We have no concrete proof.

> It's a concrete object. (real, physical)

In French, the adjective *concret / concrète* has pretty much identical meanings.

> *Pour être plus concret, que faut-il faire ?*
> – To be more concrete, what do we need to do?

> *Cela a rendu l'idée plus concrète* – That made the idea more concrete.

> *C'est un homme plutôt concret* – He's rather a pragmatic, down-to-earth guy.

However, **in English**, the <u>noun</u> concrete refers to a construction material made of gravel, sand, cement, and water. There **is no** corresponding noun *concret* in French.

To translate the construction material concrete from English to French, use *le béton*.

> *C'est un trottoir en béton* – It's a concrete sidewalk.

> *béton armé* – reinforced concrete

And in a figurative sense:

> *C'est un alibi en béton* – It's a rock-solid alibi.

la cheminée – the chimney

For our final *faux ami*, we'll tackle *la cheminée*, which can indeed mean chimney:

> *Regarde ! Cette maison a trois cheminées* – Look! That house has three chimneys.

> *La cheminée de l'usine est très grande* – The chimney / smokestack of the factory is very tall.

However *la cheminée* can also mean the fireplace:

> *Quel joli fauteuil devant la cheminée* – What a pretty armchair in front of the fireplace.

> *Ils ont même une cheminée dans leur chambre* – They even have a fireplace in their bedroom.

> *Allons allumer un feu dans la cheminée* – Lets start a fire in the fireplace.

> *La cheminée tire bien* – The fireplace is drawing well.

And finally, *la cheminée* can mean the mantlepiece:

Le livre est sur la cheminée – The book is on the mantlepiece.

C'est une cheminée en bois massif – It's a mantlepiece in heavy wood.

Don't confuse the <u>noun</u> *cheminée* which we've been discussing with the <u>verb</u> *cheminer* (which has the same pronounciation). The verb *cheminer* means to go along *un chemin* (or path), usually a long one, and often at a slow and fairly regular pace.

Sur le trottoir désert, ils cheminaient lentement dans le calme de la nuit – On the deserted sidewalk, they walked along slowly in the calm of the night.

When used more generally, *cheminer* can mean to advance slowly, and when used figuratively it can refer to pretty much anything advancing slowly.

I hope that you have found this book useful, and that it will help you with reading, writing and speaking good French. I must admit that I learned a great deal in putting it together. I really enjoyed writing it, and I especially hope that you got an equal pleasure from reading it.

List of References

I used the following reference books to supplement my knowledge from everyday reading and conversation in the preparation of this book.

Harper Collins French Concise Dictionary, Second Edition, Harper Collins, 2000

Harrap's Shorter Dictionnaire, Anglais-Français Français-Anglais, 7th Edition, Chambers Harrap, 2004

Webster's New World Dictionary, Second College Edition, Simon and Schuster, 1982

Le Petit Robert, Dictionnaire Alphabétique et Analogique de la Langue Française, Dictionnaires Le Robert, 1993

Le Petit Larousse, Grand Format, Larousse, 2001

Dictionary 1.0.1, Apple Computer 2005

Alphabetized Index

9 781604 942200